Cecilia Reclaimed

Cecilia Reclaimed

Feminist Perspectives on Gender and Music

Edited by Susan C. Cook
and Judy S. Tsou

Foreword by Susan McClary

UNIVERSITY OF ILLINOIS PRESS
Urbana and Chicago

Publication of this book was supported through the generosity of
an anonymous donor.

This book is printed on acid-free paper.

Library of Congress Cataloging-in-Publication Data

Cecilia reclaimed : feminist perspectives on gender and music / edited
   by Susan C. Cook and Judy S. Tsou ; foreword by Susan McClary.
        p.   cm.
   Includes bibliographical references and index.
   ISBN 0-252-02036-7 (cloth : acid-free paper).—ISBN 0-252-06341-4
(paper : acid-free paper)
   1. Feminism and music. 2. Women musicians. I. Cook, Susan C.
II. Tsou, Judy S.
ML82.C42 1994
780'.82—dc20   93-18463
                                                            CIP
                                                            MN

Hail! bright Cecilia, Hail to thee!
Great Patroness of Us and Harmony!
—Nicholas Brady after Dryden

Contents

Foreword: Ode to Cecilia   ix
Susan McClary

Acknowledgments   xiii

Introduction: "Bright Cecilia"   1
Susan C. Cook and Judy S. Tsou

1. Feminist Approaches to Musicology   15
   Marcia J. Citron

2. Erasing the Boundaries between Public and Private
   in Women's Performance Traditions   35
   Jennifer C. Post

3. Music and the English Renaissance Controversy
   over Women   52
   Linda Phyllis Austern

4. Quinault, Lully, and the *Précieuses:* Images of Women
   in Seventeenth-Century France   70
   Patricia Howard

5. "A Distinguishing Virility": Feminism and Modernism
   in American Art Music   90
   Catherine Parsons Smith

6. The Child Is Mother of the Woman: Amy Beach's
   New England Upbringing   107
   Adrienne Fried Block

7. Anna Maria della Pietà: The Woman Musician of
   Venice Personified   134
   Jane L. Baldauf-Berdes

8. Ladies' Companion, Ladies' Canon? Women Composers
   in American Magazines from *Godey's* to the *Ladies'
   Home Journal*   156
   Bonny H. Miller

9. Feminine or Masculine: The Conflicting Nature
   of Female Images in Rap Music   183
   Venise T. Berry

10. "Cursed Was She": Gender and Power in American
    Balladry   202
    Susan C. Cook

    Contributors   225
    Index   229

Foreword: Ode to Cecilia

Susan McClary

In October 1987 at the New Orleans meeting of the American Musicological Society, I found a note posted on the bulletin board asking me to telephone someone named Susan Cook. Susan had heard that I was interested—as was she—in the possibility of feminist music criticism. Later that day (over popcorn shrimp, as I recall), we discussed/planned/dreamed how we might facilitate the integration of such issues into musicology. Soon both of us began writing articles and giving talks that focused on questions of gender, the body, sexuality, and the politics of representation. In addition to her own research, Susan worked tirelessly to organize workshops and panels at disciplinary meetings, helping to consolidate a much-needed sense of intellectual community. She also operated as a talent scout and with Judy Tsou started planning a collection of essays that would actualize some of the ideals of feminist musicology so many of us envisioned.

A mere five years later, our dreams have become reality, for with the publication of *Cecilia Reclaimed: Feminist Perspectives on Gender and Music*, we can see already the widespread impact of feminist methods in music studies. No longer an aberration identified with one or two mavericks, gender-sensitive music criticism is currently being practiced by a large number of scholars—male as well as female—from virtually all areas of specialization. Each of the women in this volume has allowed herself to rethink her field with gender at the center, and the results are nothing short of startling: in essay after essay, matters long regarded as resolved open up again in unexpected ways, and assumptions that have defined the boundaries of the discipline come repeatedly into question.

Some of the essays continue the work pioneered by feminist musicologists seeking to recover the women who have participated in musical activities throughout Western history. Because we now have a clearer picture of the figures, their contexts, and accomplishments, it has become possible to study in greater detail the circumstances that simultaneously enabled and restricted the careers of some of these women.

Thus Adrienne Fried Block examines the severe child-rearing practices that guided the training of Amy Cheney Beach, and Jane L. Baldauf-Berdes investigates the policies of the Venetian orphanages that produced such internationally known artists as Anna Maria della Pietà. Both these essays are remarkably free of the outrage that unavoidably marked earlier research, when the patterns of systematic social exclusion that had held women back first began to be discerned. While never losing sight of those constraints, Block and Baldauf-Berdes render balanced readings of their respective historical subjects by explaining also the empowering aspects of their circumstances.

Lest anyone think that Western culture is being singled out for chastisement, Jennifer C. Post's essay locates the kinds of practices discussed by Block and Baldauf-Berdes within an ethnomusicological framework. Post reveals how women's musical activities have been similarly encouraged yet circumscribed in many other cultures; she also destabilizes the model of public/domestic spheres that has informed much interdisciplinary research on gender by including the category of the professional woman musician. (This option, as Post shows, is no utopia: while the professional leaves behind the strictures of the home, she usually must cater at least as much to the preferences of the typically male audience for which she performs or composes.)

Other writers in *Cecilia Reclaimed* focus primarily on the politics of representation: the ways in which ideologies concerning gender have influenced musical activities at various moments in history. Marcia J. Citron analyzes the gendered aspects of the sonata procedure that informs the most privileged genres of the nineteenth century and asks if women composers might have resisted writing such pieces because of the form's masculinist implications. Linda Phyllis Austern demonstrates how debates over women in the Renaissance were mirrored in debates concerning music; in showing the ways the English mapped gender-related anxieties onto music, she helps explain why England has so marginalized musical activities throughout its history. Patricia Howard traces the central topoi in the opera libretti of Quinault back to his involvement with a literary circle of women—the *Précieuses*—and reveals how he then turned those topoi around so that they coincided with the patriarchal interests of the Sun King. Susan C. Cook compares the lyrics of a widespread American ballad with the actual historical events they purport to recount and shows how the ballad's rhetorical strategies produce a misogynist moral aimed against all women. And finally, Catherine Parsons Smith draws on the work on early twentieth-century modernism by Sandra M. Gilbert and Susan Gubar to deliver an extraordinarily compelling indictment of the ways male composers of that period legitimated their own enterprises while deliberately discrediting the women artists who had begun to emerge as potential rivals.

What is remarkable in each of these essays is not that elements of misogyny are unmasked—this much is scarcely news (nor, of course, is music any more or any less guilty of misogyny than is any other area of culture), but rather that they suggest that such troubling elements often motivated some of the major transformations in musical practice. Musicologists traditionally have attempted to account for formal procedures (sonata), styles (Lully's settings of Quinault), or period shifts (the emergence of modernism) on the basis of "aesthetic" priorities or "purely musical" devices. But as in other disciplines, it now appears that such privileged concepts as the "aesthetic" or the "purely musical" hide a multitude of ideological tensions. And it is high time we began to investigate the history of music as it has participated in articulating and transmitting social beliefs, anxieties, hopes, and desires. Not because of the taint of misogyny (although we must continue to point this out whenever it occurs), but because in denying the representational dimensions of music, we also deny its very real power as a cultural medium.

One of the most exciting aspects of *Cecilia Reclaimed* is its refusal to acknowledge the old barriers between so-called Western and non-Western musics, between high and popular culture. The essays by Post and Cook would typically appear in journals devoted to ethnomusicology or folklore—not cheek by jowl with studies of aristocratic entertainments from seventeenth-century France. While the majority of pieces included here involve the European tradition, their juxtaposition with studies of other societies and oral-tradition repertories makes it clear that the West is to be understood as a specific culture among many others. In a sense, these questions concerning gender cause the spotlight of ethnography to pivot so that it now also shines on the music long hailed as universal, as having transcended social interests.

The later essays in the volume focus on musical practices of the West—indeed, of the United States—but practices that have been excluded from musicological consideration. Bonny H. Miller looks at the music distributed by means of women's journals during the nineteenth century and thereby uncovers a number of women involved in composition. She also begins to sketch the ways women's musical activities and even their understanding of their lives were shaped by such networks. And Venise T. Berry explores contemporary battles over gender imaging in Hip Hop culture, especially with the emergence of major female rap stars (Salt 'N Pepa, MC Lyte, Queen Latifah, Oakland 3 5 7) who produce their own lyrics, personae, and videos. Berry's is one of the few essays to address the issue of self-representation so crucial to today's debates within feminism.

While reading *Cecilia Reclaimed*, I was continually reminded of how in graduate school in the late 1960s we lamented that all the important projects had been completed; nothing remained for us to do except to check out a minor kapellmeister here or there. It now appears that all the really interesting work lies before us. If our predecessors in musicology brought together a massive amount of information, they avoided interpreting their data for the most part. It is that long-delayed interpretation that the contributors to this volume have undertaken in full force. As Susan C. Cook and Judy S. Tsou point out in their introduction, we no longer have to imagine what feminist music criticism would look like or to argue for its inclusion in musicology. With *Cecilia Reclaimed*, it has arrived.

Acknowledgments

In our introduction we liken the process that brought this collection together to the traditional women's work of quilting. We began this project in 1985, and over time and with the help of many hands the collection has taken shape. Numerous individuals deserve credit for their part. Foremost, we would like to thank the contributors themselves for their care and patience. For their support during the early stages of this project, Jan Bell Groh, Deborah Hayes, Barbara Garvey Jackson, JaFran Jones, Nancy B. Reich, and Elizabeth Wood deserve our gratitude as well. We are especially grateful to have been working with an editor like Judy McCulloh of the University of Illinois Press. Judy's care, professionalism, and encouragement sustained us throughout.

Both of us would like to thank certain people important to our own individual work. Susan would like to recognize the students in her 1991 theory and methods course in women's studies at Middlebury College who taught her about the power of women's communities. At the University of Wisconsin–Madison she thanks Mary Anne Long, who through the generosity of the Eugenie Mayer Bolz Fellowship Program, assisted in the completion of this collection. Others deserving special recognition for contributing questions and conversation are Kirsten H. Powell, Charles W. Dill, Shannon L. Green, Audrey Highton, Brian Hyer, Julia Eklund Koza, Margaret Miner, Lynette Roth, Susanna Watling, and Katherine Younger.

Judy would like to thank the University of California at Berkeley and Duke University for their support. She also thanks David Carlson for emotional, intellectual, and technical support.

Introduction: "Bright Cecilia"

Susan C. Cook and Judy S. Tsou

Since the late fifteenth century, the early Christian martyr Cecilia has been honored—on mistaken grounds, it now seems—as the patron saint of music. As such, she symbolized at least some kind of female identification with musical practice. Many of today's feminist music scholars may well have been inspired by Cecilian symbolism but soon learned that the source of this symbol was stereotypical and patriarchal. Cecilia was in many ways the *patronized* saint of music, limited, by her sex, to a passive role of idealized, even swooning, muse or performer, but not as an active creator. Cecilia thus presented cultural notions of acceptable female practice; she played the organ, but she did not compose organ symphonies.

Saint Cecilia presents just one example of the gendered nature of musical activity. This entire collection explores in depth other such intersections of gender and music. To reclaim Cecilia, as our title suggests, we acknowledge from the outset that gender, commonly understood as the social construction of sexual difference, has influenced all aspects of musical culture. Throughout history, changing, even contradictory, definitions of "the masculine" and "the feminine," incorporating as well cultural notions of creativity and genius, determined who did what in music and what was done in the name of music.[1] These same slippery categories of masculinity and femininity still affect how we, as scholars, critics, learned amateurs, or even disinterested bystanders, define what music is and what music does. When combined with historical analysis and criticism, contemporary gender ideology shapes scholarly opinion about what particular musical activities are of greatest cultural significance and thus most worthy of attention.

A recognition of gender as a category of analysis has come slowly and often with difficulty to the academic discipline of music. Our intention here is not to discuss why this has been the case. Rather we would note that the past several years have shown a growing willingness on the part of music scholars to take seriously what feminisms—the use of the plural indicating the lively diversity of possible approaches—can offer to their study. Indeed, in the six years that this collection has been in the making, major conferences on feminist theory and women in music have taken place, and research with a feminist perspective has received a hearing at the annual meetings of virtually all professional music societies.

This collection, however, is the first in the field to emphasize in its title the centrality of feminist perspectives and methodologies to its content. The individual essays represent some of the most recent musicological work that identifies gender and its ideology as a starting point from which to formulate any number of questions about musical activity, works, culture, and experience. The explorations provided here reveal, in their various approaches and methods, how musical activity can be reread through gender and how music likewise helps define what it means to be male or female in a given time or place.

As with other work in women's studies and feminist scholarship, these essays are political. Although the term *gender* can be used to blunt the force of the term *feminist,* identifying the cultural construction of gender means identifying women's oppression and acknowledging the many painful realities of patriarchal beliefs and practice. Believing, as historian Joan Wallach Scott has shown, that "history's representations of the past help construct gender for the present," the authors here attempt to right the inequities of male-female relations by rewriting aspects of our musical past; they ask new questions about musical practices, examine neglected primary source materials, and use gender to add untold dimensions to our previous understandings of music history and musical activity.[2]

These essays share with other work in women's studies the methodological necessity of crossing disciplinary boundaries to borrow the tools, terminology, and perspectives of other fields to explain more fully gender construction and its ramifications. Notable borrowings, evident in the notes and references for each essay, come from women's history, feminist literary criticism, and black feminist theory, as well as from new work in sociology, media studies, and anthropology.

Adopting the perspectives of new fields is necessary in feminist work, but using the specialized terminology from other disciplines can be risky. We have tried to strike a balance between relying on distinctive and crucial terms that may be unfamiliar to some and maintaining whenever possible theoretical and linguistic inclusiveness. We envision these essays as responses in an ongoing dialogue with feminist practitioners in those same fields from which we borrowed. Furthermore, we hope to show how our work in musicology can enrich their perspective and demonstrate that musicology can have its own distinctive presence in the larger realm of feminist studies.

* * *

This volume has its roots in history. The documentation in the English language of women's musical activity began, not surprisingly, with the first wave of feminism surrounding the struggle in Europe and North America for women's suffrage at the turn of the century. Of the many publications from that time, the most cited are Otto Ebel's *Women Composers: A Bibliographical Handbook of Woman's Work in Music* (1902) and Arthur Elson and Everett Ellsworth Truette's *Woman's Work in Music* (1903). These early publications, often focusing entirely on composition as the criterion for musical "work," contain short biographical listings that trivialize the women cited. George Upton's *Women in Music* (1886) discusses the role of wives of famous composers and accepts on unquestioned essentialist grounds the hopelessness of women succeeding as composers.

Although these publications may be valuable to modern scholars in understanding the power of gender ideology to distort purported scholarly objectivity, in their own time, these publications undermined women's very real musical activities and contributions and kept them invisible to future generations. It was not until 1948 that Sophie Drinker's *Music and Women: The Story of Women in Their Relation to Music* began to question presumptions about musical life and practice. A visionary work in many respects, it was marginalized in the profession and had little effect in redressing or revising patriarchal practices.[3]

The second wave feminist movement of the 1960s brought renewed interest in women's lives, activities, and experiences. Women's studies programs were well established in North American colleges and universities, however, by the time music scholars began to challenge conventional views about women's musical place and to take a fresh look at women's musical activities. The International Year of the Woman in 1975 prompted the establishment of the International League of Women Composers, an organization promoting the compositions of contemporary women. American Women Composers, Inc., another advocacy organization for women composers, was established the following year as part of the bicentennial celebration in the United States.

Like its sister discipline, women's history, the study of women in music began with compensatory history: the identification of those women—typically composers or performers of neglected concert music—whose lives and work were not part of the accepted musico-historical canon of "great work." Such was the aim of the organizers of the International Congress of Women in Music, established in 1979. The publications from this period also reflected such efforts: Don L. Hixon and Don Hennessee's *Women in Music: A Biobibliography* (1975), followed by the ambitious first edition of Aaron Cohen's *International Encyclopedia of Women Composers* (1981).

Unlike much mainstream musicology with its European bias, the study of women in this beginning period acknowledged the significant contributions of women to musical life in the United States, reflecting the influences of American and African-American Studies. Such works include Adrienne Fried Block and Carol Neuls-Bates, *Women in American Music: A Bibliography of Music and Literature* (1979); D. Antoinette Handy, *Black Women in American Bands and Orchestras* (1981); Mildred Denby Green, *Black Women Composers: A Genesis* (1983); and Judith Tick, *American Women Composers before 1870* (1983).

Several serial publications appeared as newsletters published by the International Congress on Women in Music, the International League of Women Composers, and American Women Composers, Inc. Similarly, *The Musical Woman*, with three volumes completed to date, and Da Capo Press's Women Composers Series of reprints focused on the compositional lacunae that prevented a better assessment of female agency in Western concert music.

This period also saw the beginning of studies that explored with greater specificity women's contributions to genres or cultural life, such as Christine Ammer's *Unsung: A History of Women in American Music* (1980), Carol Neuls-Bates's *Women in Music: An Anthology of Source Readings from the Middle Ages to the Present* (1982), and Sally Placksin's *American Women in Jazz, 1900 to the Present: Their Words, Lives, and Music* (1982). Jane Bowers and Judith Tick's collection of scholarly essays *Women Making Music: The Western Art Tradition, 1150-1950* (1986) became a central text for courses on women in music. Other publications in this period helped continue to identify and document women composers and their work. More recently, *Women and Music: A History* (1991), edited by Karin Pendle, presents new material concerning the work of women in Western music.

Beginning in the mid-1980s the influence of feminist research in other fields helped bring diverse approaches and methodologies to the study of what came to be called "women in music." The identification of women composers through dictionaries, biographies, and bibliographies continued with such works as Joan M. Meggett's *Keyboard Music by Women Composers: A Catalog and Bibliography* (1981) and Rose-Marie Johnson's *Violin Music by Women Composers: A Bio-Bibliographical Guide* (1989). Studies of individual women composers resulted in several Greenwood Press bio-bibliographies, including Marcia J. Citron's *Cécile Chaminade: A Bio-Bibliography* (1988), Walter B. Bailey and Nancy Gisbrecht Bailey's *Radie Britain: A Bio-Bibliography* (1990), and Deborah Hayes's *Peggy Glanville-Hicks: A Bio-Bibliography* (1990). Other in-depth scholarly biographies also appeared that identified new kinds of source materials and accounted for the differences in women's lives, notably Nancy B. Reich's *Clara Schumann: The Artist and the Woman* (1985) and Catherine Parsons Smith and Cynthia S. Richardson's *Mary Carr Moore, American Composer* (1987).

In addition to the Greenwood Press bio-bibliographies, devoted to a single woman, bibliographies on the general topic of women in music have begun to appear. Under Nancy B. Reich's editorship, the College Music Society's Committee on the Status of Women in Music published a detailed bibliography as part of its report *Women's Studies/Women's Status* (1988).[4] Margaret Ericson of the Music Library Association's Women and Music Roundtable is preparing an extensive bibliography: *Women and Music: A Selective Bibliography on the Collective Subject of Women in Music.*[5]

In the late 1980s explicitly feminist scholarship in musicology also emerged. This work identified gender as a distinct social force, sought to examine its ramifications within musical culture, and asked new questions about musical practice. Such studies extended beyond the identification and examination of compositions and works by women composers as the only ways of making women the subjects of study. Notably, essays by Susan McClary, Eva Rieger (in translation), Judith Tick, Hazel Carby, and Catherine Clément (also in translation) explored the role of gender and gender bias in musical language, institutions, and compositions, providing new interpretations of musical life and raising issues of sexual aesthetics, sexuality, and the conjoining of racism and sexism.[6] Similarly, the essays in *Women and Music in Cross-Cultural Perspective* (1987), edited by Ellen Koskoff, identified gender ideology and resulting issues of power and value at work in the genres, traditions, and activities of women's music making outside the so-called Western musical canon.[7]

* * *

Our collection, like those of Jane Bowers and Judith Tick, Ellen Koskoff, and Karin Pendle, continues to make the essay anthology the
genre of choice for feminist work. In this regard, we have much in
common with nonmusic fields, where multiauthored collections presenting a variety of feminist perspectives are commonplace.[8] These
collections do not attempt to present the unified face of a monograph
but seek to show how distinctive feminist practices can be brought to
bear on a variety of topics. Such an approach has special strengths,
particularly when authors present material partaking of a nontraditional point of view, as is still true of feminist studies, and when
scholars have had to spend the time and effort that might have produced a monograph in retraining themselves to undertake work in
women's studies.[9] Our collection presents multiple faces; it seeks to
offer something of interest to a wide readership and thus argues more
convincingly for the relevance and necessity of its perspective within
the larger discipline.

The literary critic Elaine Showalter, in her recent collection of essays
Sister's Choice, uses the metaphor of quilting to describe the writing
practices and strategies of some American women writers.[10] We too
see a kind of quilting process at work in this collection, with its many
contributors and their multiple approaches. Indeed, it was our intention from the outset to provide an idea of how wide-ranging feminist
musicological work could be, although we acknowledge that the collection is not as diverse as it should be. In particular, no essay deals
explicitly with musical activity as it pertains to lesbian identity.

Confined by the limits of a single volume as well as current musicological practice, we have nevertheless tried to show the many tex-
tures feminist research can take. Some of the essays represent primary
source studies examined through the lens of gender, while others take
theories developed in sister branches of feminist study and either adapt
them to musical ends, exploring issues of biography and stylistic development, or use them to explore musical discourse and the collusion
of musical practice and misogyny.

Although most of the authors would define themselves as musicologists, many of their theoretical perspectives show the influence of
ethnomusicology and its perception of music as a cultural system. The
musical subjects themselves come primarily from Europe and North
America; specifically represented are concert music, both instrumental
and vocal, and the vernacular genres of ballads, salon music, and contemporary African American rap. The essays raise issues of not only

gender but also race and class as they move among musical practices of the courtly ruling class and the elite discourse of the twentieth-century modernist movement to the practices surrounding marginal girls in Renaissance Venice and the largely white middle-class experiences of magazine music and balladry. While Venise T. Berry's essay on contemporary rap music is the only essay that explicitly deals with current musical activity, several articles in their explorations of female subjectivity suggest ramifications for present-day musical and even academic life.

As with a quilt, pieced together from a variety of materials as part of a collaborative process, this collection could have been organized in any number of internal patterns emphasizing different relationships between its constituent pieces. In our pattern we suspended the common practice of organizing by geography or chronology and instead chose a pattern arising from the individual author's choice of a particular focus within the larger framework of gender and music.

The opening two essays present distinctly theoretical and methodological positions coming from musicology and ethnomusicology. Marcia J. Citron's essay provides an appropriate starting point for the collection, discussing how feminist musicology has come of age and how it can continue to mature. In her presentation of two possible feminist approaches, Citron examines the sonata aesthetic and how its structures encode gender relations and roles, and discusses the possible ramifications of reader-response theories for understanding gendered listening. Jennifer C. Post, relying on contemporary anthropological thought and drawing on her cross-cultural work as an ethnomusicologist, discusses aspects that define and complicate women's professional musical activity. Several of her observations about the constraints and contestations of women's public activities are further examined in succeeding essays.

The essays by Linda Phyllis Austern, Patricia Howard, and Catherine Parsons Smith demonstrate the gendered discourse surrounding musical activities and practices in particular historical times and geographic locales. Austern shows how views of female nature and sexuality influenced English Renaissance discussions about music. Howard's essay examines the work of Lully's librettist Philippe Quinault, a beneficiary of the female literati of the French court who later came to rewrite mythology to portray women as powerless and self-destructive. Drawing on the work of the feminist literary critics Sandra Gilbert and Susan Gubar, Smith reveals that misogyny was an essential feature of twentieth-century musical modernism.

Adrienne Fried Block and Jane L. Baldauf-Berdes show that exploring gender transforms how one writes about the lives of particular women. Block explores child-rearing practices and their ramifications for the musical career of the child prodigy Amy Beach. Baldauf-Berdes, through archival study of neglected materials, sheds light on the little-known institutional practices of Venetian orphanages that accorded some women, such as the performer Anna Maria della Pietà, positions of musical and civic power.

The final three essays by Bonny H. Miller, Venise T. Berry, and Susan C. Cook demonstrate how gender ideologies shaped particular musical genres and specific works representative of those genres. Miller examines magazine music as an outlet for female creativity. While men had access to other avenues, women were often restricted to this privately public forum, with its kinds of composition acceptable for the consumption of its female readership. Berry explores contemporary African American rap music and shows how female rappers have transformed the genre to fit their own needs, defining and redefining for themselves as black women what is feminine and feminist. In their public performances Berry's subjects continue to show the uneasy relationship between female sexuality and musicality that Austern identified in her essay on the English Renaissance. Cook's essay shares with Howard's examination of libretti a focus on texts where musical settings help perpetuate ideological stances. Uncovering the particular events surrounding the creation of the popular North American ballad "Fuller and Warren," Cook provides a close reading of the ballad and its particular misogynistic message.

In a recent essay, the historian Linda Kerber examined the rhetoric of women's history, particularly the metaphor of the "sphere" as "the trope on which historians came to rely when they described women's part in American culture."[11] This trope initially acknowledged the separation of men and women in society and the specific limitations placed on women. Not surprisingly, one of the common threads connecting the work in our collection is that all the authors acknowledge the limitations, subtle and overt, familial and societal, contestable and insurmountable, that women, often regardless of race, class, geographic location, or historical time, faced as performers, as creators, and even as listeners because of the ideology of gender.

Thus Smith's examination of modernist musical discourse reveals the attempt to limit women's participation as concert music professionals in our own century. Block, in her essay on Beach, also describes the societal restraints upheld by Beach's mother that hampered Beach's career as a performer but may have allowed her work as a composer, because it could be carried out in her private home. Miller's essay demonstrates that many women and men, professionals and amateurs, published their music in magazines often intended for female readership and otherwise encouraging their limited activities. Cook examines the implications of male occupations that fostered the transmission of ballads and the formation of specifically male-identified and male-addressed texts that defined women's place.

Recent work on women's history, Kerber notes, has moved away from the rigid dualism of male/female spheres to an interactive view emphasizing social exchange and reciprocity between the sexes that may have positive as well as negative ramifications. The "woman's sphere" alone can be too easy a metaphor for describing the complex power relations between women and men and between women and women, especially when issues of race, class, and sexual orientation are taken into account.[12] To perpetuate a theoretical model of female domesticity or "the cult of true womanhood" as a universal perpetuates the often unwitting white middle-class bias of much feminist work and ignores interlocking systems of oppression experienced by women of color, poor women, and lesbians. Kerber also suggests that the sphere can be read not just as an abstract notion of a "sphere of influence" but as a literal space or place where women, whose experiences are further shaped by race, class, or sexual orientation, exercised control. She identifies one such model in the work of Jane Addams and her formation of Hull House in Chicago during the early decades of this century.

This interactive view is present in Marcia J. Citron's exploration of women listeners, and Jennifer C. Post breaks down the rigid dualism of public/private or male/female musical activity, even as she notes how some women create private performing spaces for themselves in larger mixed-sex public space. Post suggests a continuum of female activity, from amateur to professional, acting in tension with other cultural constraints. The responses and counterresponses on female nature and musicality discussed by Austern suggest the fluidity of gender boundaries and their contested interpretations. Berry shows how African American women rappers inhabit a complex place in male-dominated rap and a white-dominated feminist movement. These female performers speak to and for black women, often by talking back to black men; in their videos these rap artists may appropriate such male-defined spaces as the urban street and legitimate their presence in it. Similarly, Baldauf-Berdes presents an actual women's space, the Venetian *ospedali*, where women exercised uncommon control and excelled as bearers of a music-centered culture unique to Venice.

* * *

It is perhaps the hope of all editors that their collections not only will bring to light new work but also will encourage further explorations along the lines they have identified. We have no doubt that feminist and gender research in all areas of music scholarship is here to stay; we are likewise confident that this collection will become just one of many that maps new territory by questioning those maps already before us. In naming this volume we again invoke the name of Cecilia, and we reclaim her through the reexamination and re-visioning of our musical heritage cognizant of, yet unfettered by, the patriarchal restraint that bound Cecilia and her sisters for centuries.

NOTES

1. For an in-depth discussion of the cultural notions of genius and creativity, see Battersby, *Gender and Genius*.

2. Scott, Introduction to *Gender and the Politics of History*, 2.

3. Solie, "Sophie Drinker's History," explores Drinker's alternative to the "historiographic paradigm" in detail.

4. A large portion of Reich's *Women's Studies* is an annotated bibliography of research on women in music (with music defined largely as Western concert music) appearing between 1980 and 1987. A most worthwhile resource, it includes nonmusic as well as music reference sources, books and articles, discographies, special collections, and a list of theses and dissertations (1971–87) written on the subject.

5. Ericson's bibliography begins where the College Music Society's report left off, covering 1987 to 1992. Special features include citations to reviews of books when available, a list of papers read at conferences during the years covered, and a continuation of Reich's list of dissertations and theses on women in music. The collection excludes works about a single woman.

6. See McClary, "Beanstalk"; Rieger, " 'Dolce Semplice'?"; Tick, "Piano Girl"; Clément, *Opera*; and Carby's provocative essay " 'It Jus Be's Dat Way Sometime,' " which has been reprinted in a number of collections, most recently in *Feminisms*, edited by Warhol and Herndl.

7. Other recent publications in ethnomusicology focusing on women include Keeling, *Women in North American Indian Music*; and Herndon and Ziegler, *Music, Gender, and Culture*.The journal *World of Music* has also devoted an entire issue to women, entitled *Women in Music and Music Research*, also edited by Herndon and Ziegler.

8. A few examples of the many such anthologies include Carroll's *Liberating Women's History*; Showalter's *Speaking of Gender*; and Anzaldúa's *Making Face*. Individual authors have produced collected anthologies of their own work not unlike the anthologies already cited that also show the development of their feminist perspective. Examples include Smith-Rosenberg, *Disorderly*

Conduct; Heilbrun, *Hamlet's Mother;* and Wallace, *Invisibility Blues.* Mc-Clary's *Feminine Endings* follows this latter pattern as well.

9. While this collection has been taking shape several of the authors have started or completed monographs expanding on aspects of their feminist work presented here. Notably, Jane L. Baldauf-Berdes and Marcia J. Citron both have completed books: *Women Musicians of Venice* and *Gender and the Musical Canon,* respectively. Adrienne Fried Block and Susan C. Cook are currently working on full-length feminist biographical studies of Amy Beach and the social dancer Irene Castle, respectively.

10. Showalter, *Sister's Choice;* see especially the chapter entitled "Common Threads." Warhol and Herndl, the editors of *Feminisms,* have also invoked the imagery of quilting as an organizational strategy.

11. Kerber, "Separate Spheres," 10.

12. For a recent discussion of the particular way race confounds an easy definition of *woman's sphere,* see Higginbotham, "African-American Women's History."

REFERENCES

Ammer, Christine, ed. *Unsung: A History of Women in American Music.* Contributions in Women's Studies, no. 14. Westport, Conn.: Greenwood Press, 1980.

Anzaldúa, Gloria, ed. *Making Face, Making Soul/Haciendo Caras.* San Francisco: Aunt Lute, 1990.

AWC News. Washington, D.C.: American Women Composers, Inc., 1979–82. (Continued by *AWC News/Forum*)

AWC News/Forum. McLean, Va.: American Women Composers, Inc., 1983-present. (Continues *AWC News*)

Bailey, Walter B., and Nancy Gisbrecht Bailey. *Radie Britain: A Bio-Bibliography.* Bio-Bibliographies in Music, no. 25. Westport, Conn.: Greenwood Press, 1990.

Baldauf-Berdes, Jane L. *The Women Musicians of Venice: Musical Foundations, 1525–1855.* Oxford: Oxford University Press, 1993.

Battersby, Christine. *Gender and Genius: Towards a Feminist Aesthetics.* Bloomington: Indiana University Press, 1989.

Block, Adrienne Fried, and Carol Neuls-Bates, eds. *Women in American Music: A Bibliography of Music and Literature.* Westport, Conn.: Greenwood Press, 1979.

Bowers, Jane, and Judith Tick, eds. *Women Making Music: The Western Art Tradition, 1150–1950.* Urbana: University of Illinois Press, 1986.

Carby, Hazel. " 'It Jus Be's Dat Way Sometime': The Sexual Politics of Women's Blues." In *Unequal Sisters: A Multicultural Reader in United States Woman's History,* edited by Ellen Dubois and Vicky Ruiz. New York: Routledge, 1990.

Carroll, Berenice A., ed. *Liberating Women's History.* Urbana: University of Illinois Press, 1976.

12   Susan C. Cook and Judy S. Tsou

Citron, Marcia J. *Cécile Chaminade: A Bio-Bibliography.* Bio-Bibliographies in Music, no. 15. Westport, Conn.: Greenwood Press, 1988.
———. *Gender and the Musical Canon.* Cambridge: Cambridge University Press, 1993.
Clément, Catherine. *Opera, or the Undoing of Women.* Translated by Betsy Wing. Foreword by Susan McClary. Minneapolis: University of Minnesota Press, 1988.
Cohen, Aaron. *International Encyclopedia of Women Composers.* New York: Bowker, 1981.
———. *International Encyclopedia of Women Composers.* 2d ed. New York: Books and Music, 1987.
Drinker, Sophie. *Music and Women: The Story of Women in Their Relation to Music.* New York: Coward-McCann, 1948.
Ebel, Otto. *Women Composers: A Bibliographical Handbook of Woman's Work in Music.* Brooklyn: F. H. Chandler, 1902.
Elson, Arthur, and Everett Ellsworth Truette. *Woman's Work in Music.* Boston: L. C. Page, 1903.
Ericson, Margaret. *Women and Music: A Selective Bibliography on the Collective Subject of Women in Music.* Boston: G. K. Hall, forthcoming.
Green, Mildred Denby. *Black Women Composers: A Genesis.* Boston: Twayne, 1983.
Handy, D. Antoinette. *Black Women in American Bands and Orchestras.* Metuchen, N.J.: Scarecrow Press, 1981.
Hayes, Deborah. *Peggy Glanville-Hicks: A Bio-Bibliography.* Bio-Bibliographies in Music, no. 27. Westport, Conn.: Greenwood Press, 1990.
Heilbrun, Carolyn G. *Hamlet's Mother.* New York: Columbia University Press, 1990.
Herndon, Marcia, and Susanne Ziegler, eds. *Music, Gender, and Culture.* ICTM [International Council for Traditional Music] Study Group on Music and Gender. Intercultural Music Studies, no. 1. Wilhelmshaven, Germany: Florian Noetzel, 1990.
———. *Women in Music and Music Research.* Special issue of *The World of Music: Journal of the International Institute for Traditional Music* 33, no. 2 (1991).
Higginbotham, Evelyn Brooks. "African-American Women's History and the Metalanguage of Race." *Signs* 17 (Winter 1992): 251–74.
Hixon, Don L., and Don Hennessee. *Women in Music: A Biobibliography.* Metuchen, N.J.: Scarecrow Press, 1975.
ILWC Journal. Framingham, Mass.: International League of Women Composers, 1989– . (Continues *International League of Women Composers Newsletter.*)
International Congress on Women in Music Newsletter. Los Angeles: ICWM, 1983–89. (Discontinued. See also *Working Papers on Women in Music.*)
International League of Women Composers Newsletter. Arlington, Va.: ILWC, 1981–89. (Continued by *ILWC Journal.*)

Johnson, Rose-Marie. *Violin Music by Women Composers: A Bio-Bibliographical Guide*. Music Reference Collection, no. 22. Westport, Conn.: Greenwood Press, 1989.

Keeling, Richard, ed. *Women in North American Indian Music: Six Essays*. Society for Ethnomusicology Special Series, no. 6. Bloomington, Ind.: Society for Ethnomusicology, 1989.

Kerber, Linda. "Separate Spheres, Female Worlds, Woman's Place: The Rhetoric of Women's History." *Journal of American History* 75 (June 1988): 9–39.

Koskoff, Ellen, ed. *Women and Music in Cross-Cultural Perspective*. Contributions in Women's Studies, no. 79. Westport, Conn.: Greenwood Press, 1987; Urbana: University of Illinois Press, 1989.

McClary, Susan. *Feminine Endings: Music, Gender, and Sexuality*. Minneapolis: University of Minnesota Press, 1991.

———. "Getting down off the Beanstalk: The Presence of a Woman's Voice in Janika Vandervelde's *Genesis II*." In *Feminine Endings: Music, Gender, and Sexuality*. Minneapolis: University of Minnesota Press, 1991.

Meggett, Joan M. *Keyboard Music by Women Composers: A Catalog and Bibliography*. Westport, Conn.: Greenwood Press, 1981.

The Musical Woman: An International Perspective. Judith Lang Zaimont, editor-in-chief. 3 vols. to date. Westport, Conn.: Greenwood Press, 1983– .

Neuls-Bates, Carol, ed. *Women in Music: An Anthology of Source Readings from the Middle Ages to the Present*. New York: Harper and Row, 1982.

Pendle, Karin, ed. *Women and Music: A History*. Bloomington: Indiana University Press, 1991.

Placksin, Sally. *American Women in Jazz, 1900 to the Present: Their Words, Lives, and Music*. New York: Seaview Books, 1982.

Reich, Nancy B. *Clara Schumann: The Artist and the Woman*. Ithaca, N.Y.: Cornell University Press, 1985.

———, ed. *Women's Studies/Women's Status*. College Music Society Reports, no. 5. Boulder, Colo.: College Music Society, 1988.

Rieger, Eva. " 'Dolce Semplice'? On the Changing Role of Women in Music." In *Feminist Aesthetics*, edited by Gisela Ecker and translated by Harriet Anderson. Boston: Beacon Press, 1986.

Scott, Joan Wallach. *Gender and the Politics of History*. New York: Columbia University Press, 1988.

Showalter, Elaine. *Sister's Choice: Tradition and Change in American Women's Writing*. Oxford: Clarendon Press, 1991.

———, ed. *Speaking of Gender*. New York: Routledge, 1989.

Smith, Catherine Parsons, and Cynthia S. Richardson. *Mary Carr Moore, American Composer*. Women and Culture Series. Ann Arbor: University of Michigan Press, 1987.

Smith-Rosenberg, Carroll. *Disorderly Conduct: Visions of Gender in Victorian America*. New York: Alfred A. Knopf, 1985.

Solie, Ruth. "Sophie Drinker's History." In *Disciplining Music: Musicology and Its Canons,* edited by Katherine Bergeron and Philip V. Bohlman. Chicago: University of Chicago Press, 1992.

Tick, Judith. *American Women Composers before 1870.* Ann Arbor, Mich.: UMI Research Press, 1983.

—————. "Passed Away Is the Piano Girl: Changes in America's Musical Life, 1870–1900." In *Women Making Music: The Western Art Tradition, 1150–1950,* edited by Jane Bowers and Judith Tick. Urbana: University of Illinois Press, 1986.

Upton, George Putnam. *Women in Music.* 2d ed. Chicago: A. C. McClurg, 1886.

Wallace, Michele. *Invisibility Blues: From Pop to Theory.* Haymarket Series. London and New York: Verso, 1990.

Warhol, Robyn R., and Diane Price Herndl, eds. *Feminisms: An Anthology of Literary Theory and Criticism.* New Brunswick, N.J.: Rutgers University Press, 1991.

Women Composers Series. 23 vols. to date. New York: Da Capo Press, 1979– . (Performing editions or study scores of works by women composers of the past.)

Working Papers on Women in Music: The Journal of the International Congress on Women in Music. La Crescenta, Calif.: ICWM, 1985–

1

Feminist Approaches to Musicology

Marcia J. Citron

Feminist musicology is coming of age. The critical mass of feminist contributions that debuted at the 1988 annual meeting of the American Musicological Society, the discipline's major public forum, marked a turning point. Ideas aired in papers and panel sessions sparked a palpable feeling of excitement and fostered a sense of a vital research community.[1] Some believe the field has matured to the point that spadework exploration of overlooked women composers—so-called compensatory history, which has mostly proceeded via traditional (male-defined) epistemology and methodology—has yielded its monopoly to the possibilities offered by truly woman-centered or feminist strategies. Such strategies are in general more conceptual and more analytical from an intellectual point of view, and arguably more perceptive and telling in their potential for understanding women's musical contributions. They already boast a significant history in other disciplines. Although musicology is experiencing a remarkable proliferation of feminist work, it has made only modest gains compared with other fields, where feminism took root as early as the 1960s.

Several reasons account for the situation; they fall into two broad categories. The first encompasses structural and institutional characteristics of musicology as an intellectual discipline, as it has been practiced, that challenge and perhaps discourage feminist inquiry. I have discussed some of the issues elsewhere.[2] The second category concerns properties of music as an art form that render feminist categorization and analysis elusive, especially compared with other art forms. This elusiveness in no way spells impossibility. On the contrary, it seems to suggest a multiplicity of approaches, many involving assumptions, theories, and methodologies taken from other fields. These new modelings can infuse the traditional ways of conducting research into West-

ern art music, akin to what has been happening when feminist viewpoints are assumed in other fields.

   In this essay I explore two approaches that hold promise for feminist
musicology. The first approach, premised on the ability of Western art
music to reflect and construct social meanings and relationships, challenges the paradigm of autonomy that accompanied the rise of public
music and capitalism.[3] In particular I show how sonata form and the
sonata aesthetic, especially in the nineteenth century, encoded gendered structures that reflected and constructed relationships of gender
and power in Western society. The second approach describes how
reader-response theories might be utilized to underpin theories of gendered listening and thereby undermine the myth of universal response.
Each issue is broad and could easily fill an entire essay.[4] But even in
relatively abbreviated form they are suggestive, and it is hoped they
will lead to further feminist work.

   * * *

Aesthetic challenges confront feminist musicology: characteristics of
music that tend to inhibit the positing of woman-centered theories
and methodologies. Instrumental music creates the most obvious barrier in its seeming lack of tangible content, reality, and hence meaning.
This has become particularly evident as we have turned to feminist
colleagues in other disciplines and have attempted to apply their theories and strategies to music. We have also noted how they have generally ignored music, even in seemingly relevant studies.[5] Naturally,
the positivist emphasis in musicology is partly responsible. Not to be
discounted either is the mystique of music to the uninitiated: the arcane
notion of reliance on aural rather than visual or intellectual faculties.[6]
Add to this the ability to "hear" a score or play by ear, evoking awed
admiration, and the glass wall is erected.

   To repeat, however, it is the fundamental aesthetic attribute that
has proven the most daunting: music (textless) has no apparent content. How do we locate content, especially narrative content, in
sounds—mere acoustical phenomena? Do we locate content in the visual, the experiential—the phenomena of the notated page, the performance?[7] Do we fill in explicit content through a story line or a
succession of specific emotional states, much as the Romantics did?
Do we give up in exasperation and claim there is no content, while
still sensing that something is happening to us as we listen? Whatever
the particular strategy, we have to admit it is much easier to identify
and analyze content in other art forms: literature with its linguistic,

art with its visual signs. One can easily pick out images of women, stories of women, characters who are women and proceed to thematicism or symbolism to construct more complex analyses. Such easily accessible bases for feminist exploration make us envious. On the other hand, the very indefiniteness of instrumental music increases the potential for a greater number of interpretations. Early German Romantics, for instance, found this a major attraction. Perhaps, then, the perceived disadvantage is actually an advantage. In any case, we must dismantle the modernist impulse that implies music lacks content and meaning and ponder their interrelationship in new and varied ways. Although breaking the barrier of pure music means the destruction of a long-held ideology, it represents a crucial step for feminist musicology. It makes possible the construction of links between gender and meaning and hence affords new ways of conceptualizing women's relation to music.

Those of us who teach courses in women's music in Western society invariably encounter the question of whether a specifically woman's style in music exists. There is general agreement that women have emphasized certain genres more than others.[8] This, of course, begs the question of whether specific elements of musical language—harmony, melody, rhythm, texture—bear the identifying stamp of a female creator. Such gendered elements are not to be confused with another type of gendered element: musical language that connotes attributes linked with women, whether in pieces authored by a woman or a man. Both Eva Rieger and Susan McClary have brilliantly explored these elements from an ideological perspective in canonic works by men. McClary, for example, has analyzed the misogynistic semiotic associations of chromaticism in Bizet's *Carmen* and Tchaikowsky's Symphony no. 4. She has also explored gendered strategies in an instrumental work by the female composer Janika Vandervelde.[9] Identifying vocabulary or syntax specifically attributable to a female rather than a male composer is a formidable challenge. Elsewhere I have suggested that while we might isolate certain tendencies that could be part of a female aesthetic, I have found no specific language, style, or dynamic that every woman utilizes. Such tendencies depend on variables of culture and individual disposition and could also be utilized by men. Moreover, women are not raised in "pure" female culture and will tend to express, at least in part, aspects of masculine culture that they have internalized.[10]

The sonata aesthetic has functioned as a major creative ethos in Western music for over two hundred years. Compositions deemed the highest and the most revealing of skill and imagination, especially the symphony, have been based on the sonata aesthetic and in turn have became the concrete embodiments of that aesthetic. We are of course talking about textless instrumental music; texted music has its own hierarchies, with opera at the top. I suggest in the following discussion that the sonata aesthetic, of which sonata form is an important part, involves gendered discourse and rhetoric to a significant degree. Furthermore, these gendered aspects may have played a major role in the tendency of many women composers to eschew the sonata aesthetic in favor of other creative configurations.

In much historical work on women composers, including my own, considerable space has been devoted to the stories of women's lack of access to the professional (patriarchal) world of music. This includes educational, performing, conducting, organizational, and critical exclusion, as well as more invisible barriers. Such accounts have been absolutely necessary to reveal the heightened, unacknowledged, and often insurmountable difficulties women have faced in acquiring what was a matter of course for men. These explorations generally rest on a model of oppression and implicitly situate male culture as the norm and female culture as the Other in relation to that prevailing culture. Many feminists, however, object to that model because it perpetuates the Freudian thesis of woman as lack and simultaneously views her activities as marginal and subsidiary. This is a compelling argument and one to which I subscribe. Nonetheless, we have to exercise care lest we discard vital historical evidence in our newfound enthusiasm for theory. Ignoring received paradigms, even if rejected in principle as representative of male-centered society, can lessen our effectiveness in bringing about meaningful change.

In many respects the sonata aesthetic stands as a symbol and product of Western patriarchal values. Instead of reinforcing the notion that women avoided symphonies, sonatas, and chamber music because of some essentialist lack of skill or imagination, I will show how the conventions and subtext of the sonata aesthetic have privileged the masculine and thus held lesser meaning for women. This model enunciates difference, not oppression. Nonetheless, history has judged women composers as lesser partly because they eschewed the sonata style. We should also remember that various social circumstances prevented women from obtaining the education and professional access necessary to succeed in the many structures enmeshed in the aesthetic.[11]

The term *sonata aesthetic* includes sonata form, the sonata cycle as a multimovement form type, and the genres that deploy these plans, namely symphony, chamber music, solo sonata, and to a lesser extent concerto. It also entails their attendant rhetoric, ideology, and symbolism, a powerful cultural force. "The most prestigious of musical forms" is how Charles Rosen has characterized sonata form, which he defines broadly.[12] For the aspiring composer, the sonata style was the sine qua non of success. Beethoven, according to Rosen, "raised the prestige of the sonata form to an eminence that made it the major challenge to every composer for more than a century to come." For those successive composers, "the proof of greatness was the sonata. Only through the sonata, it seemed, could the highest musical ambitions be realized. . . . Pure music in its highest state was sonata."[13] Such statements betray the reverence accorded the aesthetic: at once an ideal, a goal, a test, a barometer of skill and success. It became an icon, a monument, a symbol of society itself. Its privileged musical status mirrored privileged social groups and thus found greater resonance in the male composer than in the female composer.

Sonata form lies at the core of the sonata aesthetic. Given musicology's traditional emphasis on formalist concerns, we have come to view sonata form, like all form types, as a neutral, abstract plan. As a neutral scheme, sonata form should be free of gendered attributes or symbols. This is certainly how it was viewed in the last modernist phase of musicology, when scholars attempted, for example, to discredit the validity of the notion of masculine and feminine themes, a concept apparently first articulated by A. B. Marx, in 1845.[14] In 1971, for instance, Charles Rosen made a valiant but unsuccessful effort at dismissal in his landmark study *The Classical Style*. Rather than state categorically that no correlation existed between bold gestures and masculinity and between lyricism and femininity, Rosen observed that he had found masculine and feminine themes in areas in the movement where they are not supposed to be, not to mention hermaphrodite themes that mix elements of both sexes.[15] He apparently did not realize that by continuing to link the designated traits with gender labels, he actually confirmed, rather than refuted, the traditional terms.

These historical gender associations reveal merely the tip of the iceberg; sonata form holds deeper, more fundamental gender associations. These ties express and privilege the masculine and consequently, like the larger aesthetic, have tended to hold less meaning as a potential creative outlet for women. The rhetoric of sonata form centers on masculine metaphors, notably power, hegemony, opposition, and competition. The opposition metaphor occurs frequently. Rosen, for example, describes classical (i.e., sonata) form "as the symmetrical resolution of opposing forces" and offers this extended summary: "The exposition of a sonata form presents the thematic material and articulates the movement from tonic to dominant in various ways so that it takes on the character of a polarization or opposition. The essential character of this opposition may be defined as a large-scale dissonance."[16]

He characterizes the difference between sonata form and ordinary ternary form (ABA) as the former's progression of opposition-intensification-resolution, presumably referring respectively to the exposition, development, and recapitulation. The opposition entails the contrasting themes of the first and second groups, as well as the contrasting tonalities of tonic and dominant.[17] Donald Francis Tovey, for example, cloaked the opposition in martial imagery in his statement that some J. C. Bach transitions have been "wittily described as 'presenting arms' to the new key." Of more recent vintage is James Webster's description of the onset of the recapitulation as "a relaxation of tension or as a triumph over difficulties."[18] In the 1950s Ernst Meyer offered a socialist interpretation that constructed links with aggressive tendencies in nineteenth-century bourgeois society: "Through the dialectical contrasting of two opposing themes (often a forward-storming and a restrained) there originates an aggressive, dramatic element, which corresponds to the love of combat [Kampfesfreudigkeit] of the progressive currents of the era."[19]

A hierarchic scheme is fleshed out in the innocuous terms *principal theme* and *subsidiary theme*. They do not indicate opposition, which in the abstract implies equality of participants, but instead suggest domination of one over the other. The nature of that domination is uncertain, however. We can imagine such pairs as more important–less important, better quality–lesser quality, stronger-weaker, and no doubt others; one correspondence involves the terms *masculine* and *feminine*. In the late eighteenth century the structure of sonata form was expressed mainly in terms of dual tonal areas, tonic and dominant. In the early nineteenth century, however, theorists began to define the form more in terms of themes than tonality, and in compositional treatises starting with Marx they began to affix gendered labels to the themes. Here is Marx's introduction of gender in 1845: "The second theme . . . serves as contrast to the first, energetic statement, though dependent on and determined by it. It is of a more tender nature, flexibly rather than emphatically constructed—in a way, the feminine as opposed to the preceding masculine."[20] Subsequent definitions— including appearances in the works of Hugo Riemann and Vincent D'Indy around 1900 and in *Die Musik in Geschichte und Gegenwart* as late as the 1950s—continued the core ideas of masculine strength and feminine tenderness and dependence.[21] The distinguishing feature seemed to be the lyricism of the feminine theme topos, presumably expressive of gentleness in women. Other metaphors could have been applied, or eschewed in favor of the existent terms *first and second themes* or *principal and subsidiary.*

The use of gendered metaphor shows how essentialist notions of male and female permeated society, at least masculine society, and how they could be utilized in the discourse of high culture. Perhaps this functioned as a means of inscribing the Romantic ideal of *das Ewigweibliche*—the eternal feminine—into the realm of supposedly abstract music. This idealization threw into greater relief the masculineness of the opening theme and thereby rendered it more important. The opening theme not only reinforced the masculinity of its male creator but also affirmed the presence of the male composer as the main compositional subject of the movement: subject as individuated person and subject as musical theme.[22] In contrast, the feminine theme conveyed metaphorically two negative portrayals of woman: woman as lack and woman as Other. Viewed patriarchally, the lyrical feminine theme lacked the completeness found in the powerful gestures of the masculine theme and thus mirrored a basic Freudian distinction between the sexes. The analysis seems particularly apt, since to many nineteenth-century and modern critics the adoption of lyricism as a thematic component in sonata form helped spell its doom. At the least it lessened its effectiveness. Another salvo at woman as scapegoat?

The metaphor of woman as Other emerges when we consider that not only does lyricism function as an introduced element of disruption to the more energetic opening but it arrives with another striking feature of disruption: a new key center. The imposition of a new tonality brings tension, even if in lyrical guise, and needs to be tamed, resolved, brought back to the original key, representative of the masculine. Thus the element of Otherness is neutralized by the prevailing masculine order. Seen this way, the opposition described above is in no way a contest between equals but a clear hierarchic relationship, with the feminine functioning as the subsidiary. How ironic that the original key of the feminine theme should be called the dominant, for in the end it is the tonic that dominates.

Gendered themes also exhibit links with social structures. One link involves the notion that the gendered thematic dichotomy reflected the gendered dichotomy between the public and private spheres, a split largely resulting from realignments in the nature and locus of production brought on by increasing industrialization. As I have argued elsewhere, however, the public-private duality is an artificial concept, whose power, nonetheless, has generally worked to the detriment of women.[23] The second hypothesis is fairly obvious: the subsidiary, feminine theme symbolized women's subordination in society, while the principal, masculine theme reflected male hegemony.[24] Overall, sonata form met the need of the newly emergent bourgeois society to validate itself and maintain social control over women. Sonata form became a metaphor for this gendered struggle, and once entrenched it acted to reinforce and reconstruct the gendered ideology in Western society at large.[25] In addition, the persuasiveness and power of gendered codes in sonata form suggest the distinct possibility of gendered systems inscribed in other structures of Western art music, particularly those that seem gender-neutral.

Rosen mentioned "pure music," or what others have termed "absolute music," music without any stated narrative or function and hence supposedly devoid of content. In the twentieth century we have tended to follow our Romantic ancestors and elevate the concept to what Susan McClary has dubbed the "Master Narrative."[26] That is, absolute music has taken on an aura of primal myth, of sanctity, of privilege, of control; it is generally accepted without question. Women composers, however, have evinced considerably less interest in absolute music. Narrative genres such as song and character piece have held a greater attraction, probably because they have provided a more direct means of female self-expression.[27] Women in the nineteenth century, increasingly relegated to the home as a result of the economic and social forces of industrialization, had few avenues for direct communication in the public sphere. Perhaps they believed abstract music too impersonal, too disembodied, or too rife with multiple meanings for the kind of directness and immediacy they desired. Women seemed to crave the potential for their own involvement or literal embodiment in the process of that communication, in other words, the performance. In addition, they may have felt alienated by masculine emphases on the metaphysical and on the transcendent ego in absolute music.

Webster's Ninth New Collegiate Dictionary defines metaphysical as "of or relating to the transcendent or to a reality beyond what is perceptible to the senses." This entails an infinite, unbounded realm of time and space. Transcendent implies not only going beyond but also moving toward the ultimate, toward the perfect, toward God, the embodiment of transcendence and perfection. God the creator is the model for man the creator, who is a likeness of God. As exclusive bearer of God's image, only man is validated as a creator, not woman. This is especially so when the type of music is deemed absolute. Metaphorically, therefore, men occupy center stage in the theater of absolute music.[28] Another link between absolute music and God is conveyed through the medium of the concert hall. Carl Dahlhaus offers the intriguing notion that concert halls of the nineteenth century, devoted largely to absolute music, especially symphonies, functioned as new temples of art.[29] Secular music was replacing sacred music, but symbolically the religious continued in these architectural monuments sanctifying the art of music. Dahlhaus's emphasis on a religious base in Western music, of which absolute music is a major component, implies another reason why women creators might shy away from absolute music: women had little power in shaping and operating religious institutions and only a limited role in them as creators.[30]

A central component of the metaphysical concerns the transcendence of the composer as subject. This situates attention on the ego, on a very strong, sometimes exaggerated notion of self, and it formed a basis for the influential cult of genius that Beethoven and his worshipers perpetuated. The mythology elevated the individuated composer above everyday concerns and tangible reality. On this view the composer's ego intruded on the art work.[31] Women composers, however, seldom injected a strong sense of ego into the art work. Many, in fact, had difficulty placing themselves in positive juxtaposition with their compositions, not to mention dominating it with an individuated self.[32] I believe women composers viewed themselves more in the tradition of craftspeople, an attitude characteristic of both sexes prior to the nineteenth century.[33] This resulted in a greater intersubjective space between the creator's ego and the created; much less of the ego was invested in the composition. With ego transcendence an important part of the symbolism of absolute music, however, women apparently preferred to gravitate toward genres free of this intrusion.

Absolute music inscribes a male psychological profile of growth that stresses quest and transcendence.[34] The socialization process encourages separateness, exploration, and adventure, which result in personal change. The quest, whose early stages resemble rites of passage, is an important component. It includes the search for knowledge, self-knowledge, and self-realization—basically an amalgam of the three great male literary themes of Faust, Don Quixote, and Don Juan. The quest also informs much vocal music—another way of saying that literature abounds in the quest theme.[35] Transcendence caps male psychological growth as the ego attains maximum separateness and goes beyond the here and now. The developmental road traversing quest and transcendence has been described as a spiritual journey, a notion applied to male creative maturation but seldom if ever ascribed to a woman.

In addition to its personal association, spiritual journey can pertain to a piece of music. For example, we commonly speak of Beethoven's spiritual journey over the span of his career or over the span of a given symphony, such as the fifth or the ninth. The conceptual overlap helps blur the divisions between the person and the art work. One interesting historical question is how much the male journey actually reflected personal psychological processes and how much it began to adopt a life of its own as an independent convention implanted in pieces of music. Perhaps in Beethoven's time the musical journey directly reflected a male psychological profile. Afterwards the journey often may have been an abstract version of an established convention. Whether original or derivative, the crucial point is that absolute music, particularly the symphony, was grounded in a gendered process reflective of one sex and alien to the other.

If the spiritual journey does not characterize a female psychological process, then what might a female profile look like?[36] While this question raises the dangers of essentializing women and obscuring individual differences, we could say that white Western women of the middle and upper classes over the past two hundred years have generally been socialized to develop close to home, to establish inclusive rather than exclusive bonds ("we" rather than "I"), and to acquire knowledge and self-knowledge through interaction with others and for the benefit of the larger group. Personal growth is important but has usually occurred in the context of interconnected systems within a tangible reality of finite time and space. Women's prescribed role as primary nurturer and caretaker of the family and other socially conceived conventions of femininity have been critical in focusing women's attention on the here and now rather than on the ambiguous beyond.[37] The metaphysical and transcendent characteristics of absolute music, therefore, might seem alien and alienating. We should not be surprised that women have evinced lesser interest than men in interacting with its ideology. Nonetheless, most women composers, performers, and listeners are also socialized in mainstream society and as a result experience ambivalence and conflict. Perhaps a psychology of contradiction aptly characterizes a crucial aspect of women's relationship with absolute music.

* * *

Music is often dubbed the universal communicator by virtue of the accessibility of sound and its ability to go beyond the kinds of barriers erected by language. The aesthetic catholicity tends to obliterate differences in transmission and reception and consequently diminishes the viability of sexual difference as a critical constitutive factor. Yet as we have seen in the sonata aesthetic, reputedly abstract musical structures encode aspects of cultural difference. Response theory, which has dramatically expanded conceptualizations of the dynamics of agency and the production of meaning in literature, can suggest ways of highlighting the importance of gender differentiation in the listening process. Effectively undermining universality of response, such an emphasis has potential in constructing feminist theories of perception.

Reader-response criticism embraces great diversity. Theories range from the strict author intentionality espoused by E. D. Hirsch, to the playful, creative role ascribed to the reader by Roland Barthes, to the primacy of phenomenological experience endorsed by Wolfgang Iser. Some theories, especially the ideas of Hans-Robert Jauss and his teacher Hans-Georg Gadamer, pay attention to historical context and its impact on the attitudes and expectations a respondent brings to a work of art. Yet major theorists have generally ignored social specificity, especially variables of class, race, gender, sexuality, and nationality. They either have been vague on the makeup of their respondent(s) or have posited some kind of idealized reader, for instance, an implied reader or an inscribed reader. In practice, these utopian constructs have probably represented the culturally empowered group of the well-educated, white, Euro-American male. Because women and other muted cultural groups tend to disappear under such universalizing views of response, it is crucial to affirm and articulate the terms of sociohistorical specificity in theories of response. Instead of limiting interpretive possibilities, specificity yields multiplicity, multiplicity in the number of theoretical models and in the kinds of responses that follow those models.

In addition to these factors, specificity entails historical grounding and a sense of the position and involvement of the individual in relation to a group or groups. This turns out to be a complex dynamic but one that calls for definition. In music, for instance, it is important to separate listening on the level of the individual from listening on the level of the audience or general public and then to relate the two. But which individual, in what temporal relationship with the composer and the performance (it could, after all, be a recording), and in what performing location with what semiotic associations? For women we must draw distinctions between a woman as a specific individual and women in general and realize that one flirts with essentialism and its potentially negative connotations when discussing the latter.[38] Women display a broad spectrum of cultural characteristics, and specificity plays as great a defining role here as it does in dealing with humankind in general. On the other hand, multiplicity comes into play through

an individual's varied response patterns to different sections of a work
and from one listening to another of a given piece. For a specific female
respondent, multiplicity also exists as a result of the conflicts and
contradictions between her sense of herself as a woman and her con-
ditioning in male-dominated society. Strategies of resistance have often
resulted.[39]

Phenomenological theories of literary response offer attractive possibilities for music. In the theories of Iser, for instance, the very experience of reading occupies primacy of position in the production of
meaning. As a temporal process that includes filling in gaps and shifting
viewpoints, it bears considerable resemblance to music. Barthes,
steeped in a very different intellectual tradition, also emphasizes performance in his view of reading as a dynamic process in which the
reader, the primary element, interacts playfully with the text: manipulating, rearranging, chopping. According to Barthes, these activities
render the respondent a creator, and he considers the respondent more
important in that regard than the author.[40] The theory opens up several
possibilities for reconceptualizing the nature and function of artistic
creativity and the cultural signs associated with the figure of the composer. In musicology this could imply a deemphasis of the traditional
focus on the figure of the composer and could result in greater cog-
nizance of the social context. Such cultural broadening enormously
benefits the exploration of women composers and their music.[41]

Although seemingly last in a process starting with creation, response
displays temporal multiplicity. It precedes creativity in the sense of
constructing the social and aesthetic conditions in which a work will
be written and thereby influencing the way the work is fashioned.
Furthermore, the conditions of response are inscribed in the work and
usually include the type(s) of intended respondents as well as intended
locale for performance. For example, I have shown elsewhere how
intended audience and place of performance may have influenced the
deployment of a particular strategy of gendered codes in Cécile Chaminade's Piano Sonata.[42] In music, response also occurs by way of the
performers, in the midst of the transmission process. While they are
responding to a complex web of cultural and aesthetic codes, they are
simultaneously creating cultural and aesthetic meanings in their playing. Compared with literary response, therefore, music provides an
additional locus of response/creativity and thus complicates the three-
fold communicative model of author-work-respondent underlying
many theories of literary response.

Patrocinio Schweickart has posited an intriguing feminist theory of
response that asserts that for a woman a sense of full meaning as a

respondent is possible only when she is responding to a work authored by a woman.[43] Without the possibility of forging ties of identification with another woman—in other words, the author—a female respondent experiences feelings of alienation and conflict;[44] Schweickart's argument implies that in music the gender of the performers would also play a role. Overall her theories raise a host of questions, including potential noncongruences resulting from a woman composer of another cultural context, the strategies a woman listener might use in listening to mostly male repertories, and whether music by a woman is always expressing femaleness.They assume that separate female traditions can and do exist and that they are desirable. Whatever the potential difficulties, however, Schweickart's theories would probably promote affiliation and identification among women and suggest some fundamental commonalities that strengthen community.[45]

Another approach to response that has elicited feminist discussion concerns the centrality of a woman's experience as a basis for response. Jonathan Culler, building on the work of Peggy Kamuf and Elaine Showalter among others, proposes in his well-known "Reading as a Woman" that a meaningful theory of response for women would be based on hypothesized female experience—that is, a woman responding as a derivative, theorized woman rather than as herself on behalf of her own experiences. Although Culler perceptively recognizes that the category of woman cannot be pure because of socialization in masculine culture, several feminists take exception to this construct because it undermines the reality and agency of actual women. For some it smacks of patriarchal tokenism packaged in goodwill.[46] Whatever one's opinion of Culler's ideas, however, the larger issue remains of conceptualizing the role of experience in female response, including music response. Experience, of course, can be defined much more broadly than mere empirical events and can encompass, for example, psychological and sexual factors. Embedded in and reflective of the social fabric, these factors demonstrate how consumption and production—response and creation—operate as two vantage points from which to deal with the same phenomena. Both are vital if we are to understand the complexities of women's involvement in Western art music.

* * *

What seems clear in light of the issues raised in this essay is that despite disciplinary and aesthetic challenges, several viable avenues lie ahead for meaningful feminist musicological work. Psychoanalysis, for example, may prove extremely important, although one major hurdle concerns its traditional disregard for historical grounding. That very property, however, allows it the freedom to structure imaginative theories that historians (including musicologists) could use yet might not posit themselves because of certain paradigms in their own field. Further work is needed on the sonata aesthetic in toto and on its individual components. I did not have space, for example, to discuss Hegelian theories or explore pieces by women that fall within the sonata aesthetic. Listener-response theory holds great potential for reconceptualizing the nature, significance, and diversity of female musical response.

Anyone writing feminist musicological work must be prepared to take a stand, to go out on a limb as it were—a serious challenge given the objectivist traditions of the discipline. The rewards, however, are many, including intellectual growth and heightened sensitivity to nontraditional viewpoints. In this regard ethnomusicology has much to teach us. We can only look forward to future work.

NOTES

1. See the summary report by Solie and Tomlinson, "Women's Studies." In June 1991 the first major conference devoted to feminist theory and music took place at the University of Minnesota; other important gatherings that summer occurred in Utrecht (Seventh International Congress on Women and Music) and London (Gender and Music Conference). See Cash, "Conference Report," on the Minneapolis conference; and Citron, "Conference Report," on the Utrecht and London conferences.

2. See Citron, "Gender, Professionalism, and the Musical Canon," especially 114–17, where I underscore the intellectual insularity of graduate musicology education and the absence of feminism as a distinct area of specialization in the field. These circumstances derive partly from roots in positivism and elitism that embrace objectivity, while feminism engages the personal and the political, emphasizing subjectivity. As time passes, I sense that graduate education is gradually incorporating theory and methodology from other fields, necessary tools for feminist inquiry. Furthermore, the proliferation of papers devoted to gender since I wrote the essay in 1988 hints at the possibility that feminist musicology might be recognized as a distinct area of specialization. It will probably be a while before this occurs, however, because disciplinary categories change slowly and with considerable resistance. Yet substantial interest exists in feminist musicology, and not merely within its circle of practitioners. Although mainstream journals and grant agencies are only beginning to support feminist work, music-book publishers' great interest in

feminist topics implies pent-up demand in the musicological population, mostly among women.

3. For more on this relationship, see Citron, *Gender and the Musical Canon*, especially chap. 1. Susan McClary has written extensively on social referentiality in music, especially in her essay "The Blasphemy of Talking Politics."

4. I offer a more detailed analysis of sonata form and the sonata aesthetic in *Gender and the Musical Canon*, chap. 4, including a reading of how the gendered codes of sonata form are configured in the first movement of Cécile Chaminade's Piano Sonata, op. 21. Chap. 5 treats issues of response.

5. Wolff, "Autonomous Art," 8–9, also discerned this trend.

6. One aspect of poststructuralism is the movement away from exclusive reliance on the visual as the medium for obtaining knowledge. The aural, for example, is gaining a foothold in some theoretical work, as philosopher Karey Harrison pointed out in her paper "Reason Embodied." See also Mowitt, "Sound of Music."

7. The visual plays a major epistemological role when musical works are treated as texts. See Kerman, "Canonic Variations," 107–25; and Citron, *Gender and the Musical Canon*, chap. 1. On the centrality of the performance, see Goehr, "Being True to the Work." The phenomenologist Wolfgang Iser considers the experience of perceiving central to his theories of response; see the discussion later in this essay.

8. One barometer of the widespread interest in the notion of a specifically woman's style is the notice inserted in the June 1989 issue of the College Music Society's *Bulletin* by the editors of *The Musical Woman*, soliciting opinions from readers on the matter. See also Citron, *Gender and the Musical Canon*, chap. 4; and the opinions of several contemporary female composers in "In Response."

9. See Rieger, *Frau, Musik und Männerherrschaft*, especially "Sexistische Strukturen in der Musik," 129–50; and McClary, "Sexual Politics," *Georges Bizet*, and "Beanstalk." See also Kallberg, "Harmony of the Tea Table." My thanks to Susan McClary and Jeffrey Kallberg for sending manuscript versions of their essays.

10. For a fuller discussion and additional bibliography, see Citron, *Gender and the Musical Canon*, chap. 4. See also Rieger, " 'Ich recycle Töne' "; and Cox, "Recovering *Jouissance*."

11. See Citron, "Gender, Professionalism, and the Musical Canon." The sonata aesthetic is more specific to Austro-Germanic culture and its attempts to exert and maintain musical hegemony in Europe.

12. Rosen, *Sonata Forms*, 1.

13. Ibid., 284, 293.

14. Marx, *Lehre*, part 3, 273.

15. Rosen, *Sonata Forms*, 81.

16. The shorter excerpt is from Rosen, *Classical Style*, 83, and the longer is from Rosen, *Sonata Forms*, 222.

17. Rosen, *Sonata Forms*, 17.

18. Tovey, *Encyclopaedia Britannica*, s.v. "sonata forms," 20:978; Webster, *The New Grove Dictionary of Music and Musicians*, s.v. "sonata form," 17:498.

19. Quoted in Rieger, *Frau, Musik und Männerherrschaft*, 141. Meyer's use of *dialectical* obviously refers to Hegel. Unfortunately, lack of space precludes discussion here of Hegelian dialectics and sonata form.

20. Translation in Bloom, "Communication," 161–62. Bloom actually translated the fifth edition (1879), but the wording of the passage in question is identical.

21. Riemann, *Katechismus*, 128; D'Indy, *Cours de composition*, 2:262; Müller-Blattau, *Die Musik in Geschichte und Gegenwart*, s.v. "Form," 4:col. 549. Subsequent editions of Marx and Riemann also contain the gendered description.

22. See Rieger, *Frau, Musik und Männerherrschaft*, 141.

23. See Citron, *Gender and the Musical Canon*, chap. 3.

24. Rieger, *Frau, Musik und Männerherrschaft*, 3.

25. Evolution, in the distorted form of biological determinism, was used in a similar way to validate the white European male of the middle to upper classes; see Gould, *Mismeasure of Man*.

26. See McClary, "Sexual Politics."

27. Kallberg, "Harmony of the Tea Table," for example, posits a feminine topos as a basic feature of the nocturne.

28. For more on absolute music and women, see Rieger, *Frau, Musik und Männerherrschaft*, 147–48.

29. Dahlhaus, *Nineteenth-Century Music*, 44.

30. Perhaps their only ecclesiastical creative power resided in the convents, as the significant accomplishments of Hildegard of Bingen, Isabella Leonarda, and other nuns attest. See, for example, Yardley, " 'Ful weel' "; and Bowers, "Women Composers in Italy."

31. Rose Subotnik, "On Grounding Chopin," 117, citing Theodor Adorno, notes the paradox of the impurity created by this personal intrusion within absolute music.

32. See, for instance, the disparaging self-images of Fanny Hensel and Clara Schumann in, respectively, Citron, *Letters of Fanny Hensel*; and Reich, *Clara Schumann*. Similarly, many nineteenth-century women writers, including Emily Dickinson and Christina Rossetti, doubted their artistic self-worth; see Gilbert and Gubar, *Norton Anthology*, 185.

33. Edith Borroff convincingly proposed this notion in a conversation we had a few years ago.

34. I am presenting generalized psychological profiles, drawn from generally accepted psychological theory. See, for instance, Gilligan, *In a Different Voice*.

35. For example, Goethe's influential *Wilhelm Meister* pair, whose poems were set by many Romantics, embodies the quest ritual.

36. See, for instance, two classic feminist tracts of psychological development: Gilligan, *In a Different Voice;* and Chodorow, *Reproduction of Mothering.*

37. In contrast to this profile, Meredith Monk's opera *Atlas,* premiered in Houston in February 1991, focuses on a woman's quest that challenges boundaries beyond the here and now, thereby challenging traditional patterns of female socialization in Western society.

38. Essentialism also lurks when *woman* is used as a transcendent signifier, without social qualification.

39. See, for instance, Gilbert and Gubar, *Madwoman in the Attic;* and Fetterley, *Resisting Reader.* Stout, *Strategies of Reticence,* has hypothesized that many women writers deployed silence as a conscious strategy of resistance.

40. Barthes, "Death of the Author," 142–48. See also Barthes, "From Work to Text," 73–82, for his distinctions between a work, which is the raw product emanating from the author, and a text, the semiotically rich entity constructed by the reader.

41. See Foucault, "What Is an Author?" 141–60. See also Wolff, *Social Production of Art,* 117–36, for a fine discussion of the decentered author; and Citron, *Gender and the Musical Canon,* chap. 3.

42. Citron, *Gender and the Musical Canon,* chap. 4.

43. Schweickart, "Reading Ourselves," 31–62.

44. Female creative traditions are also critical for a woman creator; see Citron, *Gender and the Musical Canon,* chap. 2. Georges Poulet has posited intimate relationship as a fundamental link between author and reader in literary response; see the Introduction of Tompkins, *Reader-Response Criticism,* xiv.

45. Lipking, "Aristotle's Sister," speaks of the importance of structures of affiliation among women.

46. Culler, "Reading as a Woman." Critiques emanated from Modleski, "Power of Interpretation," 121–38; Scholes, "Reading like a Man," 204–18; and Fuss, "Reading like a Feminist," 77–92.

REFERENCES

Barthes, Roland. "Death of the Author." In *Image, Music, Text,* translated by Stephen Heath. New York: Noonday Press, 1977.

——. "From Work to Text." In *Textual Strategies: Perspectives in Post-Structuralist Criticism,* edited by Josué Harari. Ithaca, N.Y.: Cornell University Press, 1979.

Bloom, Peter. "Communication." *Journal of the American Musicological Society* 27 (Spring 1974): 161–62.

Bowers, Jane. "The Emergence of Women Composers in Italy, 1566–1700." In *Women Making Music: The Western Art Tradition, 1150–1950,* edited by Jane Bowers and Judith Tick. Urbana: University of Illinois Press, 1986.

Cash, Alice. "Conference Report: Feminist Theory and Music: Toward a Common Language." *Journal of Musicology* 9 (Fall 1991): 521–32.

Chodorow, Nancy. *The Reproduction of Mothering: Psychoanalysis and the Sociology of Gender.* Berkeley: University of California, 1978.

Citron, Marcia J. "Conference Report: Beyond Biography: Seventh International Congress on Women in Music, and Music and Gender Conference." *Journal of Musicology* 9 (Fall 1991): 533–43.

———. *Gender and the Musical Canon.* Cambridge: Cambridge University Press, 1993.

———. "Gender, Professionalism, and the Musical Canon." *Journal of Musicology* 8 (Winter 1990): 102–17.

———, ed. *Letters of Fanny Hensel to Felix Mendelssohn.* New York: Pendragon Press, 1987.

Cox, Renée. "Recovering *Jouissance:* An Introduction to Feminist Musical Aesthetics." In *Women and Music: A History,* edited by Karin Pendle. Bloomington: Indiana University Press, 1991.

Culler, Jonathan. "Reading as a Woman." In *On Deconstruction: Theory and Criticism after Structuralism.* Ithaca, N.Y.: Cornell University Press, 1982.

Dahlhaus, Carl. *Nineteenth-Century Music.* Translated by J. Bradford Robinson. Berkeley: University of California Press, 1989.

D'Indy, Vincent. *Cours de composition musicale.* 2 vols. Paris: Durand et Cie, 1902–9.

Fetterley, Judith. *The Resisting Reader: Feminist Approaches to American Fiction.* Bloomington: Indiana University Press, 1978.

Foucault, Michel. "What Is an Author?" In *Textual Strategies: Perspectives in Post-Structuralist Criticism,* edited by Josué Harari. Ithaca, N.Y.: Cornell University Press, 1979.

Fuss, Diana. "Reading like a Feminist." *Differences* 1 (Summer 1989): 77–92.

Gilbert, Sandra, and Susan Gubar. *The Madwoman in the Attic: The Woman Writer and the Nineteenth-Century Imagination.* New Haven, Conn.: Yale University Press, 1979.

———. *The Norton Anthology of Literature by Women.* New York: W. W. Norton, 1985.

Gilligan, Carol. *In a Different Voice: Psychological Theory and Women's Development.* Cambridge, Mass.: Harvard University Press, 1982.

Goehr, Lydia. "Being True to the Work." *Journal of Aesthetics and Art Criticism* 47 (Winter 1989): 55–67.

Gould, Stephen J. *The Mismeasure of Man.* New York: W. W. Norton, 1981.

Harrison, Karey. "Reason Embodied." Paper presented at Rice University, April 1989.

"In Response." *Perspectives of New Music* 20 (1981–82): 288–329.

Kallberg, Jeffrey. "The Harmony of the Tea Table: Gender and Ideology in the Piano Nocturne." *Representations* 39 (Summer 1992): 102–33.

Kerman, Joseph. "A Few Canonic Variations." *Critical Inquiry* 10 (September 1983): 107–25.

Lipking, Lawrence. "Aristotle's Sister: A Poetics of Abandonment." *Critical Inquiry* 10 (September 1983): 61–81.

McClary, Susan. "The Blasphemy of Talking Politics during Bach Year." In *Music and Society: The Politics of Composition, Performance, and Reception*, edited by Richard Leppert and Susan McClary. Cambridge: Cambridge University Press, 1987.

———. *Georges Bizet: Carmen*. Cambridge: Cambridge University Press, 1992.

———. "Getting down off the Beanstalk: The Presence of a Woman's Voice in Janika Vandervelde's *Genesis II*." In *Feminine Endings: Music, Gender, and Sexuality*. Minneapolis: University of Minnesota Press, 1991.

———. "Sexual Politics in Classical Music." In *Feminine Endings: Music, Gender, and Sexuality*. Minneapolis: University of Minnesota Press, 1991.

Marx, A. B. *Die Lehre von der musikalischen Komposition*. Leipzig: Breitkopf und Härtel, 1845.

Modleski, Tania. "Feminism and the Power of Interpretation: Some Critical Readings." In *Feminist Studies/Critical Studies*, edited by Teresa de Lauretis. Bloomington: Indiana University Press, 1986.

Mowitt, John. "The Sound of Music in the Era of Its Electronic Reproducibility." In *Music and Society: The Politics of Composition, Performance, and Reception*, edited by Richard Leppert and Susan McClary. Cambridge: Cambridge University Press, 1987.

Müller-Blattau, Joseph. *Die Musik in Geschichte und Gegenwart*, s.v. "Form." 17 vols. Edited by Friedrich Blume. Kassel: Bärenreiter, 1949–79.

Reich, Nancy. *Clara Schumann: The Artist and the Woman*. Ithaca, N.Y.: Cornell University Press, 1985.

Rieger, Eva. *Frau, Musik und Männerherrschaft*. 2d ed. Kassel: Furore-Verlag, 1988.

———. " 'Ich recycle Töne': Schreiben Frauen anders?" *Neue Zeitschrift für Musik* (February 1992): 14–18.

Riemann, Hugo. *Katechismus der Musik (Allgemeine Musiklehre)*. Leipzig: Max Hesse, 1888.

Rosen, Charles. *The Classical Style*. New York: W. W. Norton, 1971.

———. *Sonata Forms*. New York: W. W. Norton, 1980.

Scholes, Robert. "Reading like a Man." In *Men in Feminism*, edited by Alice Jardine and Paul Smith. New York: Methuen, 1987.

Schweickart, Patrocinio. "Reading Ourselves: Toward a Feminist Theory of Reading." *Gender and Reading: Essays on Readers, Texts, and Contexts*, edited by Elizabeth A. Flynn and Patrocinio Schweickart. Baltimore: Johns Hopkins University Press, 1986.

Solie, Ruth, and Gary Tomlinson. "Women's Studies in a New Key." *NWSAction* 2 (Spring 1989): 6.

Stout, Janis. *Strategies of Reticence: Silence and Meaning in the Works of Jane Austen, Willa Cather, Katherine Anne Porter, and Joan Didion*. Charlottesville: University of Virginia Press, 1990.

Subotnik, Rose Rosengard. "On Grounding Chopin." In *Music and Society: The Politics of Composition, Performance, and Reception*, edited by Richard Leppert and Susan McClary. Cambridge: Cambridge University Press, 1987.

Tompkins, Jane, ed. *Reader-Response Criticism: From Formalism to Post-Structuralism.* Baltimore: Johns Hopkins University Press, 1980.

Tovey, Donald Francis. *Encyclopaedia Brittanica,* s.v. "sonata forms." 24 vols. Chicago: Encyclopaedia Brittanica, 1957.

Webster, James. *The New Grove Dictionary of Music and Musicians,* s.v. "sonata form." 20 vols. Edited by Stanley Sadie. London: Macmillan, 1980.

Wolff, Janet. "The Ideology of Autonomous Art." In *Music and Society: The Politics of Composition, Performance, and Reception,* edited by Richard Leppert and Susan McClary. Cambridge: Cambridge University Press, 1987.

————. *The Social Production of Art.* New York: St. Martin's Press, 1981.

Yardley, Anne Bagnall. " 'Ful weel she soong the service dyvyne': The Cloistered Musician in the Middle Ages." In *Women Making Music: The Western Art Tradition, 1150–1950,* edited by Jane Bowers and Judith Tick. Urbana: University of Illinois Press, 1986.

2

Erasing the Boundaries between Public and Private in Women's Performance Traditions

Jennifer C. Post

Until the 1980s few ethnographic studies in the fields of anthropology and ethnomusicology examined women's musical activities. Studies described and discussed music events without indicating the sex of the performers or included only descriptions of men's musical performances. During the last decade, though, research has appeared that presents descriptive data on women's musical activities in specific cultures and identifies some of women's musical contributions to community life.[1] These new studies provide data that allow us to test some of the gender constructs developed by anthropologists, historians, and feminist scholars during the last twenty years. A closer look at these studies and their descriptions of various traditions in which women participate reveals not only the importance of developing social constructions for each individual culture but also significant cross-cultural patterns in musical performance practice.

This study tests a model that divides women's and men's realms into private and public domains, and it discusses its applicability to women's musical performance practices in different cultural contexts during the nineteenth and twentieth centuries. While I look at the male/female dichotomy as it pertains to the public/private debate, I also examine a female/female, professional/nonprofessional dichotomy as well. This will isolate some common cross-cultural characteristics of women's music, not only in opposition to men's musical performances but also in women's performances in both the private and public spheres, especially as women experienced restrictions that affected and shaped their music before the middle of the twentieth century.[2]

Scholars in several disciplines have placed women and men into broad social spheres that they have termed private (or domestic) and public (or political). It has been shown that in many cultures women have remained in a domestic or private domain, while men have moved in a public sphere. This division of social groups into women's and men's spheres has been discussed, and often criticized, during the last twenty years. Yet most scholars have observed that the physical, psychological, and behavioral inclinations of women and men differ, and attitudes and behaviors relating to social organization and activities—such as the division of labor—separate women and men in many cultural contexts.

The private sphere can be defined broadly. Generally it encompasses activities in the household that revolve around family life, both inside and outside the home. In many cultures this world is occupied during much of the day principally by women involved in domestic tasks. In addition to daily activities related to nurturing a family, it includes wider responsibilities taken on during events surrounding marriage, birth, and death. These activities are often undertaken by women in relative isolation from men.

The public sphere usually incorporates activities that take place outside of the household. It frequently involves people who are not part of the immediate family and are in larger groups than might normally be found in the household. There is greater integration of women and men and more diverse activities and ideas in the public sphere. The public realm is occupied largely by men; while women may be present, men are the primary leaders and decision makers.

Although the division between public and private spheres suggests a two-part model, there is not a simple binary opposition in the social framework separating private and public spheres or women and men and the spheres in which they purportedly exist. These spheres exist on a continuum rather than as part of a clear dichotomy. There are contexts and cultures in which the division between women's and men's roles is extreme, but in many cases the poles are not so distinct. In fact, as will be shown here, there are numerous examples of women who have lived largely in the public sphere. It is the lack of rigid boundaries that has caused the greatest challenge for scholars desiring clear theoretical constructs.

Women and men have coexisted in separate spheres during much of their everyday lives in many cultures, yet these spheres are seldom exclusive. Women's and men's oppositional activities are a result of how women and men relate to one another, as well as women's and men's association with one another in their own spheres. As organizational categories are applied to social groups in different parts of the world, their final shape results from not only cultural and social factors, such as class, but also events in different historical periods.[3] Women's role in a specific social group can also change during their lifetime. For example, Ankica Petrović has observed that among Yugoslavian women, "at various stages of their lives, women occupy different degrees of social status within the family and the community at large."[4]

Some researchers also challenge the notion that direct relationships are to be made only between women's private realm and their nurturing responsibilities in the home. Their studies emphasize that women carry their private realm outside the home into social contexts that can, in a sense, be viewed as public. Linda Imray and Audrey Middleton believe that the public/private opposition is not related to activity inside or outside the home at all but to "power relationships" that become apparent through rituals men and women carry on in a variety of contexts.[5] Margaret Yocom, in her study of women's storytelling in Pennsylvania, has noted occasions when women create privacy in a crowded room by turning toward one another, to the exclusion of others, to share a story. In this public setting, women have "created isolation" and maintained characteristics of a more private realm.[6]

Women's and Men's Musical Traditions

The characteristics of women's musical performance traditions in some cultural contexts can be directly related to oppositions in women's and men's social roles. The private/domestic and public sphere models have been used in studies growing from research on gender beginning in the early 1970s.[7] Norma McLeod and Marcia Herndon used this model in their 1975 study of women's music in Malta to set up a framework for examining women's and men's roles in music based on the oppositions relating to differences in women's and men's orientation. More recently, in research on women and music in specific cultural contexts, dichotomies have been revealed by Jennifer C. Post, Marina Roseman, Susan Auerbach, Jane C. Sugarman, Cynthia Schmidt, Gretel Schwörer-Kohl, and others.[8]

In my studies of nineteenth- and early twentieth-century women's music in northern India I show that clear distinctions between women's and men's repertoires, musical styles, and performance contexts have existed for many generations. Similarly, my research on music of northern New England shows performance practices that clearly separate women's and men's spheres before the middle of this century. Roseman, studying the aboriginal Temiar in Malaysia, observes that "Temiar singing ceremonies dramatize distinctions between social groups in terms of gender."[9] Auerbach discusses the socially prescribed musical behavior of women, which differs markedly from that of men in traditional Greek village life. Sugarman indicates that among the Prespa Albanians gender divisions strongly affect their musical performance practices. Schmidt, reporting on her Kpelle research, isolates obvious instances where women's and men's performance practice differs in this highly polarized society. Schwörer-Kohl's study of ritual music among the Hmong and Lahu peoples of Thailand reveals that women's repertoires and performance practices are restricted in the ritual and secular music of especially the Hmong but also the Lahu.

Women's and men's realms in different cultures and over a long time period can be characterized by looking at their respective participation in musical activities. In many cultures men's work outside the home and their subsequent limited family orientation have yielded musical performances and other forms of entertainment that usually take place outside the home, mainly in the public sphere. In many cultures men have had more leisure time to perform music and greater freedom to travel between the public and the home environment for musical performances.

In contrast, women's domestic orientation in many cultures has resulted in musical performances mainly in the private sphere. The boundaries around women's work in some cultural contexts are not as defined as those of men's work, which allows women less time for leisure and thus for musical enjoyment. Social strictures placing women in the home and restricting their involvement in social events have excluded women in many cultures (partially or fully) from the public realm and entire genres of music (see table 2.1).

Women in nineteenth- and early twentieth-century rural New England, for example, took part in music in and around the home. Hierarchical structuring of the society often placed women in a dependent position in relation to men; social restrictions and traditions dictated many of their activities and limited the events they were free to attend outside the home. These restrictions necessarily also limited women's musical opportunities, growth, and diversity. Historically, music for women in New England often existed as an extension of their domestic activities. Women sang to themselves or to their children in the kitchen while they did their chores. Singing was said to make the time pass

Table 2.1. Men's and Women's Musical Spheres

Men's Sphere (Public)	Women's Sphere (Private)
Music performed outside home	Music performed inside home
Music performed during times of leisure	Music performed while working
Limited family orientation in musical performance	Music performed primarily for family
Music performed in and for large groups	Music performed alone or for small groups
Resulting in	*Resulting in*
Musical freedom	Musical restriction
Musical domination	Musical subordination
Integration in musical performance	Separation in musical performance along sexual lines

more quickly while they were completing their necessary domestic duties.

This functionality has been documented in other cultures as well. Mary P. Coote, in an article clarifying women's position in music in Serbo-Croatia in the nineteenth century, describes musical performance in the home while women worked as existing "in a time space [not] marked off from other activities."[10] McLeod and Herndon describe groups of women singing in a dialogue while washing clothes in Maltese villages.[11] Among the Mahars in Maharashtrian villages in India, Indira Junghare has observed that the greater part of village women's song repertoire consisted of songs sung while they worked—working in the fields, grinding, cleaning, caring for children.[12]

A "domestic" orientation is also found in women's musical performances outside the home. Women's performances of songs in a more public sphere generally revolve around events related to birth, marriage, and death. In villages in India, Bonnie Wade reports that women have been the primary performers of wedding and birth songs.[13] This has also been documented by Patricia K. Shehan in the Balkans and Auerbach in Greece.[14] Women have been the principal performers of funeral laments in cultures throughout the world: the Balkans and the Mediterranean islands, central and northern Europe, the former Soviet Union, Ireland, and Scotland. All these performances, although more publicly executed than those in the home, can be seen as part of a private (and especially domestic) realm, that is, events relating to the life cycle: birth, marriage, and death. These song types are often performed in gatherings of women who provide support for one another during times of change in women's (and their families') lives. In many of these performances women sing alone or gather to sing in small groups. We need to investigate further the spatial characteristics of women's singing during events relating to the life cycles of members of their family, for visual information points over and over to women singing in isolation, facing down, or in a circle, facing toward one another, rather than toward an audience in a public space. In these circumstances women create privacy for themselves or for their group.[15]

One of the major oppositions that becomes apparent when juxtaposing women's and men's realms, especially before the middle of the twentieth century, is their contrasting degree of involvement in instrumental music. The restrictions on women's instrumental performance in many cultures can often be related to their association with the private sphere. Women sang while they were doing housework or caring for children, while men sang more often during their leisure time, when their hands were free to use a musical instrument for accompaniment. Coote contends Serbo-Croatian women's infrequent performance on musical instruments (especially to accompany singing) results from their need to be working while they sang; their hands were otherwise occupied.[16] In India women seldom play musical instruments to accompany their songs. Hiromi Lorraine Sakata, in an article on Afghani women's songs, notes that those few instruments women do play are not considered "real" instruments, especially when women play them.[17] Gender restrictions in musical instrument use also have been documented by Ziegler for Turkish music and Auerbach for Greek music.

Restrictions on women's participation in instrumental music in European classical traditions have been discussed in relation to sexual stereotyping that began in the Renaissance. "Feminine" instruments in Western classical traditions, such as the keyboard, guitar, and harp, demanded "no alteration in facial expression or physical demeanor."[18] Although culture-specific reasons have been given for these restrictions, these standards do not seem unique to Europe. Visual and written information on musical performances in Eastern Europe, the Middle East, South Asia, and Southeast Asia evidences the dearth of women involved in instrumental performances, especially before the middle of this century. When women are seen with instruments, they are generally playing ones that do not alter their facial expressions or greatly change their stance.

In some instances, when women do perform on instruments, their position in an ensemble reflects a role subordinate to men. This function, though, is essential to the total performance. In the traditional New England dance ensemble, popular particularly before the middle of this century, the instrument women played most often was the piano. The pianist in this ensemble provided the harmonic framework for the male soloist. Yet she had to bend to the nuances of the solo vocalist or fiddler (who was almost always a man). In Malaysia Roseman reports that women play a crucial role as members of a female chorus, singing and playing bamboo-tube stampers behind a male lead singer (halaa? or spirit medium) during ritual singing sessions and ceremonies.[19] Lester P. Monts, writing on Vai music in Africa, states that women may play lead and subordinate rhythmic roles using the sasaa (gourd rattle) when they perform in ensembles of women, but when women use the sasaa in an ensemble with men, they are "relegated to the subordinate-pulse ostinato and pulse lines, while the lead rhythmic part is performed by a male musician."[20]

Music performed in the home sphere can be characterized by its solitary or small-group orientation and the gender segregation of the performers. Historically, in many cultures women in their home environment existed in greater isolation than did men working together in large groups outside of the home. As a result, women's songs were more often sung alone, while men's music existed as part of social gatherings. If there was an audience for women, it consisted of family, other community members, typically female, or children. Men sang more often for larger groups of other men as well as for groups consisting of both sexes. In some rural New England communities, women's audiences usually included only close family members, while men's audiences in the lumber camps or at the town hall consisted of both family and the wider community. A similar pattern can be seen in Ireland and England, where women sang songs in their families at home, while the pub was a center for men's musical performance. Songs often contained refrains that allowed large groups of men to join in. McLeod and Herndon give evidence of oppositions in group orientation and separation along sexual lines among women and men in Malta.[21] Ginette Dunn, in a study on music in a rural English community, also provides illustrations of these oppositions.[22] This separation between men and women was found by Sugarman in Albania, Sakata in Afghanistan, and Junghare in Mahar villages in Maharashtra. Junghare observes that "Mahar men and women generally do not find occasion to sing together and they do not share their repertoires."[23]

The limited opportunities for women in music generated practices that have separated them from the larger public musical sphere. Their musical style and context—including the restrictive characteristics—have defined a music culture that is separate from men's. Recent studies have pointed out there is a degree of power that can be derived from this type of restriction. Women can use this isolation to develop their own repertoire and styles and to accomplish limited social change.[24]

Broader gender and music studies have shown that men's sphere was more fully integrated. There have been fewer stigmas attached to men's performance, and men have been freer to move between the public and domestic realms for their performances. Their audience and repertoire, instruments, and performance context could change at their will.

A Musical Sanctuary

An interesting pattern in several cultures can be seen as women restricted to domestic life have found a musical sanctuary for themselves in religious practice: in the church, the temple, or other physical space where religious events take place. Through their connection with religious institutions and rituals, women have been permitted to perform in a public setting with greater freedom than they would in their home. In some cases performances in and around religious functions have provided the only opportunities for women to perform music outside the home. Nancy Woloch, in her study of American women in the nineteenth century, characterized the church as "something of a halfway house between domestic life and public life."[25] Nancy Cott reinforces this with her statements on the role women played in the New England church in the eighteenth and nineteenth centuries: "religious identity also allowed women to assert themselves, both in private and in public ways. It enabled them to rely on an authority beyond the world of men and provided a crucial support to those who stepped beyond accepted bounds—reformers, for example." She adds, "In contrast to the self-abnegation required of women in the domestic vocation, religious commitment required attention to one's own thoughts, actions, and prospects.[26]

Linda Dahl, in her study on women in jazz, discusses African American women's experience in their local churches during the nineteenth century. She describes the church as "their place of emotional release," where women who were normally "staid and hardworking" were permitted once a week to let themselves go by singing.[27]

Women in many cultures have been associated with communal rituals, many of which have religious associations. Many Hindu women in India have felt free to worship with song through group performances of *bhajans* (songs of praise). Religious and other ritual events are times when Indian women can engage in socially sanctioned public dancing.[28]

Further study is needed to clarify the characteristics of women's and men's participation in music in the context of religion and religious institutions to determine where their performances fit into the public-private continuum.

Women in the Public and Private Sphere

Women's artistic performance expressions in cultures throughout the world have not been restricted to the private sphere. Many cultures have had long-standing traditions of professional women who took part in musical as well as other artistic performances; other cultures have introduced, or permitted, women's professional performances only in the last one or two generations. For example, since at least the fourth century b.c., professional women in India were trained to perform music and dance publicly. They were allowed some social freedom that women in the private sphere were not. Similarly, Japan's geisha tradition has long supported a carefully defined public performance practice by women.[29] Sakata reports a similar tradition in Afghanistan. McLeod and Herndon report that in Malta public women sing in forms vastly different from those of women in the domestic sphere. Beginning in the early twentieth century women in Europe and North America began to have greater freedom to perform in public, which reflected concurrent social change.

One might expect that music events involving public or professional women would exhibit characteristics of the men's public sphere. Research shows that, in fact, although women in the public sphere display some social characteristics similar to men's, the performance contexts and styles of music performed by women, whether in the private or public domain, manifest women's social restrictions. Women performing in the public sphere, while shedding some of their domestic responsibilities and maintaining more of a group orientation than women do in the private sphere, remain restricted in performance context and repertoire and are placed in subordinate positions in relation to men.

If women's participation in the public sphere is examined more closely, some characteristics of the private realm are found, despite women's public orientation. The characteristics of women's public performance are not always the same as those found among men who perform in the public realm, as one might expect from models of public and private. There are numerous examples to illustrate this point.

In India restrictions on professional women who performed in public in the nineteenth and early twentieth centuries can be found in their repertoire, performance context, and media. Performance traditions among professional women before the early twentieth century existed in limited environs: the Hindu temple or the Muslim court (occasionally the theater). The songs these women were expected to sing were restricted primarily to erotic songs, very different from and more musically restrictive than the classical music in the repertoires of professional male musicians. Women seldom played musical instruments, and their performance media were therefore restricted to vocal music and dance. It is unusual to find references in written or oral history to women who performed on instruments.[30]

In Japan geishas were restricted to specific song forms, and their performances were confined largely to geisha houses or tea houses. Geishas are especially known for their dance and vocal music, and although they use other instruments, they mainly play the shamisen. This instrument was adopted to accompany professional women's songs. Yet shamisen playing by geishas, whether accompanying women or men singing, is purely accompaniment—background to the vocal line.[31] Even virtuosic playing by women is not applauded. Liza Crihfield Dalby reports that when a geisha accompanies a male patron, who is generally an amateur, on the shamisen, she must make him "sound good through skillful timing with the shamisen. . . . [She] has to know the music so thoroughly that no matter how much a customer may stretch [the song] out of its intended form, she can structure it with her judicious playing."[32]

In European and American traditions, where women's professionalism in music is considerably younger than it is in other countries, we find similar restrictions in context, media, and style. Women who performed music in public in the United States at the turn of the century, who played in women's orchestras or performed parlor songs, are described by Judith Tick as representatives of a marginal sphere in the musical world.[33] Women's musical performance was not integrated into the whole; women were not permitted to perform in a variety of genres to universal acceptance.

This is also true among women breaking into jazz traditions in the early years of the twentieth century. Dahl describes the all-women bands during these years as part of the packaging of gimmicks popular at that time for selling bands. Although women began to perform on instruments and in contexts once reserved exclusively for men, they were not accepted as peers to male musicians in the genre.[34]

The environment in which professional women have performed in the public sphere can also be seen as a limitation. This context differs from that of women in the private sphere: professional women's audience is predominantly male. They have been compelled to perform to meet men's approval, and their repertoire has been restricted by what men think they should perform. It is thus men's standards that have shaped their musical style.

In both India and Japan professional women dressed, sang, and danced in a manner dictated by male patrons over many centuries. Not until the early twentieth century did some professional performers reject the traditional performance practices. In nineteenth-century Europe and America, when women broke out of the private sphere and began to perform publicly, many of their songs (most of them were vocalists) were written by men and reflected men's view of women or the way men thought women felt. Even today the European and American music industry is largely a male-dominated structure. Women performing regularly sing, play, and dress, as well as schedule, advertise, and distribute their performances, under the primary direction of male administrators.

Until recently, women involved in public performance were regarded by others and viewed themselves as unique. Their performances were seen as exceptional. In fact, women were sometimes not identified as women. In early twentieth-century Indian musical history there were several women who stepped outside the boundaries and performed classical music in forms and styles that had been reserved for men's performance. When interviewed about separate women's musical traditions, both men and women vehemently stated that these women were outside the normal woman's role. This attitude can also be found among women who took part in the early American country bands. Often, when describing their participation in the band, they referred to themselves as "one of the boys."[35]

In India and Japan, as well as in other areas where the female professional musician was equated with the courtesan, professional women were not free to move outside their designated place. Although they were able to move in areas not open to other women and therefore had some degree of autonomy, there was little interaction between

Table 2.2. Characteristics of Public and Private Spheres

Men's Sphere	Professional Women's Sphere	Private Women's Sphere
Work outside home	Work outside home	Work in the home
Limited family contact	Limited family contact	Strong family contact
Group orientation	Group orientation	Solitary or small-group orientation
Resulting in	*Resulting in*	*Resulting in*
Freedom	Restriction	Restriction
Social	Social	Social
Repertoire	Repertoire	Repertoire
Musical medium	Musical medium	Musical medium
Domination	Subordination	Subordination
In an ensemble	In an ensemble	In an ensemble
Decisions about music	Decisions about music	Decisions about music
Integration	Segregation	Segregation

public and private women. In fact, the social stigmas attached to their positions kept them from moving freely between the public and private worlds. Although they were "professional" and their music was more "public," they too fell into a segregated sphere characteristic of the private realm because they lacked the freedom to perform at will.

We can see, then, the characteristics of private and public spheres, when applied to women performing in both public and private realms in several cultures, do not fall into a neat pattern. The characteristics of the public realm are not always applicable to women performing in the public sphere. Rather, restrictions (characteristics of the private sphere) apply to women performing professionally, both publicly and privately.

Women in the public sphere performed for an audience that included both women and men, their family orientation was generally limited, and there was a group orientation not found in private traditions. Nevertheless, some sexual separation or segregation still existed, and major areas of restriction and subordination can be found in the public sphere (see table 2.2).

Conclusion

In many cultures women in the late twentieth century have created for themselves a very different environment from what existed during the previous century. It would be easy to talk of total change for women. After all, women in Europe now perform in public with seemingly little restriction; women play a variety of instruments in public orchestras and bands in both the classical and popular spheres. Women in India, in both private and public spheres, are involved in a greater variety of musical forms, performance contexts, and styles than they would ever have been permitted a generation ago. Clear distinctions between private and public spheres in performance are not as easily drawn.

Have women successfully created a new environment for themselves that eliminates the public/private distinction? When women's social position in a culture has changed, how have women's performance practices in music been changed? What are the characteristics of women's relatively new place in music that puts them in a new sphere?

Although opportunities for women in music have greatly increased, the public often still judges women separately from men. In many cultures there continue to be clear distinctions between women's and men's musical involvement in instrumental traditions, as composers, as soloists, or as performers in the public sphere. Women's performances are often looked upon as isolated occurrences.

It is obvious that individual women cannot change women's position in music—only a group of women acting as representatives of their sex can do this.[36] I would extend this statement to say that we will be able to talk about change only when women's music making has fully integrated forms and styles permitting women to move in both private and public spheres, among women and men, integrated into the whole in the minds of scholars, audience, and other musicians.

Women have worked hard to erase boundaries between public and private during the last few generations. Efforts have been made to create a more integrated music for all women that includes characteristics of both the private and public spheres. As we look at women's music in the late twentieth century, it is important to remember the contexts from which the music has been derived. It would also be useful to ask whether the integration of musical styles and contexts in the twentieth century, the integration of women's and men's realms, has taken away from women's social status, their identity, and their power, which have been both a burden and a shield.

NOTES

An early version of this essay was read at the 1985 Annual Meeting of the Society for Ethnomusicology in Vancouver, Canada.

1. See, for example, articles in Koskoff, *Cross-Cultural Perspective;* and in Herndon and Ziegler, *Music, Gender, and Culture.*

2. Data for this essay are drawn from recent studies on women in music, feminist literature which has grown from works that present and debate concepts of private and public domains for women and men, and my own field work in India in the 1970s and in New England in the 1980s.

3. See Banner, "Reply."

4. Petrović, "Music Creation Process," 72.

5. Imray and Middleton, "Public and Private," 13–14.

6. Yocom, "Woman to Woman," 48.

7. See, for example, Rosaldo and Lamphere, *Women, Culture, and Society.*

8. See McLeod and Herndon, *"Bormliza";* Post, "Hindustani Music"; Post, "New England Ballad Tradition"; Roseman, "Inversion and Conjuncture"; Auerbach, "From Singing to Lamenting"; Sugarman, "Nightingale and the Partridge"; Schmidt, "Group Expression"; Schmidt, "Womanhood"; and Schwörer-Kohl, "Gender Balance."

9. Roseman, "Inversion and Conjuncture," 133.

10. Coote, "Women's Songs," 334.

11. McLeod and Herndon, *"Bormliza,"* 87–88.

12. Junghare, "Songs of the Mahars," 273.

13. Wade, *The New Grove Dictionary of Music and Musicians,* s.v. "India," 9:150–51.

14. Shehan, "Balkan Women," 50–52; Auerbach, "From Singing to Lamenting," 25–43.

15. It is unfortunate that so few studies have documented women's spatial and kinetic relations to their culture. In one recent study Ziegler discusses gender-specific wedding music in southwestern Turkey, stating, "Comparing the integration of the musicians among the wedding guests, one can notice that the women perform as though they were standing outside, excluded. This is true for the place where they are standing while performing, but it is also expressed in their attitude" (Ziegler, "Gender Specific Traditional Wedding Music," 96).

16. Coote, "Women's Songs," 334.

17. Sakata, "Hazara Women," 87–88.

18. Neuls-Bates, *Women in Music,* xiii.

19. Roseman, "Inversion and Conjuncture," 133–35.

20. Monts, "Vai Women's Roles in Music," 226.

21. McLeod and Herndon, *"Bormliza,"* 84.

22. Dunn, *Fellowship of Song,* 134–35.

23. Junghare, "Songs of the Mahars," 273.

24. See Joseph, "Poetry as a Strategy of Power."

25. Woloch, *American Experience,* 39.

26. Cott, *Bonds of Womanhood,* 140.

27. Dahl, *Stormy Weather,* 5.

28. Wade, *The New Grove Dictionary of Music and Musicians,* s.v. "India," 9:150–52.

29. Dalby, *Geisha*.

30. While there is evidence that there may have been an instrumental tradition among professional women seen in Persian and Indian miniature paintings from the seventeenth and eighteenth centuries, there are few written data to support this.

31. A relationship between the subordinate role of the keyboard player in the New England dance ensemble and the accompanist in Japan can thus be drawn.

32. Dalby, *Geisha*, 254–55.

33. Tick, "Women as Professional Musicians," 126–27.

34. Dahl, *Stormy Weather*, 47–48.

35. Auerbach, in her study of a Greek village tradition, also talks about women who have stepped outside the normal lament-singing roles of women to sing a variety of songs publicly. She described a festival at which three women sang "who affected the proud body stance, loud singing, and bravado typically associated with male revellers" (Auerbach, "From Singing to Lamenting," 31).

36. This important point relating to women and change is made in a study on women in British political life by Rodgers, "Women's Sphere in a Men's House," 50–71.

REFERENCES

Auerbach, Susan. "From Singing to Lamenting: Women's Musical Role in a Greek Village." In *Women and Music in Cross-Cultural Perspective*, edited by Ellen Koskoff. Westport, Conn.: Greenwood Press, 1987.

Banner, Lois W. "A Reply to 'Culture et Pouvoir' from the Perspective of United States Women's History." *Journal of Women's History* 1 (Spring 1989): 101–7.

Coote, Mary P. "Women's Songs in Serbo-Croatia." *Journal of American Folklore* 90 (July-September 1977): 331–38.

Cott, Nancy. *The Bonds of Womanhood: 'Woman's Sphere' in New England 1780–1835*. New Haven, Conn.: Yale University Press, 1977.

Dahl, Linda. *Stormy Weather: The Music and Lives of a Century of Jazzwomen*. New York: Pantheon, 1984.

Dalby, Liza Crihfield. *Geisha*. Berkeley: University of California Press, 1983.

Dunn, Ginette. *The Fellowship of Song*. London: Croom Helm, 1980.

Herndon, Marcia, and Susanne Ziegler, eds. *Music, Gender, and Culture*. ICTM [International Council for Traditional Music] Music Study Group on Music and Gender. Intercultural Music Studies, no. 1. Wilhelmshaven, Germany: Florian Noetzel, 1990.

Imray, Linda, and Audrey Middleton. "Public and Private: Marking the Boundaries." In *The Public and the Private*, edited by Eva Gamarnikow, David Morgan, June Purvis, and Daphne Taylorson. London: Heinemann, 1983.

Joseph, Terri Brint. "Poetry as a Strategy of Power: The Case of Riffian Berber Women." *Signs* 5 (Spring 1980): 418–34.

Junghare, Indira. "Songs of the Mahars: An Untouchable Caste of Maharashtra, India." *Ethnomusicology* 27 (May 1983): 271–95.
Koskoff, Ellen, ed. *Women and Music in Cross-Cultural Perspective*. Westport, Conn.: Greenwood Press, 1987.
McLeod, Norma, and Marcia Herndon. "The *Bormliza:* Maltese Folksong Style and Women." In *Women and Folklore: Images and Genres*, edited by Claire R. Farrer. Prospect Heights, Ill.: Waveland Press, 1975.
Monts, Lester P. "Vai Women's Roles in Music, Masking, and Ritual Performance." In *African Musicology: Current Trends: A Festschrift Presented to J. H. Kwabena Nketia*, edited by Jacqueline Cogdell DjeDje and William Canter. Los Angeles: African Studies Center and African Arts Magazine, University of California; Atlanta, Ga.: Crossroads Press, African Studies Association, 1989.
Neuls-Bates, Carol. *Women in Music*. New York: Harper, 1982.
Petrović, Ankica. "Women in the Music Creation Process in the Dinaric Cultural Zone of Yugoslavia." In *Music, Gender, and Culture*, edited by Marcia Herndon and Susanne Ziegler. Wilhelmshaven, Germany: Florian Noetzel, 1990.
Post, Jennifer C. "Professional Women in Hindustani Music: The Death of the Courtesan Tradition." In *Women and Music in Cross-Cultural Perspective*, edited by Ellen Koskoff. Westport, Conn.: Greenwood Press, 1987.
————. "Women in a New England Ballad Tradition, 1930–1960." Unpublished paper, 1983.
Rodgers, Silvia. "Women's Sphere in a Men's House: The British House of Commons." In *Women and Space*, edited by Shirley Ardener. New York: St. Martin's Press, 1981.
Rosaldo, Michelle Z., and Louise Lamphere. *Women, Culture, and Society*. Palo Alto, Calif.: Stanford University Press, 1974.
Roseman, Marina. "Inversion and Conjuncture: Male and Female Performance among the Temiar of Peninsular Malaysia." In *Women and Music in Cross-Cultural Perspective*, edited by Ellen Koskoff. Westport, Conn.: Greenwood Press, 1987.
Sakata, Hiromi Lorraine. "Hazara Women in Afghanistan: Innovators and Preservers of a Musical Tradition." In *Women and Music in Cross-Cultural Perspective*, edited by Ellen Koskoff. Westport Conn.: Greenwood Press, 1987.
Schmidt, Cynthia. "Group Expression and Performance among Kpelle Women's Associations in Liberia." In *Music, Gender, and Culture*, edited by Marcia Herndon and Susanne Ziegler. Wilhemshaven, Germany: Florian Noetzel, 1990.
————. "Womanhood, Work, and Song among the Kpelle." In *African Musicology: Current Trends: A Festschrift Presented to J. H. Kwabena Nketia*, edited by Jacqueline Cogdell DjeDje and William Canter. Los Angeles: African Studies Center and African Arts Magazine, University of California; Atlanta, Ga.: Crossroads Press, African Studies Association, 1989.

Schwörer-Kohl, Gretel. "Considering Gender Balance in Religion and Ritual Music among the Hmong and Lahu in Northern Thailand." In *Music, Gender, and Culture,* edited by Marcia Herndon and Susanne Ziegler. Wilhelmshaven, Germany: Florian Noetzel, 1990.

Shehan, Patricia K. "Balkan Women as Perservers of Traditional Music and Culture." In *Music, Gender, and Culture,* edited by Marcia Herndon and Susanne Ziegler. Wilhelmshaven, Germany: Florian Noetzel, 1990.

Sugarman, Jane C. "The Nightingale and the Partridge: Singing and Gender among Prespa Albanians." *Ethnomusicology* 33 (Spring-Summer 1989): 191–215.

Tick, Judith. "Women as Professional Musicians in the United States." *Anuario Interamericano de Investigacion/Yearbook for Inter-American Musical Research* 9 (1973): 95–133.

Wade, Bonnie. *The New Grove Dictionary of Music and Musicians,* s.v. "India." 20 vols. Edited by Stanley Sadie. London: Macmillan, 1980.

Woloch, Nancy. *Women and the American Experience.* New York: Alfred A. Knopf, 1984.

Yocom, Margaret R. "Woman to Woman: Fieldwork and the Private Sphere." In *Women's Folklore, Women's Culture,* edited by Rosan A. Jordan and Susan Kalcik. Philadelphia: University of Pennsylvania Press, 1985.

Ziegler, Susanne. "Gender Specific Traditional Wedding Music in Southwestern Turkey." In *Music, Gender, and Culture,* edited by Marcia Herndon and Susanne Ziegler. Wilhelmshaven, Germany: Florian Noetzel, 1990.

3

Music and the English Renaissance Controversy over Women

Linda Phyllis Austern

Many scholars have recently recognized that English Renaissance ideas about women are broadly indicative of sixteenth- and seventeenth-century cultural values. However, this rapidly growing body of scholarship has remained almost entirely limited to literary and social studies, in spite of the fact that English writers concerned with gender issues between the early sixteenth century and the mid-seventeenth considered women in all intellectual and social contexts.[1] Because music and feminine nature were widely perceived as similarly sensual, affective, and in need of strict rational control to benefit men and their narrow perception of women, fundamental ideas connecting music to feminine virtue, vice, and sexuality played a central role in the formation of early modern English attitudes toward women and gender. Nowhere are these ideas articulated with greater energy or clarity than in the formal controversy over the nature of women that flourished between approximately 1540 and 1640, which itself helps to indicate the great cultural and ideological upheavals that marked the end of the Renaissance.[2]

Throughout Europe since classical antiquity, women, like music, have been held alternately responsible for the spread of moral decrepitude and for bringing men closer to the divine. The English Renaissance inherited its tradition of literary and philosophical attack and defense of women, along with its complete intellectual canon, from previous eras; its antecedents included the highly revered and predominantly misogynist ideas of the classical poets and philosophers, the asceticism of the church fathers and early Christian scholastics, and the systematic misogyny of medieval theologians. Pre-Renaissance literary attacks on women eventually came to be answered by equally vigorous defenses, however, and by the close of the Middle Ages, a full-scale, widespread, and extremely complex debate concerning women was firmly in place, complete with a stock set of literary conventions and motifs that was handed on to succeeding eras. Participants in this disputation were cultured, intellectually versatile, and most often aristocratic, ranging from nameless misogynist monks to such paragons of female learning as the famous fourteenth-century writer and noblewoman Christine de Pisan.[3]

The Renaissance inherited the conventionalized debate over women from the preceding era, just as it incorporated medieval methods of biblical analysis, abiding respect for the church fathers, and the custom of drawing comparisons with Roman law and Aristotelian medicine and ethics. Participants continued to select examples of virtue and vice from earlier sources to suit their individual purposes, and the debate remained as much a rhetorical game as an earnest discussion of gender. Several interrelated factors altered the course of the controversy, however: the advent of print, an increased advocacy of literacy and learning, and the almost inestimable influence of Renaissance neo-Platonism that for the first time elevated all women to a position of idealized spiritual importance.[4]

The sixteenth- and early seventeenth-century English contributions to the ongoing debate on the nature of women were especially syncretic. They drew on every known discipline and every available authority for support, until original meanings were lost or irrevocably altered and seemingly incongruous evidence was combined to provide new support for ancient arguments. The practical wisdom of the growing middle classes met with arcane scholarly argument, Puritans and humanists drew similar conclusions from different evidence and opposing viewpoints, women of the literate classes came to their own defense more readily than ever before, and the printers and booksellers of London responded to a steadily increasing demand for any sort of material on women. Recent scholarship has tended to limit the formal controversy to prose works whose primary purpose is the attack or defense of women, but Renaissance topical boundaries were not as narrow as they have since become, and the issues of gender and women's place in a changing world proved tremendously popular. Aside from the central canon of specific literary attacks and defenses, works that have previously been considered part of the broad controversy and still contribute significantly to our understanding of English Renaissance attitudes toward women include sermons, stage plays, commonplace books, prose fiction, medical treatises, religious tracts, and song texts.[5]

The English Renaissance also inherited an age-old debate about the merits of music. The parallels and similarities between the two disputations are quite striking. Like the debate on women, the debate on music traced its roots to classical antiquity, relied on evidence from the most respected classical and early Christian authorities, and drew anecdotal examples from a curious blend of classical mythology, the Old and New Testament, history, and contemporary practice.[6] Similarly, both debates were constructed around a standardized pro-and-con form that allowed writers on each side to support their own viewpoints while anticipating and answering predictable objections from their opponents. Furthermore, as with the debate on women, the debate on music was broadly interdisciplinary, was as much didactic and prescriptive as descriptive, and expressed ideas found in such wide-ranging sources as stage plays and educational manuals.[7] Although the controversy over music never became as widespread as the one on women, both shared a number of ideas and by the mid-sixteenth century had become mutually influential, for underlying attitudes toward both women and music were the broad cultural issues of sensuality, morality, control, and love.

Recent cultural and historical studies have come to recognize the naiveté and futility of judging past cultures by modern standards and extrapolating information on the basis of modern cultural analogues. The early modern world was almost inestimably different from our own, and the roles of men and women of all social classes were rigidly defined by a complex set of hierarchical rules not unlike those perceived to govern the entire universe. The civic and domestic responsibilities of men and women were clear, separate, and, by modern standards, inflexible and unequal.

Especially in late sixteenth-century and early seventeenth-century England, where the Puritan reemphasis on biblical literalism and the teachings of the church fathers increasingly pervaded all levels of society, woman's place remained subordinate to man's; her sphere of existence was domestic, spousal, maternal, inspirational, and decorative. The few exceptional women of the highest social classes who stepped outside of this restricted position did so only through the denial of normal femininity and at the risk of censure.[8] These rigid social norms are especially evident in musical practice, for although English women from good families learned musical performance skills, they were far less likely than were continental women to sing or play in public or to learn what was considered the inappropriately masculine skill of composition because of Puritan views on the sensuality and moral dangers of music.[9]

One of the most important and transcendent characteristics attributed to women by nearly all Renaissance thinkers was the ability to inspire love and, by extension, to provide moral and spiritual stability for their husbands and children. The conflicting philosophies of humanism and the Reformation both praised the state of marriage. Additionally, through slightly different programs of education, both sought to produce sober, virtuous women who would run their households and oversee the early education of their children with quiet efficiency. At her best woman was universally venerated as the gentle, loving helpmate of man. English Puritans and humanists alike stressed the complete subordination of women to their husbands, but they equated the love of a woman with the love of God, an earthly reflection of the greater paradise to come.[10] Because of their ability to inspire a higher and more perfect love, women came to occupy a more prominent position in the Renaissance cosmos than they had in previous eras; indeed, it has been claimed that love stood at the center of the Renaissance cosmos and with it the female principle.[11]

Based primarily on the same ideas of neo-Platonism that helped to elevate woman's status and connect her with love, music theorists also located love at the center of their universe. Thomas Morley, the greatest music theorist of the English Renaissance, adopts the Platonic definition of music as "a science of love matters occupied in harmonie and rhythmos."[12] Thomas Ravenscroft, his younger contemporary, tells us that only music can truly express the universal passion of love and that, conversely, the power of love may teach a man music.[13] The great madrigal composer John Farmer explains that Venus, the astrological giver of love and amorous disposition, "is the Dominatrix in Musitians nativities."[14] The greatest literary names of the era also showed the inseparability of music and love. Robert Greene, one of the most musically oriented writers of Elizabethan prose fiction, introduces the great mythological musicians Orpheus and Arion as "famous in their times for their instruments and greatly experienced in love" in the only full-length English Renaissance work to feature their exploits.[15] Sir Thomas Overbury recognizes music as able to soften the heart to prepare it for love;[16] and William Shakespeare, of course, considers music "the food of love."[17]

Music theorists and others concerned with music in a specifically Christian context also emphasize its affinity with, and ability to inspire, love. As the love of a good woman can serve as the gateway to heavenly love, so can the sound of music directly inspire divine ecstasy and love of Christian piety, as Charles Butler reminds us in his *Principles of Musick in Singing and Setting.*[18] It is of no small consequence that

The Praise of Musicke, the longest and most thorough defense of music published during the English Renaissance, likens the eternal attraction between men and music to the sacred bond of marriage between men and women.[19] Conversely, it is most telling that numerous nonmusical works concerned with exemplary Christian living explain marital love most simply through the metaphor of musical harmony, sometimes even selecting words that apply principally to the sort of domestic music in which women and men were equal participants; "For it is not the outward rite onely which consummates a Spousall love: for if their hearts be not linked, before their hands be ever joyned: their *house musick* is very likely to close in *discords*."[20] For Puritan or humanist then, love, the universal passion that defines the perfect relationship between God and man or man and woman, may be controlled by music alone.

The authors and editors of English Renaissance attacks and defenses of women, mostly men but also a few erudite women from varied social and ideological backgrounds, approached their common subject for different reasons and from different perspectives. Several themes are common to most works, however. For nearly all participants, the debate was primarily a forum for demonstrating general erudition and skill in logic and rhetoric, a chance to show acquaintance with the seven liberal sciences and all textual traditions known to the era and to demonstrate mastery of the increasingly respectable skill of careful personal observation. As one author points out, to consider the nature of woman is, by extension, to consider the nature of all things.[21]

Some participants chose the subject because of its ancient respectability and current popularity, others because of its potential breadth and room for displaying the widest possible mastery of learning and intellectual dexterity, and still others in response to specific pamphlets or widespread social problems.[22] For some participants, particularly men of the highest social classes, the dazzling display of knowledge and the blinding mastery of the most subtle rhetorical devices became more important than the given topic of women; some authors demonstrated their verbal brilliance by arguing both sides with equal imagination, conviction, and dexterity, while others produced brilliant rhetorical paradoxes that present the most notorious villainesses of all time and all known traditions in new heroic light.[23] For other participants, who appear no less learned in their handling of the finer points of logic and topical knowledge, the debate was an earnest discussion of current social malaise and an opportunity to identify and correct some of the moral problems then plaguing English society.[24] For all, music became one of the topics through which an author could support a central argument for or against women's equality with men, because the dual practical and speculative nature of music allowed it to represent learned accomplishment and symbolize the capacity for love or lust.

Music was generally introduced into these arguments either as one of the academic liberal sciences or as a performing art practiced by men and women from ancient to modern times. Nearly all writers limited their discussions to historical and theoretical aspects of the discipline rather than to the practicalities of performance in Renaissance England, for these demonstrated the greatest erudition. A few, especially the more vituperative moralists or those with more practical intent, added descriptive comments that help increase our understanding of music's function in Renaissance life. In spite of the great musical and political changes that took place during the hundred-year span between the first and last works generally accepted as part of the English Renaissance controversy over women, musical references remained surprisingly similar and consistent, more prescriptive than descriptive and with strong moral or allegorical implications. Concern about women's use of this most sensual art clearly outweighed any actual changes in musical practice in England between 1540 and 1640.

At the very center of the musical part of the debate on women was the widespread belief that music, as the other inspiration to love, enhanced feminine attractiveness and therefore became a powerful agent of seduction unless it was placed strictly under masculine control. No matter what approach to the topic each author takes, whether instructive, descriptive, historical, rhetorical, moral, earnest, or playful, women's music is invariably related to men in some capacity and is very carefully linked to or separated from feminine sexuality in a firm division between flesh and spirit. Perhaps because of the parallel sensual affect attributed to both women and music, all antiwomen authors are likewise antimusic. Prowomen authors, however, are clearly divided into opposing camps on the issue of music and on how and why music may or may not be allowed to women for the benefit of men.

The English Renaissance condemnations of women represent the culmination of centuries of misogyny and are among the most malicious works published anywhere during the sixteenth and seventeenth centuries. They are generally the least erudite works of the controversy, and perhaps for this reason they tend to include fewer references to music or other cultured arts than do those works written in defense of women. When such virulently misogynist authors do introduce music, it is invariably as a dangerous, sex-enhancing artifice, a representative of the destructive power of feminine sexuality, or an illustration of feminine frailty. The anonymous author of the *Hic Mulier*, a rabid condemnation of female cross-dressing, compares the false attractiveness of women in men's clothing to the sirenlike enchantment of a musical whore, a grotesque symbol combining mythology with the darker side of Renaissance life to reveal the frighteningly destructive, monstrous nature of the sexually empowered, independent woman.[25] Joseph Swetnam's *Arraignment of Lewd, Idle, Froward, and Unconstant Women*, probably the most infamous and widely resented attack on womankind of the entire seventeenth century, presents music as one of the whore's common enticements by historical example. Once again music is placed in a context of sexual excess and inversion of the established hierarchy in which masculine power and authority become threatened by feminine talent, accomplishment, and an attendant lack of reliance on men.[26]

Even when women's musical performance was not perceived as a dangerous, sex-enhancing artifice used for the destruction of masculine morality and self-control, it was condemned by many of these same writers as a useless feminine vanity. As Swetnam points out, Englishwomen of all classes actively participated only in the superfluous music of pure entertainment and leisure pastime: "Is it not strange that men should be so foolish to dote on women, who differ so farre in nature from men? For a man delights in arms, & in hearing the rattling drums, but a woman loves to heare sweet musick on the Lute, Cittern, or Bandora: A man rejoyceth to march among the murthered carkesses, but a women to dance on a silken carpet: a man loves to heare the threatnings of his Princes enemies, but a women weepes when she heares of wars."[27] Perhaps taking a cue from the dissenting voice of Lord Gaspar (Gasparo Pallavicino) in the most influential manual of courtly conduct from the entire Renaissance, Baldessar Castiglione's *Il libro del cortegiano* (translated into English by Thomas Hoby as *The Booke of the Courtyer*), Swetnam perceives all sounding, melodious music as feminine and feminizing.[28] Woman's frail, sensual nature delights in the soft, artificial music of stringed instruments and in the dance, not in the useful music of war. In the strongest condemnations, then, music has no place in the ideal woman's life, for either it enhances her dangerous, destructive sexuality or it reinforces her weaker nature.

The idea that music primarily augments feminine sexual attractiveness and therefore poses moral danger to men was so pervasive that a number of defenses of women published in England between 1540 and 1640 blindly condemn the art in all feminine contexts, while others temper cautious discussions of women's use of music with graphic warnings of its destructive capabilities. Daniel Tuvil, a strong advocate of liberal education for women, completely dismisses music from his defensive *Asylum Veneris* in an epistle addressed "To the looser sort of Women," in which it figures with other adulterous arts like cosmetics and sorcery:

> Stand of[f] you foule adulterate brats of Hell,
> Whose lunges exhale a worse then sulph'rous smell
> Do not attempt with your prophaner hands
> To touch the Shrine, in which chast Virtue stands . . .
> Hence frisking Faeries, that like *Herods* Niece,
> Esteeme of dancing, as your chiefest piece,
> And with *Sempronia* care not, so your Lute
> Delight the Hearers, though your Soules be mute. . . .
> For Women only is this Place ordain'd,
> But you are Monsters, and their Sex have stain'd.
> Hence therefore, hence, you base, unhallowed crew,
> Hope for no shelter heere, All such as you,
> That hitherwards for helpe, and succor flie,
> Pluckt from the Altar, must abjure, or die.[29]

The grotesque imagery and horrifying context for music are completely unambiguous; the female musician becomes one with the monstrous, deformed, soulless figures of the whore, the murderess, the sorceress, and all other unnatural creatures that hide behind deceptively attractive feminine forms. Again, the strong association between music, sexual promiscuity, and the promise of death to men is quite evident and effectively used; nothing in this context is even remotely natural, and music simply takes its place among other poisonous artifices used for the fatal attraction of men. Music must indeed have been one of the most powerful arts available to women for such profeminist writers as Tuvil to include such gruesome descriptions in their works.

One of the clearest and most poignantly logical condemnations of music as an enhancement to feminine sexual attractiveness appears in a pseudonymous treatise entitled *The Women's Sharp Revenge*. Its authors not only protest the shaping of women's education to men's needs or men's desires but also recognize that if female musicians are considered provocative, the fault lies with the men who encourage them only in the decorative, less intellectually challenging aspects of the art:

When we [women], whom they stile by the name of weaker Vessells, though of a more delicate, fine, soft, and more plyant flesh, and therefore of a temper most capable of the best Impression, have not that generous and liberall Ed-

ucations, lest we should bee made able to vindicate our owne injuries . . . or
if (which sometimes happeneth) wee be brought up to Musick, to singing, and
to dancing, it is not for any benefit that thereby wee can ingrosse unto our
selves, but for their own particular ends, the better to please and content their
licentious appetites, when we come to our maturity and ripenesse: and thus
if we be weake by Nature they strive to make us more weak by our nurture.[30]

This work, for the first time, questions the limits traditionally imposed on English women's musical education and questions the origin
and meaning of the bond between music and women's sensuality. For
these authors, as for Tuvil, music underscores feminine licentiousness;
but, unlike Tuvil, they address actual musical practice and the cause
of the immorality presumed by so many of their male contemporaries.
For them, theory and practice are separable, linked only by masculine
desire, sexuality, and standardized ideology. The moral danger and
licentiousness of music performed by women is perceived here to be
a strictly masculine construct, related not to feminine nature but to
women's upbringing and the formation of gender in a masculine world.

Other defenses of women are more moderate in their condemnations of music in a feminine context. Most writers who find limited
virtue in music demonstrate familiarity with classical and biblical references to its great spiritual benefits and with continental conduct
books that recommend it to both sexes; however, they fail to discuss
the actual Renaissance practices that may have influenced their conclusions. These writers, whose ideologies are ultimately influenced
more by the conservative aspects of the Reformation than by the more
liberal ideas of humanism, admit music into the lives of women only
with great reluctance, because its moral danger very nearly outweighs
its benefits. Some of these treatises, such as G. M. Bruts's (Giovanni
Bruto's) influential *Necessarie, Fit, and Convenient Education of a
Yong Gentlewoman*, which appeared in an additional English version
as Thomas Salter's *Mirrhor of Modesty*,[31] are translations or editions
of continental works that articulate the predominately conservative
English attitude more strongly than do most foreign conduct books
and more elegantly than do many native writers:

Most men are of opinion, that to a gentlewoman of honor and reputation, it
is a great grace and ornament if she (among other things) beco[m]eth expert
to sing and play upon divers instruments, and to shew her selfe excellent and
famous therein, which (although it be confirmed by strong and good reasons)
I can not altogether praise, but I esteeme that as things of no great moment,
she may as well learne them. . . . Nevertheless, under a colour of vertue . . .
it hath in it a secret baite that leadeth to grievous mischiefs, and those of
greater consequence. . . . Our gentlewoman then shall abstaine wholly from

using musicke: and seeing that under the honest couverture of vertue it open-
eth the gate to many vices. . . . Let us graunt the use of singing, and of this
curious harmonie, to such as being wearied with great and important affaires,
have need of recreation: to which wee read in Homer was done to Agamemnon:
and in the scriptures to king Saul, who by the harpe and songs of David was
mooved out of a fierce and cruell passion, to peace and quietnes of mind . . .
[but] by the false harmonies of the Sirens, Ulysses (so much renowmed both
by Greeke and Latine Authors, and nourished with celestiall meat in the bo-
some of sapience, Jupiters daughter) could hardly assure himselfe: and should
wee then be so well persuaded of a weake and delicate young gentlewoman,
tenderly bred up, that as not to feare, that shee not only hearing but learning
so pleasant an Art, should not in time become licentious, delicate, and effeminate?[32]

While the male musicians of antiquity moved their masculine listeners to noble passions, their female counterparts only destroyed the
men who listened, according to this account. Furthermore, women,
more delicate and vulnerable by nature, were likely to be perverted by
music even as they allured their listeners as their ancient forebears did.
What is most striking about Bruto's description is its ambiguity and
double standard; he recognizes musical skills as trivial enough that
women might as well acquire them and praises the ability of music to
soothe a troubled mind, but he becomes adamant about its moral threat
and recommends that women abstain from using whatever skills they
have acquired. As an extension of the contemporary double standard
for the sexes, music is beneficial in the hands of men and destructive
in the hands of women. Music is not an equalizer of the sexes, nor
does it serve them similarly; its rational, beneficial side belongs to men,
while its sensual, devastating side belongs to women. It therefore il-
luminates contemporary gender ideology by functioning as an artistic
reflection of the perceived natures of men and women.

Many defenses of women praise both music and the women who
perform it, but they almost invariably perceive feminine musicians as
a source of masculine pleasure or inspiration and therefore concentrate
solely on men's responses to them. The works that praise both women
and their music are generally the most learned of the controversy, the
most arcane, and the most indebted to the ideas of humanism. These
are the works whose authors demonstrate the most thorough mastery
of the widest range of subjects and styles of inquiry. These are also
the works in which the controversy most strongly resembles a game
of wit and rhetorical skill; consequently, many of these authors seem
quite remote from their subject and unconcerned about the actual
inferior status of contemporary women.

The approach to female musicians in C. Pyrrye's relatively brief but cleverly constructed *Praise and Dispraise of Women* is typical of this sort of work. Pyrrye treats Sappho, presented by numerous other writers of the era as the archetypal musical whore, as an admirable woman. To prevent her from seeming lascivious, her music is placed in a double masculine context emphasizing its spirituality: its power is compared with David's, and the soothing effect of her music comes to represent the pleasure women offer to men.[33] The strength and beneficence of the most worthy feminine music is here at least equal to the best masculine; and music itself is again compared obliquely to the pleasurable and restorational love of a woman. Pyrrye's Sappho is clearly presented as David's match, for her music provides the same spiritual transformation as his in precisely the same way.

Anthony Gibson's erudite paradox, *A Womans Woorth, Defended against All the Men in the World*, takes an even more extreme approach to defending female musicians and equating their abilities to the best of men's. In a lengthy and learned section devoted to the art, he proves women's musical ability superior to men's by comparing famous musicians of both sexes point by point in such a way that women's music is given almost infinite power over the elements while men's remains humanly limited. His comparison of the sirens and the tritons is typical; the latter not only are placed in the former's debt but also are proved to be inferior musicians. The same sensuality that is condemned in the more negative discussions of women and music is made virtuous here; and unlike Pyrrye, Gibson equates the benefit of women's music with the same physical qualities that most often elicit disparagement, culminating in his reminder that Venus was often considered patroness of music:

The *Syrens*, so much described by the Grecians, had songs so wonderfully sweete and melodious: as they could out-eare the windes, and rob all mouthes of their natural offices. . . . Perhaps some one will say unto me, that the Tritons are verye excellent Musitians, but he must withall confesse, that they never had like power and vertue as the Syrens have, of whom they learned their very deepest knowledge. . . . The Astronomers do holde, that Venus is the patronesse of Musique, and that the influence of her planet brings most speciall felicitie to such as deale in that facultie.[34]

The notorious sirens, slayers of men through unrestrained sensuality, are here vindicated of all wrong because of the intense power of their music, a power that remains contextually and morally neutral. In opposition to Pyrrye's description, the inevitable and often-condemned sensuality of feminine music here becomes its principle source of delight, judged for its own sake and not for its ethical affect.

The Worming of a Mad Dogge, written anonymously under the feminine pseudonym of Constantia Munda ("elegant constancy"), takes a completely different though no less clever approach to vindicating women's music of charges of malignancy. Like Gibson, the unknown author relies on her wit and her knowledge of classical legends; but unlike him, she writes entirely in earnest, without the rhetorical technique of paradox. For her, music becomes a performing art of the sort that real women practice, not simply the stuff of myth and history. Her contribution to the debate on women allows an educated female voice to prove the true equality of her sex through both erudition and humor. In a direct response to Joseph Swetnam's pernicious accusation that women's sweet, passive music is useless, she addresses him by saying:

I would give a *supersedas* to my quill: but there is a most pregnant place in your booke which is worthy of laughter that comes to mind where you graphically describe the difference and apathie of man and woman, which being considered, you thinke it strange there should be any reciprocation of love, for a man you say delights in armes, and hearing the rattling drum, but a woman loves to heare sweet musicke on the Lute, Cittern, or Bandora: I prethee who but the long-eard animall had rather heare the Cukoe than the Nightingale? Whose eares are not more delighted with the melodious tunes of sweete musick, then with the harsh sounding drum? Did not *Achilles* delight himselfe with his harpe as well as with the trumpet? Nay, is there not more men that rather affect the laudable use of the Citterne, and Bandore, and Lute for the recreation of the mindes, than the clamorous noyse of drums? Whether it is more agreeable to humane nature to march amongst murthered carkesses, which you say man rejoyceth in, than to enjoy the fruition of peace and plenty, even to dance on silken Carpets, as you say, is our pleasure? What man soever maketh warres, is it not to this ende, that he might enjoy peace?[35]

In a clearly reasoned argument Munda makes Swetnam seem the long-eared ass. Like her male counterparts, she recognizes that feminine music is the sweet, delicate music of pleasant pastime, but with impeccable logic she points out that all humanity may delight in such pleasing sensuality. Again, women become inspirational figures, able to elevate men from the depths of war to enjoy the feminine fruits of peace. Woman's noblest function is to provide peaceful domestic stability for man; here Munda shows her delight in the sensuality of music as a quiet extension of the passive beauty and goodness to which men will always return from the instabilities that the world has to offer.

The musical aspect of the English Renaissance controversy over women clearly reflects the dominant misogyny of an era that regarded with extreme suspicion women's accomplishments in all but the most

narrowly defined domestic sphere. In particular, the creative, intellectual process of composition was never even considered as something
a woman might attempt, and it is notable only in its absence. Moreover,
as both auditors and performers, women are judged almost entirely
by narrow standards of masculine morality and propriety. Music becomes connected to what was widely perceived as the dangerous and
even deadly threat of feminine sexuality or to the supposedly useless
world of feminine passivity and desire for frivolous musical entertainment. Several men, however, do manage to find merit in the very
aspects of women's music that others disparage as invariably destructive; and, most important, a small but vocal female presence in this
century-long debate comes to question for the first time why men have
discredited and limited women's participation in music.

NOTES

This essay was made possible by the generosity of the Newberry Library, to
which I am eternally grateful for the 1987 award of a summer resident fellowship.

1. A representative sample of works since 1980 includes Davies, *Feminine
Reclaimed;* Henderson and McManus, *Half Humankind;* Hull, *Chaste, Silent,
and Obedient;* Willen, "Women's Education in Elizabethan England"; and
Woodbridge, *Women and the English Renaissance.* Works to date that have
considered English Renaissance women and their music, however briefly, are
Austern, " 'Sing Againe Syren' "; Camden, *Elizabethan Woman,* 158–60; Har-
ris, "Musical Education in Tudor Times," 132–33; and Westrup, "Domestic
Music," 50–52.
2. The clearest introductions to this controversy are Camden, *Elizabethan
Woman,* 239–71; Henderson and McManus, *Half Humankind;* Woodbridge,
Women and the English Renaissance, 13–113; and Louis B. Wright, *Middle-
Class Culture,* 465–507; see also Crandall, "Swetnam Anti-Feminist Controversy"; and Utley, *Crooked Rib.* For a comparison with continental attitudes
and controversies, see Bornstein, *Distaves and Dames;* Bornstein, *Feminist
Controversy;* Kelly, "Early Feminist Theory"; and Kelso, *Lady of the Renaissance,* 306–465.
3. Kelly, "Early Feminist Theory," 76, argues that most masculine defenses
of women were spontaneous literary works while most feminine defenses of
their own sex were angry retorts to specific misogynist attacks.
4. See Davies, *Feminine Reclaimed,* 3–4; Hull, *Chaste, Silent, and Obedient,* 7, 140; Maclean, *Renaissance Notion of Woman,* 24–25; and Louis
Wright, *Middle-Class Culture,* 465–66.
5. As early as 1935 Louis Wright, *Middle-Class Culture,* 473, suggested
that a significant proportion of English publications of the final quarter of the

sixteenth century contributes to the topic of women's nature and position in society. More recently Woodbridge, *Women and the English Renaissance*, 1, pointed out that so many English Renaissance works consider women's nature in one manner or another that attempting a thorough study of the topic remains quite perilous. The most inclusive descriptions of English controversial literature on women are Hull, *Chaste, Silent, and Obedient*, 117–19; and Louis Wright, *Middle-Class Culture*, 465–507. For the more conservative and easily defined limits I have generally observed in this essay, see Camden, *Elizabethan Woman*, 241–71; Henderson and McManus, *Half Humankind*, 11–19, 99–130; Hull, *Chaste, Silent, and Obedient*, 117; Utley, *Crooked Rib*; and Woodbridge, *Women and the English Renaissance*, 13–17.

6. The most comprehensive summary of the concurrent English debate on the merits and uses of music still remains Boyd, *Elizabethan Music and Musical Criticism*, 13–36; see also Hollander, *Untuning of the Sky*, 104–22.

7. Not only do such works as *The Praise of Musicke* and Butler's *Principles of Musick* reach as far afield as natural philosophy and military history to support defenses of the art, but such diverse works as Mulcaster's *Training Up of Children*, Peacham's *Compleat Gentleman*, Shakespeare's *Merchant of Venice*, and Thomas Wright's *Passions of the Minde* include material in defense or disapproval of the contemporary theory or practice of music.

8. See Dusinberre, *Shakespeare and the Nature of Women*, 200; Jordan, "Feminism and the Humanists," 252; Kelly, "Early Feminist Theory," 88; and King, "Book-Lined Cells," 75–76.

9. For further information, see Austern, " 'Sing Againe Syren.' "

10. Although Puritan and humanist ideas of love are based on radically different antecedents and are rarely compared or discussed together, they are remarkably similar. See, for example, Bullough, *The Subordinate Sex*, 203; Davies, *Feminine Reclaimed*, 4; Haller and Haller, "Puritan Art of Love," 237–39; Maclean, *Renaissance Notion of Woman*, 24–26; and Travitsky, *Paradise of Women*, 7.

11. Davies, *Feminine Reclaimed*, 4.

12. Morley, *Plaine and Easie*, 195. In this essay I have modernized the shape of the long *s* of sixteenth- and seventeenth-century usage and have interchanged the complementary pairs of letters *i/j*, *u/v*, and *w/vv* to accord with modern usage. The original punctuation has been retained except where noted.

13. Ravenscroft, *Charact'ring the Degrees*, sig. A3v. See also Allott, *Wits Theater*, fol. 69v; *Arte of English Poesie*, 36; Burton, *Anatomy of Melancholy*, 540; and Meres, *Palladis Tamia*, fols. 287v-288.

14. Farmer, *First Set of English Madrigals*, cantus partbook, sig. A4v. See also Austern, "Love, Death, and Ideas of Music," 22–24.

15. Greene, *Greenes Orpharion*, 9.

16. Overbury, *Remedy of Love*, sig. B6.

17. Shakespeare, *Comedies, Histories, and Tragedies*, 109.

18. Butler, *Principles of Musick*, 109.

19. *Praise of Musicke*, 3.
20. Brathwaite, *Art Asleep Husband?* 35.
21. Gibson, *Womans Woorth*, fols. 1–1v.
22. See, for example, *Haec-Vir;* More, *Defence of Women;* and Speght, *Mouzell for Melastomus*. Kelly, "Early Feminist Theory," 74–79, points out that women were more likely than men to write specific responses to slanderous publications about their own sex.
23. See, for example, in addition to the works cited in note 22, Gosynhyll, *Scholehouse of Women;* [Gosynhyll], *Prayse of All Women;* and Pyrrye, *Praise and Dispraise of Women*. For contrasting modern views of these paradoxes and their purposes, see Hull, *Chaste, Silent, and Obedient,* 139; and Louis Wright, *Middle-Class Culture,* 479.
24. See, for example, *Hic Mulier;* and Knox, *First Blast*.
25. *Hic Mulier*, sigs. B3v-B4.
26. Swetnam, *Arraignment,* 20–21, 31.
27. Ibid., 38.
28. See [Castiglione], *Courtyer of Count Baldessar Castilio*, sig. 12v.
29. Tuvil, *Asylum Veneris*, sigs. A6-A6v.
30. Tattle-Well and Hit-Him-Home, *Women's Sharp Revenge,* 40–42.
31. Salter, *Mirrhor of Modesty*.
32. Bruto, *Education of a Yong Gentlewoman*, sigs. H4v-I. See also Salter, *Mirrhor of Modesty*, sigs. C6-C7, which provides another translation of the same passage.
33. Pyrrye, *Praise and Dispraise of Women*, sigs. C3-C3. See also [Gosynhyll], *Prayse of All Women*, sig. A4v, which is remarkably similar.
34. Gibson, *Womans Woorth*, fols. 24v-25.
35. Munda, *Worming of a Mad Dogge,* 31–32.

REFERENCES

Allott, Robert. *Wits Theater of the Little World*. London: J.R. for N.L., 1599.
The Arte of English Poesie. London: Richard Field, 1589.
Austern, Linda Phyllis. "Love, Death, and Ideas of Music in the English Renaissance." In *Love and Death in the Renaissance*, edited by Kenneth R. Bartlett, Konrad Eisenbichler, and Janice Liedl. Dovehouse Studies in Literature, no. 3. Ottawa: Dovehouse Editions, 1991.
———. " 'Sing Againe Syren': The Female Musician and Sexual Enchantment in Elizabethan Life and Literature." *Renaissance Quarterly* 42 (Autumn 1989): 420–48.
Bornstein, Diane, ed. *Distaves and Dames: Renaissance Treatises for and about Women*. Delmar, N.Y.: Scholar's Facsimiles and Reprints, 1978.
———. *The Feminist Controversy of the Renaissance*. Delmar, N.Y.: Scholar's Facsimiles and Reprints, 1980.
Boyd, Morrison Comegys. *Elizabethan Music and Musical Criticism*. 2d ed. Philadelphia: University of Pennsylvania Press, 1962.

Brathwait[e], Richard. *Art Asleep Husband? A Boulster Lecture.* London: R. Bishop for R.B., 1640.

Bruto, Giovanni [G. M. Bruts]. *The Necessarie, Fit, and Convenient Education of a Yong Gentlewoman.* Translated by W.P. London: Adam Islip, 1598.

Bullough, Vern L. *The Subordinate Sex: A History of Attitudes toward Women.* Urbana: University of Illinois Press, 1973.

Burton, Robert. *The Anatomy of Melancholy.* 4th ed. Oxford: Henry Cripps, 1632.

Butler, Charles. *The Principles of Musick in Singing and Setting.* London: John Haviland, 1636.

Camden, Carroll. *The Elizabethan Woman.* New York: Elsevier, 1952.

[Castiglione, Baldessar]. *The Courtyer of Count Baldessar Castilio.* Done into Englyshe by Thomas Hoby. London: Willyam Seres, 1561.

Crandall, Coryl. "The Cultural Implications of the Swetnam Anti-Feminist Controversy in the Seventeenth Century." *Journal of Popular Culture* 2 (1968): 136–47.

Davies, Stevie. *The Feminine Reclaimed: The Idea of Woman in Spenser, Shakespeare, and Milton.* Lexington: University Press of Kentucky, 1986.

Dusinberre, Juliet. *Shakespeare and the Nature of Women.* London: Macmillan, 1975.

Farmer, John. *The First Set of English Madrigals: To Foure Voices.* London: William Barley for Thomas Morley, 1599.

Gibson, Anthony. *A Womans Woorth, Defended against All the Men in the World.* London: John Wolfe, 1599.

Gosynhyll, Edward. *Here Begynneth a Lytle Boke Named the Scholehouse of Women.* N.p., 1541.

[Gosynhyll, Edward]. *The Prayse of All Women, Called Mulierum Pean.* N.p., n.d.

Greene, Robert. *Greenes Orpharion.* London: Edward White, 1599.

Haec-Vir, or the Womanish-Man: Being an Answere to a Late Booke Intituled "Hic-Mulier." London: J[ohn] T[rundle], 1620.

Haller, William, and Malleville Haller. "The Puritan Art of Love." *Huntington Library Quarterly* 5, no. 2 (1941–42): 235–72.

Harris, David G. T. "Musical Education in Tudor Times (1485–1603)." *Proceedings of the Royal Musical Association* 65 (1938–39): 109–39.

Henderson, Katherine Usher, and Barbara F. McManus. *Half Humankind: Contexts and Texts of the Controversy about Women in England, 1540–1640.* Urbana: University of Illinois Press, 1985.

Hic Mulier, or, the Man-Woman: Being a Medicine to Cure the Coltish Disease[e of] the Staggers in the Masculine-Feminine of Our Times. London: J[ohn] T[rundle], 1620.

Hollander, John. *The Untuning of the Sky: Ideas of Music in English Poetry, 1500–1700.* Princeton, N.J.: Princeton University Press, 1961.

Hull, Suzanne W. *Chaste, Silent, and Obedient: English Books for Women, 1475–1640.* San Marino, Calif.: Huntington Library, 1982.

Jordan, Constance. "Feminism and the Humanists: The Case of Sir Thomas
    Elyot's *Defence of Good Women*." In *Rewriting the Renaissance: The
    Discourses of Sexual Difference in Early Modern Europe*, edited by Mar-
    garet W. Ferguson, Maureen Guilligan, and Nancy Vickers. Chicago: Uni-
    versity of Chicago Press, 1986.
Kelly, Joan. "Early Feminist Theory and the *Querelle des Femmes*, 1400–
    1789." In *Women, History, and Theory: The Essays of Joan Kelly*. Chi-
    cago: University of Chicago Press, 1984.
Kelso, Ruth. *Doctrine for the Lady of the Renaissance*. 1956. Reprint. Urbana:
    University of Illinois Press, 1978.
King, Margaret L. "Book-Lined Cells: Women and Humanism in the Early
    Italian Renaissance." In *Beyond Their Sex: Learned Women of the Eu-
    ropean Past*, edited by Patricia H. Labalme. New York: New York Uni-
    versity Press, 1980.
Knox, John. *The First Blast of the Trumpet against the Monstruous [sic]
    Regiment of Women*. N.p., 1558.
Maclean, Ian. *The Renaissance Notion of Woman*. Cambridge: Cambridge
    University Press, 1980.
Meres, Francis. *Palladis Tamia: Wits Treasury*. London: P. Short for Cuthbert
    Burbie, 1598.
[More, Edward]. *A Lytle and Bryefe Treatyse, Called the Defence of Women,
    and Especially of Englyshe Women, Made agaynst the Schole Howse of
    Women*. N.p., 1560.
Morley, Thomas. *A Plaine and Easie Introduction to Practicall Musicke*.
    London: Peter Short, 1597.
Mulcaster, Richard. *Positions wherein Those Primitive Circumstances Be Ex-
    amined, which Are Necessarie for the Training Up of Children*. London:
    Thomas Chare, 1581.
Munda, Constantia. *The Worming of a Mad Dogge*. London: Laurence Hayes,
    1617.
Overbury, Thomas. *The Remedy of Love*. London: Nicholas Okes for John
    Wels, 1620.
Peacham, Henry. *The Compleat Gentleman*. London: Francis Constable, 1622.
The Praise of Musicke. Oxford: Joseph Barnes, 1586.
Pyrrye, C. *The Praise and Dispraise of Women*. London: William How,
    [1569?].
Ravenscroft, Thomas. *A Briefe Discourse of the True (but Neglected) Use of
    Charact'ring the Degrees*. London: Edw. Allde for Tho. Adams, 1614.
Salter, Thomas. *A Mirrhor Mete for all Mothers, Matrones, and Maidens,
    Intituled the Mirrhor of Modesty*. London: Edward White, [1579].
Shakespeare, William. *Comedies, Histories, and Tragedies*. London: Isaac Jag-
    gard for Edward Blount, 1623.
———. *The Merchant of Venice*. London: Thomas Heyes, 1600.
Speght, Rachel. *A Mouzell for Melastomus*. London: Nicholas Okes for
    Thomas Archer, 1617.

Swetnam, Joseph. *The Arraignment of Lewd, Idle, Froward and Unconstant Women*. London: Printed for Richard Meighen, 1620.

Tattle-Well, Mary, and Joane Hit-Him-Home. *The Women's Sharp Revenge*. London: J.O. for James Becket, 1640.

Travitsky, Betty. *The Paradise of Women: Writings by Englishwomen of the Renaissance*. Westport, Conn.: Greenwood Press, 1981.

Tuvil, Daniel. *Asylum Veneris, a Sanctuary for Ladies*. London: Edward Griffin for Laurence L'isle, 1616.

Utley, Francis Lee. *The Crooked Rib: An Analytical Index to the Argument about Women in English and Scots Literature to the End of the Year 1568*. Columbus: Ohio State University Press, 1944.

Westrup, J. A. "Domestic Music under the Stuarts." *Proceedings of the Royal Musical Association* 68 (1941–42): 19–53.

Willen, Diane. "A Comment on Women's Education in Elizabethan England." *Topic: The Elizabethan Woman* 36 (Fall 1982): 66–73.

Woodbridge, Linda. *Women and the English Renaissance: Literature and the Nature of Womankind, 1540–1620*. Urbana: University of Illinois Press, 1984.

Wright, Louis B. *Middle-Class Culture in Elizabethan England*. Chapel Hill: University of North Carolina Press, 1935.

Wright, Thomas. *The Passions of the Minde in Generall*. Corrected and augmented. London: Valentine Simms for Walter Burre, 1604.

4

Quinault, Lully, and the *Précieuses:* Images of Women in Seventeenth-Century France

Patricia Howard

Seventeenth-century aristocratic Frenchwomen were famous in their day for their political power and literary judgment, but representations of such women in the theater (whether in, for example, Racine's *Phèdre* or Lully's *Armide*) show them as powerless, their judgment warped, and their careers destroyed by the perverse intensity of their own emotions. Catherine Clément has argued that stage representations of women, particularly in opera, where the medium of music encourages a suspension of rational analysis, profoundly affect an audience's perception of gender and help create a cultural mythology that identifies women with tragedy, failure, and death.[1] How can the highly artificial structures of opera bring about so powerful an effect? And how far can a cultural myth be seen to interact with the real world?

The power of some mid-century Frenchwomen is historical fact. Upper-class women played an active part in the political revolutions, known as the Frondes, which took place during the minority of Louis XIV. They not only intrigued against the throne but also rode at the head of armies and held cities against the regency government of Anne of Austria and Cardinal Mazarin.[2] The king's cousin, Mademoiselle de Montpensier, was among these revolutionary women.[3] She was also the first patron of France's foremost composer of the century, Jean-Baptiste Lully (1632–87). The connection is a significant one, linking, if paradoxically, life with art. La Grande Mademoiselle, while clearly modeling her own conduct on the Maid of Orleans, helped nurture the talent that was later to create the tragically ineffectual operatic heroines who held the stage in the last three decades of the century.

The role of women, aristocrats and commoners, in public life and in the family, was a lively literary topic in the seventeenth century. Both the legal question of authority (of fathers and husbands) and the more fundamental issue of woman's essential nature (the conflicting icons of Eve and Mary, the temptress and the saint) were strenuously debated in the forum of the arts. Novels, portraits, poems, plays, and eventually opera all attempted to define what it was to be a woman, throughout a broad spectrum of society, from queen to servant.[4] In the mid-century an important voice in the debate was a small group of high-born literary women, known as *Précieuses*, who undertook an analysis of women's roles in life and literature, focusing on their own class and experience.[5] They met the charge that woman was innately inferior to man, a charge articulated by the influential theologian André Valladier, who questioned whether woman could be said to be made in the image of God by asserting that "all that is strongest in the male body has been used to make the female."[6] They also used the romantic novel to represent women in roles denied them in the ordinary course of real life, where a few women might don armor and command soldiers, but most had little say in the disposition of their heart and fortune. The best known of these novelists is Madeleine de Scudéry, author of *Le Grand Cyrus* (1649–53) and *Clélie* (1654–61).

The *précieux* movement was not exclusively female. Indeed, its aim was to admit men who conformed to the submissive models represented in Scudéry's novels. Many male novelists (for example, Abbé Michel de Pure), poets (Tristan l'Hermite), and playwrights (Pierre Corneille) frequented the *ruelles*, or salons, and received publicity and perhaps financial backing, in addition to the less tangible benefits of a warmly interested readership.[7]

The *Précieuses* aspired to more than literary influence. Some of them, having tasted power in the Frondes, wanted to become involved in the wider social and political upheavals of the seventeenth century, not least the intellectual revolutions in which the foundations of modern science and philosophy were laid. But their aspirations to scientific activity on the whole were comically mistargeted. Their sphere was love; their thesis was that love relationships were controllable and should be controlled by the woman. They mimicked the work of cartographers with their fantasy maps of the kingdom of the heart, and they parodied scientific classification with their analysis of eight degrees of love, twenty kinds of sighs, and forty categories of the smile.[8] Their real achievements were in filtering the concepts of polite manners and good conversation first to the men of their own class who frequented the salons and then, by admitting the bourgeoisie, to women from a lower social stratum; they encouraged reading among less-educated men and women and made this fashionable activity more widely accessible by supporting the reform of orthography. Above all they made women noticeable. Heroic, frivolous, or pedantic, if seventeenth-century Frenchwomen of all classes are impossible to ignore, it is the *précieux* movement that made them so.

The poet and dramatist Philippe Quinault (1635–88), who was later to become Lully's librettist and to play a key part in creating a theater of memorable women, began his writing career under the patronage of the *Précieuses*, accepting their thesis of female power and recording it faithfully in his early plays. He was widely recognized by his contemporaries as both ambitious and astute, and it is clear that he sought *précieux* backing as a step on the ladder leading to literary and social success. A caustic biographical note in Antoine-Baudeau de Somaize's *Grand dictionnaire des Prétieuses* (1661) attributes his rapid rise to fame to his skillful plagiarism of other *précieux* poets, especially his teacher Tristan l'Hermite, his "amorous disposition," and his "galant manners."[9] In 1657 Quinault abandoned the salons for the court, where he seems to have been regarded as a kind of expert in preciosity, and where a few years later we find him playing a fashionable *précieux* word game, *Questions d'Amour*, on behalf of the king.

This game offers another illustration of the *précieux* obsession with pseudoscientific analysis of the realm of love. A player would propose a question involving a delicate dilemma of the heart, replies in verse or prose would then be forthcoming and their various merits debated by the company. The game was played in both real life and fiction. Contemporary novels were full of such debates, sometimes referred to as "the dialectic of love," and they were particularly relished by women because the questions articulated the *précieux* belief that love was a voluntary emotion, subject to reason, and firmly under the control of lovers of both sexes.

We have a record of one particular game, played at court in 1666. Five questions were posed by the countess Charlotte de Brégy and answered by Quinault at the king's command: (1) whether there was more joy to be had in the presence of a loved one than pain caused by evidence of their indifference, (2) what one should do when one's heart dictated one course of action and one's reason another, (3) whether one should hate someone who does not return one's proffered love, (4) whether it makes for greater happiness to love in vain someone who is altogether indifferent to love rather than someone who loves a rival, and (5) whether the *mérite* (loosely translatable as "prestige") of being loved outweighs the pain of rejection.[10]

The topics raised in the questions resurface in the following decades in the opera libretti that Quinault wrote for Lully. The predicaments that puzzled de Brégy's lovers torment the characters in Lully's and Quinault's operas, and the operas act out the *précieux* word game with concrete examples of each dilemma. The first question, for example, is debated in the opera *Alceste*, when the hero Alcide weighs the pleasure he experiences by being in Alceste's company against the pain of seeing her wed Admète: "Imagine if you can the uttermost torment of seeing your beloved possessed by a happy rival! . . . How dearly I shall pay for the pleasure of seeing her again!" (1.1).[11] The head/heart dilemma of question two is experienced by the nymph Sangaride in *Atys*. When she believes her lover Atys has been unfaithful, she tries to deny her love, singing, "Come back, Reason, come back and never leave me again; join with my anger to extinguish my love" (4.1). In *Persée* the lover Phinée, who has been jilted by Andromède, answers question three in explaining how his love has turned to hate: "Love dies in my heart; fury replaces it: I'd rather see a terrible monster devour the ungrateful Andromède, than see her in the arms of my fortunate rival" (4.3). De Brégy's fourth question is addressed in *Proserpine*, where Mercure consoles Cérès with the argument that although Jupiter neglects her, at least she need not attribute his neglect to infidelity: "A lover who is busy running a great empire hasn't always got time for love!" (1.2). Again in *Persée* the fifth question, which turns on the *précieux* preoccupation with *mérite*, is answered: Andromède reveals she has been persuaded to transfer her affections from Phinée to Persée because of the prestige of the new relationship; she cannot resist "tant de mérite . . . tant d'amour" (3.5).[12]

The correspondence between the issues raised in this set of *Questions d'Amour* (they are typical of many) and Quinault's libretti cannot have gone unnoticed. Opera was the most prestigious art form of the age. In France a single opera would be performed repeatedly over a long period before a regular audience, among which would be found many *Précieuses*. Moreover, Quinault's libretti were sold at the door of the theater, read by candlelight while the opera was in progress, and studied and debated by connoisseurs familiar with these and similar sets of *Questions* long after the performance.

The questions and the terms in which they were debated were superficially trivial, dealing with manners rather than feelings, but below their surface lay a real dilemma for seventeenth-century women: how to prolong the period of courtship to defer the biologically enforced servitude that marriage and constant childbearing imposed on the majority of women.[13] No wonder the women who reigned in the salons of the first half of the century had encouraged a return to the medieval ideal of courtly love, which kept the lover firmly on his knees and at a safe distance. In the second half of the century the *Précieuses'* crusade against marriage offered a choice of behavior, distinguishing between the *Précieuses prudes* and the *Précieuses coquettes.* The prudes advocated a secularization of the religious vow of chastity; they proposed a life of celibacy and took as their role model the dispassionate intellectual *précieuse* novelist Madeleine de Scudéry. The coquettes admitted many admirers but imposed a long and arduous courtship on them, and, inspired by the thirteen-year-long engagement of another celebrated *Précieuse,* Julie d'Angennes, they claimed the right to defer submission almost indefinitely.

The *Questions d'Amour* implied a cardinal tenet of *précieux* belief: the woman ought to be free to remain indifferent to all lovers. Celibacy was a burning issue in the literature of this age. Male authors, who often feared female celibacy or at least the self-sufficiency that it implied, betrayed their bias when they referred to the celibate woman as *ingrate* and *inhumaine;* women writers invariably spoke of celibacy as a state of *innocence, paix,* and *liberté.* Quinault's position appears at first glance to be ambivalent; he gave a voice to both views. He retained enough of his *précieux* apprenticeship to allow the majority of his female characters to acknowledge the pleasures of celibacy. For example, Proserpine develops at length the proposition that "true happiness comes from resisting love" (2.8), and Lybie, in *Phaëton,* sings, "Happy the disengaged heart" (1.1). But he also showed the failure of women to remain celibate—the often tragic failure, as in the cases of Médée and Armide, who are seen struggling in vain against their own (supposed) nature to preserve their roles as *inhumaines.* The word implies, and in these characterizations Quinault endorsed the view, that celibacy is unnatural, a dehumanizing state, not only working against the future of the human race but also denying men their pleasurable part in its continuance. That this was a common male response to the *Précieuses prudes* is suggested by Molière's satire on the position of the bigoted and pretentious Armande in *Les femmes savantes* (1672).

Whatever his own beliefs about women's capabilities and rightful ambitions, Quinault found the fate of women who fail in their attempt to live independently of men strong material for drama. For example, the fable of Pan and Syrinx, introduced into act 3 of *Isis,* acts out the *refus d'amour* as the would-be celibate Syrinx flees from the importunate Pan. Quinault and Lully could hardly soften or avoid the outcome of the myth—Syrinx is metamorphosed into a bed of reeds—but they collaborated to give dramatic emphasis to a woman's desire for celibacy and strongly articulated her preferred word for that state: the word *liberté* is heard some ninety-five times in a sequence of scenes containing just thirty-three lines. *Liberté* is also the theme of the Abbé de Pure's germinal novel *La Prétieuse*, which consistently associated the term with an all-female social environment: it is the absence of men that confers *liberté*. He also invoked the word to represent escape from the *épouvantable servitude* of marriage.[14] Likewise, Somaize not only defined marriage as *l'amour fini* and *l'abyme de la liberté* (the destruction of liberty) but also wrote that the state of *liberté* was "necessary" to the *Précieuse*.[15]

A number of characters in Quinault's operas might agree with Syrinx, "Je déclare à l'Amour une guerre immortelle" (3.6), but that is only one side of the complex *précieux* response to love. Jean-Michel Pelous identifies a rebellion among male lovers in literature and in life, dating from around 1660, which constituted a reaction to the perfect submission that the *Précieuses* expected from their chivalric lovers.[16] Contending that in the second half of the century it became inadmissible for a man of fashion to be unsuccessful in his courtship for long, Pelous traces the growth of a hedonist code of behavior, summed up ironically by Molière's Don Juan as "all women have the right to charm us."[17] Pelous, however, argues that at least some women chose to attempt to regain their former dominance by adopting the corresponding role of coquette. Berelise in de Scudéry's novel *Clélie* expresses the aspiration of the coquette: "to be loved extremely, and not to love at all, or very little."[18] The male hedonist and female coquette cynically confronted the disregard for genuine feelings displayed in the way in which women were disposed of—the Abbé de Pure would have said "bought and sold"—in seventeenth-century marriage. The *précieux* bid for emancipation, whether through celibacy or hedonism, involved denying the power of love. The sexes competed to claim the right to reject an unwanted lover and sought to defend themselves against a loss of face if they themselves were rejected.

The role of the *précieuse prude* is to refuse, that of the *précieuse coquette*, to choose. Quinault continued to show that he had mastered his salon lessons by depicting authentic examples of the coquette. Dorine in *Thésée* warns, "It's dangerous to love too much" (2.5). Charite in *Cadmus* divides love from the suffering with which it had been synonymous in past decades: "Love is no longer agreeable when it ceases to be a game" (2.1). The most fully drawn example is Céphise, the confidante in *Alceste*, who keeps two suitors dangling throughout the opera before dismissing both of them in the last act. However, all Quinault's hedonists are gods, and all his coquettes are servants. He never attempted to represent a heroine as a coquette. He subverted the *précieux* bid for emancipation by refusing his heroines the power to choose, for he perceived sexual passion in women as a force that removes mental autonomy.[19]

The issue for the *Précieuses* was social: aspiring to emotional independence, they credited women with moral strength and thought their unhappiness stemmed from the nature of the society in which they lived. The issue for Quinault was biological: he portrayed women's unhappiness as the result of what he perceived to be their innate nature, and he dramatized their presumed moral weakness. The *Précieuses* prided themselves on the freedom achieved by their *refus d'amour*, but Quinault represented them as powerless to refuse; his women characters constantly excuse their capitulation to passion with the phrase *malgré moi*—"despite myself." Manipulating literary sources, which were after all common to all seventeenth-century librettists, Quinault overturned *précieux* images of women's aspirations, punishing the celibate and marginalizing the coquette, to construct an interpretation of female sexuality that Joyce Scott calls "the fatality of love"[20] and that Catherine Clément has shown to be as enduring as it is tragic.

Quinault inherited as subject matter a world of myths in which male and female are consistently in opposition. The role of the classical mythmakers was to justify the social position of women in the ancient world and to give grounds for the popular opinion that held them to be not only inferior to men but also dangerous to the stability of society. The subjugation of women had been seen as a necessary step in establishing civilization; and so in myth the Earth goddess was replaced by the male hierarchy of Olympus, and Dionysus, Heracles, and Theseus are seen to overcame the Amazons. Woman as the root of all evil appears in classical as well as many other mythologies, and, more disturbingly, myths tend to portray the first woman as the means of introducing evil into a hitherto perfect world. Like Eve in the Garden of Eden, Pandora with her magic box was held responsible for all the miseries of the human condition.

In this context Quinault's selection of subject matter is revealing. He soon rejected the male-centered myths and legends so popular in Italian opera of the seventeenth century—the stories of Jason, Hercules, Achilles, Ulysses, and, above all, the Orpheus myth.[21] He chose instead stories that focus on women, but instead of representing the independent women of *précieux* aspirations, he portrayed women who either submit to male dominance or are destroyed by their bid for freedom in *Cadmus* (1673), *Alceste* (1674), *Thésée* (1675), *Atys* (1676), *Isis*

(1677), *Proserpine* (1680), *Persée* (1682), *Phaëton* (1683), *Amadis* (1684), *Poland* (1685), and *Armide* (1686).

The male-centered nature of Italian opera is evident in the first two libretti. The action is dominated by the hero or heroes, and Cadmus and Admète win their brides through the performance of heroic deeds, though Admète delegates his heroism to a proxy, Alcide, and Quinault removes Alceste from the center of attention in the story that tells of her heroic sacrifice in offering her life to save her husband's. The middle group of operas gives women greater prominence, but when we look at some of the principal women of these operas—Médée and Aeglé; Cybele and Sangaride; Io, Cérès, and Proserpine; Mérope and Andromède; Lybie and Théone—it is immediately apparent that although the focus of the action is on them, they are represented as unhappy and powerless pawns in the game of love. Either—like Médée, Cybele, Mérope, and Théone—they are unable to marry the hero of their choice, or—like Io, Proserpine, Andromède, and Lybie—they submit to being transferred from one suitor to another at the whim of a god or prince. The last two operas present an even bleaker picture. Roland learns that love is a cheat, and Renaud is taught that it is an illusion.

We can take the characterization of the tragic goddess Cybele in *Atys* as an example of Quinault's manipulation of his sources. In this libretto, Quinault represents the goddess as a woman out of control; she is in love with a mortal, her own high priest, Atys, and she is quite unable to "master" her own emotions. The emphasis is Quinault's own. In the classical myth, the goddess Cybele is a powerful and triumphant figure. In the rituals associated with her cult, it is the death of her high priest that is mourned, not Cybele's loss of a lover. The classical Cybele overcomes the disappointment of losing Atys's love by an act of powerful vengeance—she causes him to castrate himself—but none of the many variants of the myth puts a wholly tragic interpretation on the episode; Cybele has her revenge and, unlike Atys, lives happily ever after. The classical myth exalts the power of the female over the male, giving substance to that primitive fear of woman's sexuality that caused later classical mythmakers to replace Earth-goddess figures like Cybele with the hierarchy of sky gods, ruled by Jupiter. Quinault, however, chose to emphasize not Cybele's transcendent supernatural power but rather what he interprets as her womanly frailty—her lack of self-control—and its tragic consequences: "Hélas! par tant d'attraits falloit-il me surprendre! Heureuse si toujours j'avois pu me défendre! [Alas! was it necessary to catch me unawares by such handsomeness? How happy I would be if I could have remained immune!]" (3.8).

Quinault selected subjects that enabled him to depict women as essentially powerless, unable fully to control either events or their own conduct, and he was prepared to reinterpret earlier stories to propound this point of view. He even reversed the male and female roles represented in earlier literature by replacing the subservient male with a more assertive model; this change removed the woman's power to initiate action. When, for example, in the medieval romance *Amadis de Gaul*, a popular work with the *Précieuses*, the knight Amadis believes his mistress Oriane to be unfaithful, he still remains enslaved; he declares that he loves even her hatred of him.[22] Quinault found this implausible. He made Amadis attempt to reject Oriane when he believes her to be unfaithful, allowing Amadis to pursue military glory while Oriane is forced into waiting on events to restore her reputation. Quinault deviated from a more recent model when he adapted the story of Perseus from Corneille's play of 1650 by adding a new character, Mérope, a woman who is passed over by Persée in favor of Andromède and who perfectly exemplifies the suffering female victim of unrequited love.

Quinault's heroines are essentially passive characters who experience mental turmoil in a state of physical inaction. He elevated psychological drama to an importance previously reserved for action. We can appropriately borrow a phrase from Roland Barthes's study of Racine, in whose works he found that "to love is an intransitive state,"[23] and apply it to Quinault's heroines, for Quinault, Racine's precursor in this respect, tended to represent the state of being in love by concentrating on the subject of the emotion to the exclusion of any object at all.

Opera does not rely on plot alone to make a point. Dramatic form and musical style play an important part in articulating its message. To explore the uneasy conjunction of violent emotions and social restraint, Quinault devised a dramatic monologue, typically in three sections, with a short, heartfelt aspiration that expresses the *précieux* desire for the celibate state, a middle paragraph that either explains the wish or explains why it cannot be granted, and a return to the initial aspiration. (Sometimes the aspiration occurs three times, at the beginning, middle, and end, giving the short first line a particularly brooding and obsessive effect.) The monologue focuses exclusively on the divided state of mind of a woman who cannot help herself, who aspires to *liberté* but who succumbs to passion. In *Thésée* Médée's first monologue opens with a wish for "Sweet tranquility, undisturbed peace! Happy the heart that never loses you!" She then explains her dilemma, and the would-be celibate disappears under the complaint

Borders
Books & Music

512 E. Liberty, Ann Arbor (313) 668-7652

952   1/0010/10   000216   SALE

EH   TX RETAIL DISC   SPEC   EXTND

   2.98 NORTON PAPER 2.98

IR 1449422 1   2.98 33%   2.00   2.00

   CECILIA RECLAIMED

SP 0848450 1 12.95 33%   8.68   8.68

                 SUBTOTAL   10.68

   6.000%   TAX1   .64

Items   AMOUNT DUE   11.32

                 VISA   11.32

4430018200701963 0199 006834 7111

                 CHANGE DUE   .00

      04/06/96   08:17 PM

Returns within 30 days with receipt

of the woman who loses control of her emotions: "Pitiless love has always hounded me. Hasn't he done me enough harm already? Why does this cruel god arm himself with new arrows to trouble the remainder of my life?" Then there is a return to the opening, underlining the poignancy of the unattainable *liberté:*

res-te de ma vi - e?   Doux re - pos,   in-no-cen - te
paix,   Heu-reux, heu-reux un   coeur   qui ne vous perd ja - mais!

Doux repos, innocente paix,
Heureux, heureux un coeur qui ne vous perd jamais!
L'impitoyable Amour m'a toujours poursuivie.
N'étoit-ce point assez des maux qu'il m'avoit faits?
Pourquoi ce Dieu cruel, avec de nouveaux traits,
Vient-il encore troubler le reste de ma vie?
Doux repos, innocente paix,
Heureux, heureux un coeur qui ne vous perd jamais!
Thésée (2.1)

[Sweet tranquility, undisturbed peace!
Happy the heart that never loses you!
Pitiless love has always hounded me.
Hasn't he done me enough harm already?
Why does this cruel god arm himself with new arrows
To trouble the remainder of my life?
Sweet tranquility, undisturbed peace!
Happy the heart that never loses you!]

It is relevant to ask whether Lully's settings of the monologues offer a critique of Quinault's perception of women or reinforce it. Lully's "reprise monologue"[24] matches Quinault's structure of aspiration, explanation, and aspiration with a form that uses measured style, free style, and a return to measured style. The opening *précieux* aspiration gains in rhetorical force from this juxtaposition of styles, and it is often given further weight by a *ritournelle,* underlining the first-section material. But Lully also clearly grasped the expressive potential of the tormented emotions that appear in the middle section. Because of the way he conventionally used recitative in his operas, we cannot infer that the composer deliberately matched Quinault's portrayal of a breaking out of uncontrollable emotion with a breaking into unmeasured style. Recitative in Lully's operas does not automatically imply disabling passion; rather, it is the basic narrative and transactional medium of the drama. It always carries more expressive weight than an air, however, and in choosing recitative style for the middle portion of the monologues, Lully emphatically represented the "fatality of love."

Lully's own bias is most evident when he tampered with the musical framework Quinault offered him. Médée, contemplating killing Thésée whom she loves (and simultaneously addressing de Brégy's third *Question d'Amour*), sings, "Ah, must I avenge myself in losing the one I love?" Lully set the aspiration, explanation, and reprise of the aspiration as a lyrical rondeau air with a low emotional temperature. After it has apparently finished, he set the following three lines in recitative, but he wrenched the common-time recitative back to a semblance of the measured triple-meter air for the final reprise, which exchanges the aspiration for a resolve: "No, no, I must avenge myself by losing the one I love." The effect of the musical setting is to weight the conclusion, giving greater dramatic force to Médée's uncontrollable jealousy of her happy rival than to her strength of character in attempting to suppress her passion:

rai de dou - leur, Je trem - ble d'y son - ger, Ah!

Ah! faut - il me ven - ger, En per - dant ce que

Ritournelle

j'ai - me!

Médée

Ma Ri- va - le tri -

om - phe, et me voit ou - tra - ger; Quoi! lai - sser son am-

our sans peine et sans dan - ger, Voir le Spec-tac- le af -

freux de son bon-heur ex - tre - me! Non!

non, il faut me ven-ger, En per- dant ce que j'ai - me!

Ah! Ah! faut-il me venger,
En perdant ce que j'aime?
Que fais-tu ma fureur, où vas tu m'engager?
Punir ce coeur ingrat, c'est me punir moi-même;
J'en mourrai de douleur, je tremble d'y songer,
Ah! Ah! faut-il me venger,
En perdant ce que j'aime?

Ma Rivale triomphe, et me voit outrager;
Quoi! laisser son amour sans peine et sans danger,

Voir le Spectacle affreux de son bonheur extreme?
Non! non, il faut me venger,
En perdant ce que j'aime!

Thésée (5.1)

[Ah! must I avenge myself
by losing the one I love?
What are you doing, my anger?
What are you involving me in?
To punish this ungrateful lover is to punish myself.
I shall die of grief over it,
I tremble to think of it.
Ah! must I avenge myself
by losing the one I love?]

[My rival will triumph and see me insulted.
What, to leave her love untroubled, unthreatened,
and to see the dreadful spectacle of her perfect happiness?
No, I must avenge myself
by losing the one I love!]

The monologues form the expressive high points of Lully's operas. Clearly, the composer realized what opportunities for musical riches were offered by the unhappy situations of Médée and her sisters. In these settings Lully, too, can be seen to have played a part in constructing the seventeenth-century myth of the uncontrollable woman. The enduring popularity of his works ensured that his perception of the innately tragic nature of woman's sexuality would persist and become, as Clément has shown, the dominant genre for nineteenth-century librettists.

Why did Quinault turn from his *précieux* schooling to construct a world that offered so little prospect of happiness and self-determination to half of its inhabitants? His opera libretti carry a harsh warning: unsought, uncontrolled love, from a woman, is a shameful emotion; love can only bring happiness when it is offered in response to the suit of a hero. The ideal heroine offers the hero an ideal love that does no more than reflect a mirror image of his own inclination—the lesson of the operas is a reversal of the doctrine of the *précieux* salon.

Such a biased picture is less bizarre, however, when we consider the circumstances in which Quinault's work was produced. In his opera libretti he was not writing for an exclusively *précieux* circle; indeed, as Patrick Smith reminds us, Quinault's operas constituted "a product directed towards a specific audience of one."[25] Quinault's heroes were perceived to be allegories of Louis XIV. The heyday of the *Précieuses* had been the mid-century regency, when images of womanly power or at least of male weakness and insufficiency were general. Under Louis's eminently patriarchal reign, the male-centered hierarchy of classical gods, heroes, and servants was reborn in the strata of king, nobles, and the people. Scrutinized and decoded by court gossips eager to detect parallels between the plots and the king's amorous adventures, the operas represent a society that acknowledged the divine right of the king—and institutionalized the role of the king's mistress.[26]

Quinault's heroines are taught that their only prospect of a happy ending is to behave as those selected for the position of royal mistress should. Like Andromède, they must reject a lower hero for the higher; like Alceste, they must renounce any thought of heroic stature for themselves; like Aeglé, they must be faithful under trying circumstances; and like Io and Lybie, they must be receptive to love, not, like Médée, force it on an embarrassed monarch. Like Cérès and Théone, they must expect to be passed over or replaced. Above all, when their moment of reflected glory is past, they must take warning from the examples of Cybele and Junon and refrain from jealousy. Quinault's libretti, then, constitute nothing less than a school for royal mistresses.[27]

Louis himself, at the height of his hedonist career, recorded his attitude to the snares of love:

If it should happen that we fall inspite of ourselves into [the follies common to the rest of humanity] it is important, at least, to minimize the consequences—to observe the precautions that I have always practiced . . . the first is that the time we give to our love affairs must not prejudice our political affairs, because our first object should always be the preservation of our *gloire* and authority . . . the second consideration, more delicate and more difficult, is that in abandoning our heart we must preserve our mind; that we separate the tenderness of a lover from the resolutions of a sovereign; that the beauty who gives us pleasure never has the liberty to discuss our affairs nor the people who serve us: these two things must be separate.[28]

No clearer statement exists of the marginalization of women in the seventeenth century.

Furthermore, from the year in which Louis abandoned hedonism for a morganatic marriage with Madame de Maintenon, Quinault changed the context of his dramatic world. He replaced the amorous hierarchy of classical mythology with the quasi-historical medieval romances. In these romances, however, Quinault's lesson is even more pessimistic. The pursuit of even as poor a thing as "ideal love" is abandoned in the last two operas. Indeed, love is portrayed as an illusion. The whole of the strange, frustrating fourth act of *Armide* (in which two knights are in turn ensnared by and escape from the blandishments of women) is constructed to teach the irrelevance of love for the hero (and, by implication, for the king). Amadis, Roland, and Renaud, to a man, reject love in favor of glory (though Amadis later opts to have his cake and eat it too). From 1684 Quinault no longer had any need to enroll submissive pupils in his school of love, and there is no place for the role of love in his school for heroes.

In the century following Quinault and Racine, French opera became irreversibly woman-centered. As revivals of Lully's operas, which played a major role in the early eighteenth-century repertory, waned in popularity, they were followed in the last quarter of the century by a spate of resettings of Quinault's libretti, of which the most famous is Christoph Gluck's version of *Armide* in 1777. Quinault's influence extended even beyond this, with resettings by Niccolo Piccinni of *Roland* in 1778 and *Atys* in 1780, *Persée* by André Danican Philidor in 1780, *Thésée* by François Joseph Gossec in 1782, and, remarkably, *Proserpine* by Giovanni Paisiello in 1803. By 1803 Quinault's theater of tragic women had permanently entered the mainstream of European opera, perpetuating an artistic tradition in which woman, rather than man, serves as the hub of the action and the focus of psychological interest, which would have pleased the *Précieuses,* but also perpetuating a tradition that interprets woman's sexuality as fated, leading inevitably to tragedy and death.

NOTES

All translations have been supplied by the author.

1. Clément, *Opera.*
2. The Parlementary Fronde took place in 1648–49, the Princely Fronde in 1651–52.
3. In 1652 Mademoiselle de Montpensier led an army against the king. When the city of Orleans closed its gates to both factions, she entered the town unescorted through a back gate, captured the city, and took over its government on behalf of the rebel cause.
4. The debate on women's nature, known as the *Querelle des Femmes,* was an old one, dating from the late Middle Ages. See Kelly, "Early Feminist Theory"; for a fuller discussion of seventeenth-century women's roles and images, see Maclean, *Women Triumphant.*
5. The forms of the adjective change: *précieux* in association with a masculine or mixed-sex noun, singular or plural; *précieuse* with a singular feminine noun; *précieuses* for the feminine plural. The form *Précieuses,* then, applies to the female members of the *précieux* movement. The adjective was

originally applied as a compliment, meaning literally precious or unusually talented, but already by 1659 it had become associated with affectation, as Molière's trenchant parody *Les Précieuses ridicules* demonstrates. It is difficult to be precise about any aspect of the *précieux* movement. Scholars even disagree over its date (the earliest suggested date is 1605); many see two generations of *Précieuses*, before and after the Frondes. The first metaphorical use of the adjective, however, has been traced to 1654, and Somaize published the first edition of his dictionary, which lists members of the *précieux* circles, in 1660. The arguments over dating the movement are sifted in Zimmer, *Die literarische Kritik am Preziösentum.* Kelly, "Did Women Have a Renaissance?" 34, points out how patronage of the arts became, for aristocratic women, a substitute for governmental power during the Renaissance.

6. Valladier, *Saincte philosophie,* 813–14; Buffet, *Nouvelles observations,* 200.

7. *Ruelle* was the more common term in the seventeenth century for the meeting place of the *précieux* circle. It referred to the space between the bed (in which the hostess reclined) and the wall and implied an atmosphere in which intimate conversation flourished.

8. Backer, *Precious Women,* 163. For more scholarly evidence of the educational limitations of seventeenth-century women, see de la Barre, *Égalité des sexes.*

9. Somaize, *Grand dictionnaire des Prétieuses,* s.v. "Quirinus," 1:203–4.

10. De Brégy, *"Cinq questions d'amour,"* 97–100. The first question and answer run as follows:

> *Question:* Sçavoir si la presence de ce que l'on aime cause plus de joye, que les marques de son indifference ne donnent de peine.

> *Response:* C'est un tourment d'aimer, sans estre aimé de méme, Mais pour un bel objet, quand l'amour est extreme, Quels que soient ses regards, ils sont toujours charmans, Et si l'on s'en rapport a tous les vrais amans, C'est un plaisir si doux de voir ce que l'on aime, Qu'il doit faire oublier les plus cruels tourments.

The questions had a distant ancestry in the twelfth-century Provençal poetic genre known as the *joc-partit (jeu-parti),* which debated, for example, "Is it better to be a wife or a mistress?"; the genre seems to have disappeared between approximately 1450 and 1650. A stimulus for its reintroduction might have been a deliberately bathetic imitation of the ethical debates in Italian Renaissance academies. See Crane, *Société française.*

11. Parenthetical references to operas designate act and scene; for example, (1.2) means act 1, scene 2.

12. For a variety of definitions of *mérite,* see de Pure, *Prétieuse,* 1:159, 311; 2:105, 167, and many other instances.

13. Adam, *Histoire de la littérature,* 2:23, attributes a powerful role to fear of the physical consequences of marriage: "la crainte devant l'amour et

le mariage, qui est l'essence de la préciosité." For a detailed discussion of concepts of marriage in the seventeenth century, see Büff, *Ruelle und Realität*.

14. "Je veux travailler . . . a la liberté de mon sexe . . . et a la destruction de cette épouvantable servitude" (de Pure, *Prétieuse*, 2:269).

15. Somaize, *Grand dictionnaire des Prétieuses*, 1:51, 172–73. See also du Bosc, *Femme heroïque*, 2:684: "L'honneur et la chasteté des Dames font leur veritable liberté. La Dame qui a consenty s'est rendue esclave."

16. Pelous, *Amour précieux*, 195–224.

17. Molière, *Don Juan* (1665), (1.2): "Toutes les belles ont droit de nous charmer."

18. De Scudéry, *Clélie*, 5:1188: "D'estre fort aimée, et de n'aimer point, ou de n'aimer guere."

19. The concept of the "uncontrollable woman" was a Renaissance extrapolation from woman's physical "weakness." The imbalance of cold and moist humors were said to give her greater imaginative powers and a better memory, and consequently a capacity for implacable hatred and a tendency to pursue vengeance. This characterization was reinterpreted during the middle decades of the seventeenth century, when the concept of the heroic woman was constructed. Associated with the period of the regency of Anne of Austria (1643–52), the heroic woman is documented in the portraits in Le Moyne's *Gallerie des femmes fortes* and the heroines of Corneille's *tragédies*. Compare the resurgence of militant women during the rule of the British Queen Anne, when "all the evidence of sense and reason argued against male superiority. Not only was every man not superior to every woman; one woman was now superior to every man in the realm" (Kelly, "Early Feminist Theory," 93).

20. Scott, "Philippe Quinault."

21. It is inconceivable that Quinault should have written an Orpheus opera—or if he had, he would surely have given Eurydice a previous lover and created another nymph repining for Orpheus's lost love; such a scenario is not altogether farfetched in view of the violence he did to the Alcestis story.

22. De Lobeira, *Amadis de Gaul*.

23. Barthes, *Racine*, 58.

24. The term is my own. As with so many aspects of Lully's operas, there can be no straightforward definition. The recurrence of brief, measured phrases is a common device in Lully's operas, and the resulting structures vary from short, lyrical rondeaux to whole recitative scenes, which are given some unity by the recurrence of a single line. Between these extremes falls the reprise monologue, which differs from a passage of recitative because it is clearly identifiable as a closed form and is distinguishable from the air by its essentially declamatory style. The reprise monologue, which may derive ultimately from the lament in seventeenth-century Italian opera, is usually a soliloquy and most often opens scenes. It is generally accompanied by the continuo alone, though two examples in *Armide* are accompanied by five-part strings. It is much more likely to be given to a female than to a male character; of some thirty reprise monologues I have identified in Lully's operas, only five are sung

by men, and those are sung either by "effeminate" men or by men in "feminine" circumstances (e.g., suffering unrequited love).

25. Smith, *Tenth Muse*, 50.

26. Louis's mistresses are too numerous to list. The following liaisons are the best documented: Louise de la Vallière (1661–67), Françoise-Athénaïs de Montespan (1668–76), Gabrielle de Thianges (circa 1670–76), Mademoiselle des Oeillets (circa 1675–79), Marie Isabelle de Ludres (1676–77), Anne de Soubise (1676–78), Maris-Adélaïde de Fontanges (1678–79), and Mademoiselle Doré (circa 1679–80). It is instructive to compare the dates (necessarily approximate) of each favorite's "reign" with those of the operas.

27. For a more detailed structural analysis of Quinault's heroines, see Howard, "Women in Quinault's World," 193–99.

28. Wolf, *Louis XIV*, 307.

REFERENCES

Adam, Antoine. *Histoire de la littérature française au XVIIe siècle*. 5 vols. Paris: Domat, 1951.

Backer, Dorothy Anne. *Precious Women*. New York: Basic Books, 1974.

Barthes, Roland. *Racine*. Paris: Seuil, 1963.

Büff, Renate. *Ruelle und Realität*. Heidelberg: Carl Winter, 1979.

Buffet, Marguerite. *Nouvelles observations sur la langue françoise*. Paris: I. Cusson, 1668.

Clément, Catherine. *Opera, or the Undoing of Women*. Translated by Betsy Wing. Foreword by Susan McClary. Minneapolis: University of Minnesota Press, 1988.

Crane, Thomas Frederick. *La société française au dix-septième siècle*. 2d ed. New York: G. P. Putnam's Sons, 1907.

De Brégy, Charlotte de Saumaize. *"Cinq questions d'amour."* In *Lettres et poësie*. Paris: n.p., 1666.

De la Barre, François. *De l'égalité des sexes: Discours physique et moral où l'on voit l'importance de se defaire des préjugés*. Paris: J. du Puis, 1673.

De Lobeira, Johann, attrib. *Amadis de Gaul*. Translated by Nicholas de Herberay. Paris: Denys Ianot, 1540; Lyon: François Didier, 1577.

De Pure, Michel. *La Prétieuse*. [1656–60]. Edited by Émile Magne. Paris: Droz, 1938–39.

De Scudéry, Madeleine. *Clélie*. 8 vols. [1654–61]. Reprint. Geneva: Slatkine, 1973.

———. *Le Grand Cyrus*. 3 vols. Paris: n.p., 1649–53.

Du Bosc, Jacques. *La femme heroïque, ou les heroïnes comparées avec les héros en toute sorte de vertus*. Paris: n.p., 1645.

Howard, Patricia. *"The Positioning of Women in Quinault's World Picture."* In *Jean Baptiste Lully: Actes du Colloque*, compiled by Jerome de la Gorce and Herbert Schneider. Kongressbericht, Saint-Germain-en-Laye, Heidelberg, September 1987. Neue Heidelberger Studien zur Musikwissenschaft, 18. Laaber: Laaber-Verlag, 1990.

Kelly, Joan. "Did Women Have a Renaissance?" In *Women, History, and Theory: The Essays of Joan Kelly*. Chicago: University of Chicago Press, 1984.

———. "Early Feminist Theory and the *Querelle des Femmes*." In *Women, History, and Theory: The Essays of Joan Kelly*. Chicago: University of Chicago Press, 1984.

Le Moyne, Pierre. *Gallerie des femmes fortes*. Paris: Antoine de Sommaville, 1647.

Maclean, Ian. *Women Triumphant*. Oxford: Oxford University Press, 1977.

Molière, Jean-Baptiste Poquelin. *Oeuvres*. Edited by Eugène Despois and Paul Mesnard. 13 vols. Paris: Hachette, 1873–1900.

Pelous, Jean-Michel. *Amour précieux, amour galant, 1654–1675*. Paris: Klingsiek, 1980.

Quinault, Philippe. *Théâtre*. 5 vols. [1778]. Reprint. Geneva: Slatkine, 1970.

Scott, Joyce Alaine. " 'Douceur' and 'Violence' in the Tragedies and Tragi-Comedies of Philippe Quinault." Ph.D. diss., Duke University, 1972.

Smith, Patrick. *The Tenth Muse: A Historical Study of the Opera Libretto*. London: Gollancz, 1971.

Somaize, Antoine-Baudeau de. *Le grand dictionnaire des Prétieuses: Historique, poétique, cosmographique, cronologique, et armoirique*. 2d ed., 1661. 2 vols. Edited by M. Ch.-L. Livet. Paris: Jannet, 1856.

Valladier, André. *La saincte philosophie de l'ame*. Paris: L. Gautier, 1614.

Wolf, John B. *Louis XIV*. London: Golancz, 1968.

Zimmer, Wolfgang. *Die literarische Kritik am Presiösentum*. Meisenheim am Glan: Anton Hain, 1978.

5

"A Distinguishing Virility": Feminism and Modernism in American Art Music

Catherine Parsons Smith

The first wave of feminism had a powerful influence on American composers in the late nineteenth century and the first half of the twentieth century. Another strong influence, musical Americanism in its romantic and modernist phases, has been explored in recent years, but discussion of the role of feminism is only beginning.[1] I argue in this essay that while many middle-class white women emerged as composers before World War I, the period of romantic Americanism, an antiwoman reaction developed simultaneously with their appearance. Misogyny became an essential feature of American modernism as it developed after 1918. Antiwoman attitudes achieved or reestablished their cultural hegemony, effectively suppressing the work of women as composers of art music, shutting them out of the modernist movement, or silencing them completely. At the same time, hostility toward women stimulated and enabled contemporary male composers.[2]

Feminist literary critics, such as Sandra M. Gilbert and Susan Gubar in the first two volumes of *No Man's Land: The Place of the Woman Writer in the Twentieth Century*, argue that antifeminism was a fundamental, motivating factor for modernism in twentieth-century literature. They propose that modern American and English literature can be understood as a complex and productive reaction by both male and female writers to the feminist movement of the nineteenth century, which reached its apex with the granting of suffrage to women in England and the United States in 1920. In their preface they point out that "the ongoing battle of the sexes . . . was set in motion by the late nineteenth-century rise of feminism and the fall of Victorian concepts of 'femininity.' " They speculate that " 'modernism' in literature was for men and women both a product of the sexual battle." Gilbert and Gubar argue that the role of feminism in literary modernism has not been obvious because the contributions of female authors have been suppressed; thus, "many readers and teachers failed to perceive the sexual struggle that . . . influences much of the literature written between the mid-nineteenth century and the present."[3]

The sexual struggle that influenced modern literature also affected the modernist movement in American music, where its presence has also been difficult to perceive. Gilbert and Gubar's thesis provides a powerful tool to illuminate the previously unseen gendering of musical modernism. Their main points include (1) the use of "sexual linguistics" by men as a means to distance themselves from and exclude women as authors; (2) the ambivalence of literary women toward their female literary forebears, which Gilbert and Gubar call, using Freudian terms, a "female affiliation complex"; and (3) the early prominence, and later suppression, of antiwoman statements, which they characterize as "masculinism," in literary modernism.[4] This essay explores these three points as they apply to music.

In their discussion of "sexual linguistics," Gilbert and Gubar distinguish between *materna lingua,* the primal mother tongue, which is the everyday, vernacular speech that both women and men acquire in infancy as they are nurtured by their mothers, and *patrius sermo,* the formal discourse intended for the conduct of public affairs, transmitted by males to other males and serving to distance them from women and to exclude women from the conduct of those affairs. Latin functioned in the eighteenth and nineteenth centuries as the *patrius sermo* for literary men, long after it had lost its role as the exclusive language for learned and public discourse. Gilbert and Gubar point out that in the nineteenth century, as women began to gain access to the schools and universities previously closed to them, the study of Latin began to lose this privileged function and, as a result, its central place in the curriculum.[5] Uneasy over this new situation in which male and female writers shared a common language, male authors undertook to appropriate, mystify, or transform the *materna lingua,* in order to create or restore the lost exclusionary power of the *patrius sermo.* Ezra Pound's and T. S. Eliot's interest in neoclassicism, a summoning of "antique" authority conveniently predating the emergence of women in the nineteenth century, is cited as one example in literature; James Joyce's experiments with language are another.

The musical language of nineteenth-century romanticism may also be seen, from the point of view of the early twentieth century, as having become a *materna lingua.* The array of experimental, modernist musical usages devised in those years are examples of new *patrii ser-mones*. Serialism, with its claim to have superseded romantic concepts of melody and harmony, is an obvious example of a new *patrius sermo*, although it was not widely adopted by American modernist composers until after Arnold Schoenberg's arrival in the United States in 1934. Another *patrius sermo* is neoclassicism, which was marked in music by a new interest in pre-1800 compositional models. The intention of neoclassicism to transform musical speech is widely recognized, though without its antifeminist connotation.[6] Neoclassicism affected most modernist composers in both Europe and the United States. The machine-inspired music of the futurists is a third *patrius sermo*. When Aaron Copland made his infamous remark about Nadia Boulanger ("But had she become a composer, she would of biological necessity have joined the automatically inferior ranks of the 'woman com-poser' "), he was reserving the creation and use of the *patrius sermo* to men, even as he acknowledged Boulanger's teaching ability, which had led him far beyond the *materna lingua*.[7]

Gilbert and Gubar's second point, a more complex one, deals with the ambivalence of literary women toward their female literary fore-bears, described in Freudian terms as a "female affiliation complex," and the varied consequences of this ambivalence. The "feminization of women" (i.e., the attachment of biological sex to culturally defined gender roles in the period of romantic Americanism) was in their view "a pernicious influence in American culture," resulting in "a fatally feminized literary matrilineage."[8] In music numerous middle-class white women of the generation of romantic Americanism, the most famous being Amy Beach, were able, like their male contemporaries, to build constructively on the nineteenth-century American tradition of domestic music that preceded them.[9] But the modernist generation firmly turned away from the domestic tradition, identifying it with "feminization." The younger women thus rejected their romantic Americanist foremothers, alienating themselves from female role models along with their "feminized" heritage. Simultaneously, they themselves were rejected and isolated as composers by the male mod-ernists. Cut adrift through choices such as these, composer Peggy Glan-ville-Hicks could imagine herself as a pioneer without precedent among women. As a consequence, she could ignore most of the women whose music she had reviewed in the *New York Herald Tribune* and could even apply higher standards to women than to men when she added the names of ninety-eight American composers, ninety-six of them male, to the 1954 edition of *Grove's Dictionary of Music and Mu-sicians*.[10]

Even when it went unrecognized, the blind alley created by this double rejection may have helped deflect many women from creative careers in music. Ruth Crawford Seeger, the best known, abandoned the development of her own modernist compositional language in the early 1930s, just as she seemed to have gained creative maturity.[11] Evelyn Berckman, Marie Bergersen, and Katherine Ruth Heyman are examples of women who channeled their talent away from composition.[12] Others, such as Elizabeth Sprague Coolidge, Minna Lederman, and Claire Reis, turned to careers as patrons, impresarios, or literary advocates of the modernist movement, thus helping to reinforce the sexual hierarchy of their discipline, as did the female patrons of the literary modernists.[13] As a result of this deflection, the female romantic American composers had few creative descendants, and very few female composers of the modernist generation are well known today.[14]

    * * *

Gilbert and Gubar speak of the close association of "modernist male sexual anxiety and women's entrance into the public sphere."[15] This anxiety is widespread in writings on music by male authors during the modernist period, even those who were not themselves modernists. Women, T. J. Jackson Lears points out, provided "a convenient target" for male artists who, "distrusting their own usefulness in an activist society, . . . traced enervation to feminization because they equated masculinity with forcefulness."[16] In a 1918 article by T. Carl Whitmer called "The Energy of American Crowd Music" in the *Musical Quarterly*, we read, "Even now we are so artistically reticent or intellectually snobbish that our large output of ladylike works tied with baby ribbon is entirely out of proportion to our other qualities, so elemental for the most part."[17] When the virtuoso pianist Josef Hofmann presented an entire recital of music by American composers in January 1919, a prominent male critic pronounced it "wearisome" and elaborated: "most of the pieces said so little to the hearer. Soft, mushy stuff most of them were, painfully devoid of virility, strength, and originality. We had not before been aware of the fact—if it is a fact—that the American composer is so effeminate."[18]

Male music teachers felt particularly threatened by the feminine gender associations of their work. In 1918 the *Music Supervisors' Journal* of the Music Teachers National Association carried an article entitled "Music and Manliness," which addressed the question:

Are you one of those people who consider Music effeminate? If so, do you know that:—

1. All the great *composers* were *men*.
2. The great Symphony Orchestras of the world are composed of *men players* and are conducted by *men*. . . .
3. Many *churches* in the larger cities have their music supplied by choirs of *men* and *boys* under a *male organist and director.*
4. The *men* who are playing and singing on the Concert stage and in Grand Opera have to be and are men of splendid physique and considerable intellectual attainment. They are the *physical equals* of the best football and baseball players.[19]

A few years later "The Feminization of Music" was decried in the *Music Teachers National Association Proceedings:* "How has it come about then that in present-day America eighty-five per cent of the music students are girls; seventy-five per cent (at least) of the concert audiences are women, and even the promoting and managing of musical enterprises is getting more and more into their hands?"[20] Mary Herron Dupree has shown that the critical vogue of the 1920s that asserted the failure of romantic Americanism is in fact antifeminist. She quotes composer-critic Deems Taylor to the effect that "this well-nigh complete feminization of music is bad for it." Taylor blames women for the cultural role assigned to them by men: "Women have undertaken to be the moral guardians of the race . . . their predominance in our musical life aggravates our already exaggerated tendency to demand that art be edifying."[21]

References to the importance of "virility" and the dangers of effeminacy in music are also found in modernist discussions of art music. Irving Weill wrote in *Modern Music* that "one begins to sense a distinctively American quality in some of the American music that has been written recently. One senses it in a distinguishing virility—the virility with which it so constantly seeks to express its ideas and its feelings."[22] Henry and Sidney Cowell remarked on Charles Ives's "lifelong insistence that a preoccupation with art . . . [has] nothing about . . . [it] that is incompatible with a rugged masculinity and all the heroic pioneer virtues."[23]

The quintessentially original, iconoclastic, and "American" Ives functioned as a parent of American modernism and as father figure and role model for modernist composers in the 1920s and 1930s. Judith Tick recently characterized his writing as "the most extraordinary use of gendered language in the public testimony of an American composer."[24] In his *Memos*, which were dictated in 1931–32, Ives remarked, "As a boy I was partially ashamed of it [i.e., music]— an entirely wrong attitude, but it was strong—most boys in American country towns, I think, felt the same. When other boys, Monday a.m.

on vacation, were out driving grocery carts, or doing chores, or playing ball, I felt all wrong to stay in and play piano. And there may be something to it. Hasn't music always been too much an emasculated art?"[25] *Memos* is full of comments about "sissy," "emasculated," "old lady" music, projecting hostility that clearly influenced Ives's approach to his art.[26]

As Tick makes clear, Ives's language was an expression of his perceived powerlessness as an artist. His principal targets were both the received European art music tradition and its commercial exploitation in the United States in the period of modernism.[27] She points out that Ives's charges of "effeminacy" were aimed at these two male-dominated targets rather than directly at women, but even those remarks that seem to suggest a fear of male effeminacy in fact reflect hostility toward women, as Gilbert and Gubar argue in a discussion of transvestism that concludes the second volume of their study.[28]

When in the nineteenth century the separate roles of women and men were clearly defined, romantic literary (and musical) heroes could safely engage in occasional transvestism ("sexchanges"), with a strengthening and humanizing effect. Later, in Ives's day, when the "separate spheres" conception of the roles of women and men was being challenged, any appearance of effeminacy, however superficial or fleeting, was perceived as a sign of weakness rather than as a source of enhanced expressiveness for male authors and composers. Gilbert and Gubar point out that both transvestism and the appearance of anomalous sexual characteristics are used as metaphor for fundamental social disorder in T. S. Eliot's *Wasteland*, one of the most privileged of all the texts of literary modernism. Ives's attacks on the effeminacy of Mozart, Beethoven, and the Kneisel Quartet, among others, would seem to conform to this pattern.

In another interpretation of Ives's role, Lawrence Kramer asserts that Ives's language, far from being a "private eccentricity," actually expresses "an entrenched political and esthetic position." He argues that Ives's "musical space is structured so as to articulate the domination of immigrants by natives, blacks by whites, and women by men," thus encoding xenophobic and racist messages to go along with misogyny.[29]

Whatever his purpose, Ives's language contributed to an antiwoman atmosphere among musical modernists that was highly destructive to women's creativity, although it was also enabling for some men. Moreover, the seemingly endless chorus of voices requiring that music be "virile" and "masculine" served literally to transform the meaning of the phrase "American music" to exclude biological females entirely in the modernist period, along with the "feminine."

Finally, Gilbert and Gubar explore the association of modernism with a strongly antiwoman attitude that they call "masculinism," subsequently suppressed along with feminist texts from the modernist period. They emphasize Italian futurism, which was influential for its declarations of principle more than for its actual literary or musical achievements. They quote Filippo T. Marinetti's "Futurist Manifesto" of 1909, which "links male militarism with misogyny": "We will glorify war—the world's only hygiene—militarism, patriotism, the destructive gesture of freedom-bringers, beautiful ideas worth dying for, and scorn for women (*disprezza della donna*)!"[30] Marinetti, the movement's chief spokesman, was particularly crude in another of his declarations: "To possess a woman one does not rub against her but penetrates her! A knee between the buttocks? It should be mutual! You will say, this is barbarism! All right then, let us be barbarians! . . . Hail the savagery of brusque possession . . . and the fury of muscular, exalting, and fortifying dance! In the name of health, force, willpower and virility."[31] Given this context, B. F. Pratella's phrase in still another of the futurists' manifestos, "exalting the man-symbol everlastingly renewed by the varied aspects of modern life," cannot possibly refer to humankind in general.[32] In at least one instance Marinetti, this time along with Maestro Giuntini, added racism to misogyny: "We condemn the use of popular songs. . . . We condemn imitations of jazz and negro music, killed by rhythmic uniformity and the absence of inspired composers."[33] Marinetti, the leader of the futurists, was closely associated with the composer Pratella and the painter-composer Luigi Russolo, whose "Art of Noises" is often quoted in textbook accounts of musical modernism in Europe and the United States for its musical ideas. The male supremacism, racism, and militarism are not mentioned in the music histories.[34]

The expatriate literary, artistic, and musical circle in Paris, to which Ezra Pound and Virgil Thomson introduced George Antheil in 1923, flirted strongly with futurism and futurism's more lighthearted successor, Dadaism. George Antheil often styled himself a "futurist," even though he took exception to the Italian futurists' specific conception of music.[35] He wrote in 1923, "I . . . took this name temporarily because certain ground principles of the now passé Italian futurists were enormously sympathetic to me." Much later Antheil displayed one aspect of his futurist sympathies when he explained the title of his most notorious work: "The words 'Ballet Mécanique' were brutal, contemporary, hard-boiled."[36] He went much further in an unpublished letter, describing his second sonata for violin and piano in terms that include sexual violence against women: "fifteen minutes of complete disillusion, and death to all that was called music. I pride myself with the fact that most of the themes are not original. 'In the shade of the Old Apple Tree, Hochee Chooche[,] Darling, you are growing older,' and all the most vomiting, repulsive material possible. This sonata is like Joyce, and like spew—nevertheless it is electrical. For the first time in the history of the concert stage, the world is allowed to gaze raptuously [sic] into an open cunt."³⁷

Antheil became a close associate of the poet and amateur composer Ezra Pound, who is considered preeminent among the moving spirits of literary modernism. In 1924 Pound authored a tract in support of Antheil, whom he then believed was Stravinsky's equal or superior; later Antheil helped Pound with his opera "The Testament of François Villon."³⁸ Pound's literary work includes a translation of a pseudo-scientific treatise on sexuality, *The Natural Philosophy of Love* by Remy de Gourmont, with a postscript that includes the following:

it is more than likely that the brain itself, is ... only a sort of great clot of genital fluid ... man [is] really the phallus or spermatozoid charging, head-on, the female chaos. ...

Without any digression on feminism ... one offers woman as the accumulation of her hereditary aptitudes, but to man, given what we have of history, the "inventions," the new gestures, the extravagance, the wild shots, the new bathing of cerebral tissues.

... man has for centuries nibbled at this idea of connection, intimate connection between his sperm and his cerebration.³⁹

Antheil himself selected a gendered stereotype when he characterized himself as "The Number One Bad Boy of Music." Certainly the urge to pull "bad-boy" tricks, such as the famous 1927 Carnegie Hall performance of *Ballet Mécanique*, is something he made little attempt to play down in his later autobiography. The stereotypical image of "real" boys as being expected to defy authority, while girls are to accept it, is abundantly clear in Antheil's career, as it is in Thomson's later evaluation of him. Perhaps the "truculent, small-boy" image that Antheil projected encouraged Thomson to evaluate him as "the first composer of our generation." When Antheil did not live up to his promise, Thomson wrote that "the 'bad boy of music' ... merely grew up to be 'a good boy.' "⁴⁰

Nicolas Slonimsky, musical modernism's most thorough chronicler and one of its most ardent admirers, targets women for verbal abuse, when he mentions them at all. His characterization of Marion Bauer (quoting Edgard Varèse) as "crystalized urine" in a 1984 interview is repeated in his autobiography, though without the translation.[41] He described Mary Carr Moore's opera *David Rizzio* as "abecedarian" in the fourth edition of *Music since 1900* and characterized her *Los Rubios* with the same word in his 1986 supplement. His description of Cécile Chaminade's work in his notice of her death uses the not uncommon device of ridicule-by-feminization: "French composeress of ingratiatingly harmonious piano pieces adorned with endearingly sentimental titles, possessing a perennial appeal to frustrated spinsters and emotional piano teachers."[42]

The substantial professional gains made by women musicians and teachers of music in the period of romantic Americanism before World War I probably strengthened the fear that American art music had become, or was inherently, effeminate. Indeed, population trends reinforce the hypothesis that modernism was a reaction against the emergence of women as musicians. Between 1870 and 1910, a period when the number of musicians grew much faster than the overall population, the proportion of women among working musicians had grown from 3 percent to 29 percent, and the proportion of women among teachers of music had grown from 41 percent to 81 percent. The reversal of this thirty-year trend coincides with the first appearance of modernism in the decade between 1910 and 1920, for the census reveals that 1910 was a high point for women in the music professions. By 1920 women had left the professions, especially teaching, in droves.[43] After 1920 there was little justification for the often-expressed fear that women would literally take over the field.

The gains of middle-class white women were thus well under way at the time "American music" suddenly became a hot topic for musical polemicists, after the Boston Symphony Orchestra performed works by Margaret Ruthven Lang (1893) and Amy Cheney Beach (1896, 1900) and the visiting Czech nationalist composer Anton Dvořák wrote on the subject.[44] That the concept of "American music" had been proposed some decades earlier without attracting much attention invites the conclusion that nationalism and feminism are closely intertwined.[45] "American music" became an issue only after women had successfully entered the field as composers. In addition to the racial issues raised in this debate, part of it was really about whether a national music might include, and perhaps even be partially defined by, the work of women.[46]

Social changes wrought by immigration also played a problematic part in the interaction of feminism and modernism in American music. Turn-of-the-century romantic Americanist composers, both women and men, characteristically sprang from the ranks of the U.S.-born whites rather than directly from the great pre–World War I wave of central European immigration.[47] They were thus rooted in the nineteenth-century American tradition of domestic music as well as in the borrowed European romantic tradition. Foreign-born musicians and teachers of music were predominantly male; U.S.-born musicians and teachers of music were predominantly female. After World War I the steady in-migration of male musicians from Europe may have helped deepen the cultural division between women and men, enhancing gender stereotyping during the period when modernism emerged as an artistic force in American music. The battle of the sexes in American music had nativist, national implications from the start that complicate a feminist interpretation of musical Americanism.

Carl Dahlhaus in his 1969 essay on modernism in music, recently translated as " 'New Music' as Historical Category,"[48] makes two points that powerfully reinforce the hypothesis of this essay. First, Dahlhaus thought that a background of social change was a necessary accompaniment to the introduction of the "new" in music history. Overlooking the first feminist movement entirely, he was unable to identify such a background in support of the modernist period of the twentieth century. The general suppression of women's work during the modernist period and of the modernists' antiwoman attitude, by, in Gilbert and Gubar's words, "privileging certain . . . twentieth-century works as purely aesthetic or philosophic objects and repressing significant aspects of the history in which the authors of these works were engaged," was remarkably successful in music.[49] Dahlhaus wrote that literary advocacy "forms an integral part of music as a historical event, and even as a perceived object." "Musical perception . . . is permeated with reminiscences of what one has read, with traces of literary memory." His assertion that modernism was established through the circulation of polemical proclamations that "sometimes resemble a self-fulfilling prophecy" is entirely consistent with the feminist assertion that women have been selected out of history quite deliberately.

It appears that modernism in music, as in literature, may indeed be understood as a reaction to the first wave of feminism. One must painfully conclude that while this reaction was productive for many males, it was profoundly destructive for female composers. In the end it may have contributed to the relative isolation of the modernists from concert audiences, for an intuitive understanding of modernist male hostility toward women may be a major reason why these largely female audiences rejected modernism so viscerally. The aftereffects of this long-unacknowledged gendering of modernism in American music in the period between the two world wars have lingered into our own day. They have nevertheless dwindled enough so that we may now acknowledge that the hostility of the modernists toward women continues to underlie critical discourse on the art music of the twentieth century. We may now examine in detail how women composers of the modernist period dealt with their own ambivalences and with the male modernists' attempts to exclude them, literally and linguistically, from the possibility of creativity. We must surely confront, rather than pass tacitly by, the violent antifeminism of the futurists. Most important, we may begin to investigate whether there was a different, more broadly defined, perhaps less hostile or more gender-inclusive form of modernism in American music that until now has been wholly hidden from view.[50]

NOTES

The author gratefully acknowledges comments and suggestions from many individuals, beyond those cited in the endnotes, who have either read or heard this essay in its several earlier versions.

1. Zuck, *Musical Americanism;* Levy, *Musical Nationalism;* and Tischler, *American Music,* are concerned with musical Americanism in various of its aspects. The role of women is discussed in Tick, "Women as Professional Musicians"; see also Tick, "Charles Ives." The situation of an individual woman composer in the period under discussion is documented in Smith and Richardson, *Mary Carr Moore.* The term *romantic Americanism* to describe the pre–World War I generation is taken from Chase, *America's Music.*
2. Lears, *No Place of Grace,* xv, credits Antonio Gramsci with the concept of "cultural hegemony . . . winning the 'spontaneous' loyalty of subordinate groups to a common set of values and attitudes," which are determined by the dominant social group.
3. Gilbert and Gubar, *No Man's Land,* 1:xii, xiv.
4. Gilbert and Gubar treat the futurists' masculinism first; here it is treated last.
5. Ong, *Fighting for Life,* especially 36–37, on *patrius sermo* versus mother tongue and on the role of "learned Latin" in male education. Discussed in Gilbert and Gubar, *No Man's Land,* 1:252–53.
6. See, for example, Albright, "Stravinsky's Assault on Language."
7. Copland, *Copland on Music,* 84–85.
8. Gilbert and Gubar, *No Man's Land,* 2:178, 174.
9. The anonymous domestic tradition was first described by Tick, "History of American Woman Composers"; also in Tick, *American Women Composers.*

10. Hayes, *Peggy Glanville-Hicks*. In a letter of 19 March 1990 Hayes calls attention to the "surprising lack of misogynist criticism" at the *Herald Tribune* in Glanville-Hicks's years there, 1947–55. More recently, Carter, "Thomson's *Herald Tribune* Writings," has shown that Virgil Thomson, the *Tribune*'s chief critic at the time, altered his "usually critical descriptive apparatus and approach to discourse" when he wrote about music composed by women.

11. Wilding-White, "Ruth Crawford Seeger." For Charles Seeger's initial reluctance to accept a woman as a student, see Gaume, "Ruth Crawford." Tick, " 'Spirit of Me,' " offers rich insights into Crawford's "decision born of indecision."

12. Luening, *Odyssey*, 387, 389, mentions Berckman as a composer active in New York in the late 1930s, but her name does not appear in the index. Luening's book is free of misogynist language, though he clearly had many opportunities not open to women. On Bergersen, see Borroff, "Marie Bergersen," 492. For Heyman, see Bowers, "Memoir within Memoirs."

13. Gilbert and Gubar, *No Man's Land*, 1:147. See also Whitesitt, "Role of Women Impresarios"; Barr, "Style of Her Own"; and Oja, "Women Patrons and Crusaders."

14. Miriam Gideon (b. 1906), Louise Talma (b. 1906), and Elinor Remick Warren (1900–1991) are among the best known of these few. Vivian Fine (b. 1913) was a member of a circle of composers that met regularly in 1933 in New York, with Copland as moderator.

15. Gilbert and Gubar, *No Man's Land*, 1:98.

16. Lears, *No Place of Grace*, 104.

17. Whitmer, "American Crowd Music," 98.

18. Henry T. Finck in the *New York Evening Post*, quoted in "American Composers Tested by Hofmann," 28–29.

19. Smith, "Music and Manliness," 12.

20. Randolph, "Feminization of Music," 194.

21. Taylor, "Music," 211, quoted in Dupree, "Failure of American Music," 311.

22. Weill, "American Scene Changes," 7.

23. Cowell and Cowell, *Charles Ives*, 9. The statement is the Cowells' formulation of Ives's preoccupation, in words that echo but do not actually quote their subject.

24. Tick, "Charles Ives," 83.

25. Ives, *Memos*, 130.

26. Solomon, "Charles Ives," raises this as well as other questions.

27. Tick, "Charles Ives."

28. Gilbert and Gubar, *No Man's Land*, 2: chap. 8, "Cross-Dressing and Re-Dressing: Transvestism as Metaphor."

29. Kramer, "Ives's Misogyny"; the quotations are taken from the abstract. Like Gilbert and Gubar, Kramer is a literary critic; unlike them, he has brought recent critical developments in literature to bear on musicological questions.

30. Marinetti, "Futurist Manifesto," 22.

31. Marinetti, "Down with the Tango," 1302.

32. Pratella, "Manifesto," 37.

33. Marinetti and Giuntini, "Aeromusic," 1304.

34. Russolo, "Art of Noises." For appearances of Russolo's manifesto in standard texts, see, for example, Hansen, Introduction to Twentieth Century Music; and Hitchcock, Music in the United States. Articles discussing Italian futurism as a musical phenomenon include Payton, "Music of Futurism"; Radice, "Futurismo"; and Waterhouse, "Futurist Mystery."

35. Antheil, "Musical Neofism," quoted in Whitesitt, George Antheil, 69. On the same page Whitesitt also quotes an undated typescript in the Antheil Estate: "I entirely discount the futurists, because their music was not composed but improvised—and improvisation is the very antithesis of composition."

36. Antheil, Bad Boy of Music, 139.

37. George Antheil to "Dearest good old Stan[ley Hart]," [4 May? 1925], Music Division, Library of Congress, Washington, D.C. I am indebted to Wayne Shirley for calling this letter to my attention and to the Antheil Estate for permission to quote it.

38. Pound, Antheil. Pound's interest in music and his attempts at composition were an outcome of his ideas about the relationship between poetry and music, based on his study of the medieval Provençal poets—an example of a modernist's invention of a new patrius sermo.

39. Pound, translator's postscript to Natural Philosophy of Love, 169, 170, 180; an earlier edition appeared in 1931. It must be added that, unlike Charles Ives, Pound supplied important critical support to female modernist writers, including H.D., Mina Loy, and Marianne Moore.

40. Thomson, Virgil Thomson Reader, 48. See also note 11 above.

41. Slonimsky, Perfect Pitch, 204 ["une pipi crystallisée"). I interviewed Slonimsky in Los Angeles on 29 November 1984; he added in the interview that Bauer was "the damnedest fool I ever knew."

42. Slonimsky, Supplement, 274. The first Moore citation appears in Music since 1900, 550; the second is in the Supplement, 261. Between the two volumes, Moore became a "composer" rather than a "composeress." The entry marking Chaminade's death, which appears in both the fourth edition and the supplement, is even more offensive than that in the third edition (New York: Coleman-Ross, 1949), which has her as "French composer of unpretentiously semi-classical and—to the unfastidious ear—ingratiatingly attractive piano pieces with charmingly descriptive titles."

43. These data on musicians and teachers of music are from decennial reports of the United States Census:

	No.	Male (%)	Female (%)	Total Population
1870	16,010	10,257 (64)	5,753 (36)	38,000,000
1890	62,155	27,636 (44)	34,519 (56)	63,000,000
1910	138,243	54,832 (39)	83,851 (61)	92,000,000
1930	165,128	85,517 (52)	79,611 (48)	123,000,000

	Musicians	% Female	Teachers of Music	% Female
1870	6,346	3	9,491	41
1910	54,832	29	83,851	81

For contemporary discussions of these figures, see Harris, "Occupation of Musician"; and Hill, *Women in Gainful Occupations.*

44. Dvořák, letter to the *New York Herald,* 21 May 1893, reprinted in the *Boston Herald,* 28 May 1893; see also "Music in America." Block, "Boston Talks Back to Dvořák," points out that Dvořák generated controversy partly because of his insistence that "the negro melodies . . . must be the real foundation of any serious and original school of composition to be developed" in this country.

45. Chmaj, "Fry versus Dwight." See also Dupree, "Failure of American Music."

46. Historians of the Progressive Era argue that expressions of nationalism appeared in American culture as a reaction to pressure on the white, male, native-born population from the first feminist movement, the wave of immigration from central Europe, and accelerating technological change. See Hobsbawm, "Inventing Traditions," and "Mass-Producing Traditions"; see also Glassberg, *American Historical Pageantry.*

47. Clara Kathleen Rogers (b. 1844) and Helen Hopekirk (b. 1856) are two early exceptions. Both were born in the British Isles, and both settled in Boston.

48. Dahlhaus, " 'Neue Musik.' "

49. Gilbert and Gubar, *No Man's Land,* 1:xiv.

50. Building on Gilbert and Gubar's work, feminist literary critics have begun to explore this concept. See, for example, Scott, *Gender of Modernism.*

REFERENCES

Albright, Daniel. "Stravinsky's Assault on Language." *Journal of Musicological Research* 8, nos. 3–4 (1989): 259–79.
"American Composers Tested by Hofmann." *Literary Digest* 60 (15 February 1919): 28–29.
Antheil, George. *Bad Boy of Music.* Garden City, N.Y.: Doubleday, Doran, 1945.
———. Letter to Stanley Hart, [4 May 1925]. Antheil Collection, Music Division, Library of Congress, Washington, D.C.
Barr, Cyrilla. "A Style of Her Own: Reflections on the Patronage of Elizabeth Sprague Coolidge." In *Cultivating the Muse: Women Music Patrons and Activists in the United States* [tentative title], edited by Ralph P. Locke and Cyrilla Barr. Berkeley: University of California Press, forthcoming.
Block, Adrienne Fried. "Boston Talks Back to Dvořák." *Institute for Studies in American Music Newsletter* 18 (May 1989): 10–11, 15.

Borroff, Edith. "Marie Bergersen." In *Anthology for Music in Europe and the United States*, edited by Edith Borroff. 2d ed. New York: Ardsley House, 1990.

Bowers, Faubion. "Memoir within Memoirs." *Paideuma: A Journal Devoted to Ezra Pound Scholarship* 2 (Spring 1973): 53–66.

Carter, Karen. "Virgil Thomson's *Herald Tribune* Writings: Fulfilling the 'Cultural Obligation'—Selectively." Paper presented at the Sonneck Society for American Music Conference, February 1992.

Chase, Gilbert. *America's Music: From the Pilgrims to the Present*. Rev. 3d ed. Urbana: University of Illinois Press, 1987.

Chmaj, Betty. "Fry versus Dwight: American Music's Debate over Nationality." *American Music* 3 (Spring 1985): 63–84.

Copland, Aaron. *Copland on Music*. Garden City, N.Y.: Doubleday, 1960.

Cowell, Sidney, and Henry Cowell. *Charles Ives and His Music*. 2d ed. New York: Oxford University Press, 1969.

Dahlhaus, Carl. " 'Neue Musik' als historische Kategorie." In *Das Musikalisch Neue und die Neue Musik*, edited by H.-P. Reinecke. Mainz: Schott, 1969. Translated by Derrick Puffett and Alfred Clayton as " 'New Music' as Historical Category." In *Schoenberg and the New Music*. Cambridge: Cambridge University Press, 1987.

Dupree, Mary Herron. "The Failure of American Music: The Critical View from the 1920s." *Journal of Musicology* 2 (Summer 1983): 305–15.

Gaume, Matilda. "Ruth Crawford: A Promising Young Composer in New York, 1929–1930." *American Music* 5 (Spring 1987): 74–84.

Gilbert, Sandra M., and Susan Gubar. *No Man's Land: The Place of the Woman Writer in the Twentieth Century*. Vol. 1, *The War of the Words* (1988). Vol. 2, *Sexchanges* (1989). Vol. 3, *Letters from the Front* (forthcoming). New Haven, Conn.: Yale University Press, 1988– .

Glassberg, David. *American Historical Pageantry: The Uses of Tradition in the Early Twentieth Century*. Chapel Hill: University of North Carolina Press, 1990.

Hansen, Peter. *An Introduction to Twentieth Century Music*. 4th ed. Boston: Allyn and Bacon, 1978.

Harris, Henry J. "The Occupation of Musician in the United States." *Musical Quarterly* 1 (April 1915): 299–311.

Hayes, Deborah. *Peggy Glanville-Hicks: A Bio-Bibliography*. Westport, Conn.: Greenwood Press, 1990.

Hill, Joseph A. *Women in Gainful Occupations: 1870–1920*. Census Monographs, no. 9. Washington, D.C.: U.S. Department of Commerce, 1929.

Hitchcock, H. Wiley. *Music in the United States: A Historical Introduction*. 3d ed. Englewood Cliffs, N.J.: Prentice-Hall, 1988.

Hobsbawn, Eric J. "Introduction: Inventing Traditions." In *The Invention of Tradition*, edited by Eric J. Hobsbawn and Terence Ranger. Cambridge: Cambridge University Press, 1990.

———. "Mass-Producing Traditions: Europe, 1870–1914." In *The Invention of Tradition*, edited by Eric J. Hobsbawn and Terence Ranger. Cambridge: Cambridge University Press, 1983.

Ives, Charles E. *Memos.* Edited by John Kirkpatrick. New York: W. W. Norton, 1972.

Kramer, Lawrence. "Ives's Misogyny and Post-Reconstruction America." Paper presented at conference, Feminist Theory and Music: Toward a Common Language, University of Minnesota, June 1991.

Lears, T. J. Jackson. *No Place of Grace: Antimodernism and the Transformation of American Culture, 1880–1920.* New York: Pantheon, 1981.

Levy, Alan. *Musical Nationalism: American Composers' Search for Identity.* Westport, Conn.: Greenwood Press, 1983.

Luening, Otto. *The Odyssey of an American Composer.* New York: Charles Scribner's Sons, 1980.

Marinetti, Filippo T. "Down with Tango and Parsifal!" Translated by Nicolas Slonimsky in *Music since 1900.* 4th ed. New York: Charles Scribner's Sons, 1971.

———. "Futurist Manifesto." Translated by R. W. Flint in *Futurist Manifestos,* edited by Umbro Apollonio. New York: Viking, 1973.

Marinetti, Filippo T., and Maestro Giuntini. "Futurist Manifesto of Aeromusic: Synthetic, Geometric, Curative." Translated by Nicolas Slonimsky in *Music since 1900.* 4th ed. New York: Charles Scribner's Sons, 1971.

"Music in America." *Harper's Magazine,* February 1895, 423–28.

Oja, Carol. "Women Patrons and Crusaders for Modernist Music in New York." In *Cultivating the Muse: Women Music Patrons and Activists in the United States* [tentative title], edited by Ralph P. Locke and Cyrilla Barr. Berkeley: University of California Press, forthcoming.

Ong, Walter J. *Fighting for Life: Contest, Sexuality, and Consciousness.* Ithaca, N.Y.: Cornell University Press, 1981.

Payton, Rodney J. "The Music of Futurism: Concerts and Polemics." *Musical Quarterly* 62 (January 1976): 25–44.

Pound, Ezra. *Antheil and the Treatise on Harmony, with Supplementary Notes.* 1924. Reprint. New York: Da Capo Press, 1968.

———. Translator's postscript to *Natural Philosophy of Love,* by Remy de Gourmont. New York: Willey, 1940.

Pratella, F. Balilla. "Manifesto of Futurist Musicians 1910." Translated by Caroline Tisdall in *Futurist Manifesto,* edited by Umbro Apollonio. New York: Viking, 1973.

Radice, Mark A. "Futurismo: Its Origins, Context, Repertory, and Influence." *Musical Quarterly* 73, no. 1 (1989): 1–17.

Randolph, Harold T. "The Feminization of Music." *M.T.N.A. Proceedings,* 17th series (1922): 194–200.

Russolo, Luigi. "The Art of Noises: Futurist Manifesto." Translated by Stephen Somervell in Nicolas Slonimsky's *Music since 1900.* 4th ed. New York: Charles Scribner's Sons, 1971.

Scott, Bonnie Kime, ed. *The Gender of Modernism.* Bloomington: Indiana University Press, 1990.

Slonimsky, Nicolas. *Music since 1900.* 4th ed. New York: Charles Scribner's Sons, 1971.

———. *Perfect Pitch*. New York: Schirmer Books, 1988.

———. *Supplement to Music since 1900*. New York: Charles Scribner's Sons, 1986.

Smith, Catherine Parsons, and Cynthia S. Richardson. *Mary Carr Moore, American Composer*. Ann Arbor: University of Michigan Press, 1987.

Smith, Fred T. "Music and Manliness." *Music Supervisors' Journal* 5 (September 1918): 12.

Solomon, Maynard. "Charles Ives: Some Questions of Veracity." *Journal of the American Musicological Society* 40 (Fall 1987): 443–70.

Taylor, Deems. "Music." In *Civilization in the United States: An Inquiry by Thirty Americans*, edited by Harold E. Stearns. New York: Harcourt, Brace, 1922.

Thomson, Virgil. *A Virgil Thomson Reader*. Boston: Houghton Mifflin, 1981.

Tick, Judith. *American Women Composers before 1870*. Ann Arbor, Mich.: UMI Research Press, 1983.

———. "Charles Ives and the 'Masculine' Ideal." In *Musicology and Difference: Gender and Sexuality in Music Scholarship*, edited by Ruth Solie. Berkeley: University of California Press, 1993.

———. " 'Spirit of Me . . . Dear Rollicking Far-gazing Straddler of Two Worlds': The 'Autobiography' of Ruth Crawford Seeger, 1901–1953." Paper presented at the Music and Gender Conference, King's College, London, July 1991.

———. "Towards a History of American Women Composers before 1870." Ph.D. diss., City University of New York, 1979.

———. "Women as Professional Musicians in the United States, 1870–1900." *Anuario Interamericano de Investigacion Musical/Yearbook for Inter-American Musical Research* 9 (1973): 94–133.

Tischler, Barbara L. *An American Music: The Search for an American Musical Identity*. New York: Oxford University Press, 1987.

Waterhouse, John C. G. "A Futurist Mystery." *Music and Musicians* 15 (April 1967): 26–30.

Weill, Irving. "The American Scene Changes." *Modern Music* 6 (May-June 1929): 3–9.

Whitesitt, Linda. *The Life and Music of George Antheil, 1900–1959*. Ann Arbor, Mich.: UMI Research Press, 1983.

———. "The Role of Women Impresarios in American Concert Life, 1871–1933." *American Music* 7 (Summer 1989): 159–80.

Whitmer, T. Carl. "The Energy of American Crowd Music." *Musical Quarterly* 4 (January 1918): 98–116.

Wilding-White, Ray. "Remembering Ruth Crawford Seeger: An Interview with Charles and Peggy Seeger." *American Music* 6 (Winter 1988): 442–54.

Zuck, Barbara. *A History of Musical Americanism*. Ann Arbor, Mich.: UMI Research Press, 1980.

6

The Child Is Mother of the Woman: Amy Beach's New England Upbringing

Adrienne Fried Block

Leon Edel, the biographer of Henry James, wrote an essay entitled "The Figure under the Carpet" that traces one biographer's search for the hidden but powerful patterns shaping a creative life.[1] No influence is as profoundly formative as that of the primary caretaker during the first few years of a child's life. Because a child's memory usually begins with events in the fourth year, few influences are more hidden—except the influences that shaped a mother's attitudes and beliefs.

There are significant revelatory hints about the childhood experiences of Amy Marcy (Cheney) Beach (Mrs. H. H. A. Beach, 1867–1944), but no hints remain about the childhood of her mother, Clara Imogene (Marcy) Cheney (1846–1911). The received information about Beach's childhood was that it was an ideal and idyllic one.[2] A newly discovered autobiographical sketch by Amy Beach, however, exposes the intergenerational conflicts between the child and her mother.[3] Written years later, when Beach was able to distance herself from her family and home, this autobiography, with its unprecedented candor, made it imperative that I revise the story of her early life.

I found Clara Cheney's child-rearing methods, as described by her daughter in that autobiography, troubling by my standards because of their harshness and rigidity. Although neither Clara Cheney nor anyone else ever suggested that her way of raising her only child was based on traditional religious beliefs, prescriptive writings describing normative child-rearing practices among New England Protestants of the middle to late nineteenth century make sense of her methods.[4] In this reconstruction of Beach's childhood I will cite significant events and practices from her early life, using her own words wherever possible; show how they may have stemmed from standard New England practice; and demonstrate their influence. Instead of being ideal, Beach's childhood was a conflicted one, with music—the very center of her life—the area of contention.

Clara Cheney was especially influential in the life of her prodigiously gifted daughter because for the first few years she was the child's main source of musical gratification. Beach wrote that her mother "was a brilliant pianist, and it was the joy of my life to listen to her playing, as it had been (so they tell me) the joy of my babyhood to listen to the singing of my aunt and grandmother as well as my mother. My demands were so insistent that they had to be supplied in relays. When one throat became exhausted, the other took up the strain, otherwise there was a crying spell on my part."[5] When Amy was six, Clara Cheney became her child's first piano teacher and provided her general education until age ten. She continued to exercise control over her daughter's life until Amy's marriage at eighteen.

Amy Beach's parents both came from colonial stock. Her father, Charles Abbott Cheney (1844–95), was born in Ashland, New Hampshire. His parents were Free-Will Baptists, a liberal sect that did not believe infants were born depraved. Because he traveled frequently as a salesman of imported paper stock, Charles Cheney seems to have had less direct influence on his daughter than his wife had. Clara Imogene Marcy, born in Hillsborough, New Hampshire, was a Congregationalist, a Calvinist sect noted for its stringent child-rearing practices aimed at taming the devil in the flesh. These practices underwent ameliorating changes during the middle of the nineteenth century, when Clara Marcy was growing up.

Clara Cheney became aware of her only child's musical gifts quite early; she reported that the one-year-old could sing forty tunes correctly and exactly as she heard them. Months later she was stunned when Amy, not yet two, joined her in singing a lullaby by improvising an alto to her soprano. Her mother's response to these feats was twofold. The first was a long-term decision that, as Amy recounted, "I was to be a musician, not a prodigy; that I was to be as carefully kept from music as later I would be helped to it." The second and immediate response was to keep the piano out of bounds, for her mother feared the toddler might tire of music: "I had begun to coax to play before I could reach up and touch the ivory keys. My mother, who was a fine musician and wanted to raise one, had no faith in the prodigy principle of forcing, or indulging. She believed rather in what Gerald Stanley Lee calls the 'top drawer principle,'—the principal [sic] of withholding. I was not allowed to climb up on her lap, or on the music stool. I could only hear music, think music. I could not help thinking music. It was in my blood, it was the daily talk."

Gerald Stanley Lee was an ordained Congregationalist minister who later became a popular essayist. In his book *The Lost Art of Reading,* he recommends the following method to encourage children to read:

First. Decide what the owner of the mind most wants in the world.

Second. Put this thing, whatever it may be, where the owner of the mind cannot get it unless he uses his mind. Take pains to put it where he can get it, if he does use his mind.

Third. Lure him on. It is education.[6]

The essay appeared in 1903, many years after it might have informed Clara Cheney's child-rearing methods. Therefore she must have had other reasons for declaring the piano out-of-bounds. Two groups of Protestants, the Presbyterian Evangelicals and the more moderate Congregationalists, agreed that children must learn submission and learn it early. (The third group, genteel, upper-class Protestants, usually Unitarians or Episcopalians, tended to be more indulgent. Like the moderates, they did not believe infants were born depraved, but, uniquely, they allowed their children to enjoy life's pleasures while also looking to their heavenly reward.)

Regarding submission to parental will, Evangelicals and moderates agreed on ends but parted company over means. The Evangelicals followed John Wesley's injunction to " 'break [children's] wills that you may save their souls,' . . . the crucial step toward a lifelong experience of submission and self-denial."[7] During the nineteenth century moderates condemned the breaking of a child's will as unnecessarily cruel. Like the Evangelicals, moderates wished to train their children in "obedience to laws and authority," but through temperate self-denial.[8]

Horace Bushnell's influential book *Christian Nurture,* in which he preached moderation, was an important agent of change. It appeared between 1847 and 1863, the very years when Clara Cheney was growing up.[9] Rejecting the doctrine of infant depravity, Bushnell condemned harsh discipline as "a piety of conquest rather than love,"[10] which brutalizes "the delicate and tender souls of their children."[11] He instead recommended genial warmth and love, "a good life, the repose of faith, the confidence of righteous expectation, [and] the sacred and cheerful liberty of the spirit."[12]

Nevertheless, Bushnell believed in discipline. The infant, he asserted, has

blind will, as strongly developed as any other faculty, and sometimes most strongly of all. The manifestations of it are sometimes even frightful. And precisely this it is which makes the age of impressions, the age prior to language and responsible choice, most profoundly critical in its importance. It is the age in which the will-power of the soul is to be tamed or subordinated to a higher control; that of obedience to parents, that of duty and religion. . . . everything most important to the religious character turns just here. Is this infant child to fill the universe with his complete and total self-assertion, owning no superior, or is he to learn the self-submission of allegiance, obedience, duty to God? Is he to become a demon let loose in God's eternity or an angel and free prince of the realm?[13]

Moderates like Bushnell as well as Evangelicals recommended that training a child to submit to the parent's will begin around ten months[14] and be accomplished by the age of three[15]—a practice Clara Cheney apparently followed. Her methods, however, seem closer to those of the Evangelicals, who used not only the rod but also other means to achieve submission: shaming the child, playing on the child's greatest fears, and withholding the most desired objects, including food, playthings, and love.

A recommended procedure for establishing parental authority could have been a model for Clara Cheney; it appeared in print in 1864, three years before Amy Cheney was born. I quote it in extenso because of the way it parallels Clara Cheney's withholding of music:

The infant was to be placed in the parent's lap before a table. On that table, within easy reach, was one of the baby's toys. The child was instructed not to touch the toy. When it did, the parent was to strike the child sharply on the hand. Alcott suggested that procedure continue until the toy could be placed within the baby's reach without him taking it. Once this obedience to the parent's will had been secured, the child was to be offered the toy. The child would, quite naturally, respond by looking with some confusion at the parent's face. The parent then must smile and continue to offer the toy to indicate that it was all right with the parent if the baby handled the toy. The lesson to be learned from that exercise was that the parent's will was supreme. According to the author, once that lesson was learned, a parent need never strike the child again.[16]

This method has ramifications for all pleasures of the senses—handling a toy, wearing fine clothing, or eating delectable food. One mother wrote that she taught her young child to resist gluttony by having the child serve forbidden sweets to adult guests. The moderate Horace Bushnell warned that "a child can be pampered in feeding, so as to become, in a sense, all body; so that, when he comes into choice and responsible action, he is already a confirmed sensualist."[17]

Similarly, the child must first learn to do without the powerful medium of music; later, she could be offered limited experiences without risking the possibility that as an adult she might make music the center of her life rather than home, husband, and children. In the light of nineteenth-century Protestant rearing practices, Clara Cheney also used music as a means of establishing control over the child, that is, teaching submission to parental authority by withholding what the gifted toddler wanted most. The Cheney household was saturated with music, and there was no way of limiting what the child heard without limiting what others played and sang. Short of that, the only possibility was to control the child's music making by applying the withholding principle. As in the example of the infant and the toy, Clara Cheney's authority and control over her daughter's musical life was first established by withholding the piano and later by relaxing the ban.

Meanwhile the resourceful and determined toddler found other outlets for her musicality:

I was very anxious to play the piano when scarcely more than a baby, but my mother kept me from the instrument. . . . So, if I could not play on the piano, I was not to be deprived of my music, but set my Mother Goose book up on the stairs, knelt on one of the stairs below it and, using another stair as my keyboard, played and sang original melodies or tunes for the Mother Goose rhymes pictured before me. My mother said that some of the little tunes were very fresh and original—I wish she might have taken them down.[18]

One of Beach's earliest recollections concerned her favorite book, Charles Dickens's *Child's Dream of a Star*, chosen soon after teaching herself to read at age three. In a nutshell the book deals with dying and traveling the shining path to a star, that is, to heaven. The first to die in a family of four was the youngest, a little girl. Undoubtedly Amy Cheney read the book many times, as little children do. There is no way of knowing if her joy in the hope of heaven was also mingled with terror at the thought of death.

Its message and its imagery, however, seem to have reverberated through her life and music. In 1894 Beach set to music a poem by Cora Fabbri entitled "My Star," her op. 26, no. 1. The brief text parallels that of the Dickens story:

> I dreamt I loved a star, A star so far above me;
> She said, "It is in vain Men seek to know and love me."
> I dreamt that I was dead. Methought that I was lying
> Deep in a grave, deep down, The winds above me sighing.
> In the darkness of the grave I saw my Star below me.
> She said: "My name is Peace, And only here men know me."[19]

The piano accompaniment consists of successive, rising broken chord figures traversing two to three octaves, suggesting, as do the words, the shining path to heaven of the Dickens tale.

This emphasis on heavenly reward, coincident with the high rate of infant and child mortality, helps explain what may appear to us today as a morbid fixation on death in nineteenth-century children's literature. Fundamental to the approach of conservative Protestants was the belief that this life is only a preparation for the afterlife, a brief sojourn before eternal salvation or damnation. From this flowed an insistence on children's total submission to God's will as interpreted by parents, as well as a spartan life-style for children that denied sensuous pleasures as a defense against temptation.

This belief placed substantial burdens on parents, whose first responsibility was to teach their children submission to the earthly father as the ultimate authority and the "viceregent of God" in the home,[20] in preparation for submitting to God's will. During the middle years of the nineteenth century, however, religious leaders began to stress the importance of mothers, whose role reflected the doctrine of separate spheres—the public for men, the private for women.

Because the husband's work was separated from the home, the home became a refuge from the corruption and immorality of public life, and the mother rather than the father became the transmitter of moral and religious education. When John Abbott wrote "On the Mother's Role in Education" in 1833, he confirmed this separation: "It is maternal influence, after all, which must be the great agent, in the hands of God, in bringing our guilty race to duty and happiness."[21]

The mother's duty was to teach her young children that God not only "looks upon sin . . . with abhorrence" but also promises salvation to the righteous. Mothers were told to "excite the gratitude of the child by speaking of the joys of heaven. . . . There is enough in the promised joys of heaven to rouse a child's most animated feelings." This was the message the Dickens tale delivered with clarity. But mothers were also advised to "reserve the terrors of the law for solemn occasions, when you may produce a deep and abiding impression."[22]

The belief in this life as a preparation for the afterlife, plus high mortality among infants and young children, also explained the urgency of religious involvement of very young children. Although there is no record that Amy Cheney attended Baptist services with her father, Beach did recall the first time her mother took her to the Congregationalist church in her native town of Henniker. She described what happened: "I was not three when I was first taken to a church or Sunday School. I sang with the rest. I was lifted to the table, and gradually the singing stopped, and the congregation turned to see and listen to the infant singing to the accompaniment of the big organ." The Cheney family, like many others of the time, probably sang hymns

at home, an important way to bring a child—especially a musical one—
to piety. While Clara Cheney may have been gratified at how well her
child had learned the hymns, she probably was not pleased about the
public display of her child's musical gifts; children must be kept from
the cardinal sin of pride.

Amy Cheney finally got to the keyboard at age four, but it was
despite her mother and through the intervention of her mother's older
sister, Emma Frances "Franc" (Marcy) Clement (1842–1925), who had
been sent to Boston by San Francisco musical groups to sing in the
Bouquet of Artists at the Peace Jubilee of 1872—an honor not accorded
Clara Cheney.[23] Beach describes the signal event, her first vivid memory of her beloved aunt Franc: "At last, I was allowed to touch the
piano. My mother was still opposed, but I can remember my aunt
coming to the house, and putting me at the piano. I played at once
the melodies I had been collecting, playing in my head, adding full
harmonies to the simple, treble melodies. Then my aunt played a new
air for me, and I reached up and picked out a harmonized bass accompaniment, as I had heard my mother do." Beach also recalled the
very first piece she played on that occasion: "I began at once a difficult
Strauss waltz that my mother had been playing. The difficulty for me
was the tiny size of my hands which made it necessary to omit octaves
and big chords, but I seemed to have an uncanny sense of knowing
just which notes to leave out, so that the result sounded well."[24] There
were times, though, when the frustration of not being able to re-create
the sounds she heard in her head made her fly "into a rage."[25] Otherwise, from that day on she played whatever she heard, including her
own improvisations. She also transposed with ease. Her mother, however, still maintained control over music by limiting her time at the
piano.

Clara Cheney also withheld music as punishment, the way other
parents might withhold food or love. If Amy Cheney misbehaved, her
mother refused her access to the instrument. Or, since "music in the
minor keys made her sad and disconsolate," Clara Cheney would play
something in the minor mode. "No other punishment was needed, for
the little hands that were occasionally mischievous than the playing
of Gottschalk's *Last Hope*."[26] Here was a child whose most sensitive
attribute, her musical gift, was turned into her greatest vulnerability.

There is evidence that the sin of pride was an issue during Amy
Cheney's childhood.[27] Beach herself described an incident in her mother's campaign to prevent her from taking pride in her own abilities.
The child was four at the time: "I can remember weaving my first
compositions. . . . I had been visiting my grandfather's farm in Maine

one summer, and when I reached home I told my mother that I had 'made' three waltzes.[28] She did not believe me at first, as there was no piano within miles of the farm. I explained that I had written them in my head, and proved it by playing them on her piano."[29] Clara Cheney controlled not only her own response but those of others as well: "No more was made of the [three waltzes] than there would have been had I exhibited a paper doll of my own cutting. I learned afterward from my mother herself, and her friends, that it was a part of her theory of education not to discuss before me my precocity; no one was permitted to make my accomplishments appear to me anything out of the expected or normal."

Beach remembered a related incident when she was five. Her father mentioned to her mother that a leading singer, Clara Louise Kellogg, could identify any pitch she heard. Beach recounted, "My father rebuked me for pertness when I turned and said, 'Oh, that's nothing. Anybody can do that, I can do that.' They continued the discussion. I was again reproved for interrupting. Then my mother . . . suggested that they would see if I knew what he was talking about. They made several experiments, and it was discovered that I really did have, untaught, absolute pitch."

Of this discovery, Amy Beach wrote, "It helped [my mother] to patience later, when her child appeared only pert." Patience? One needs patience to educate a slow child, but here was a child who soaked up everything around her, whose musical feats, on top of intellectual gifts, kept family and friends amazed. Patience, however, may be needed to train a child to accept the limits parents impose. For her part the child learned to cloak her self-assurance and pride in her achievements in a modest mien.

Such modesty was particularly important for a girl to learn. According to early nineteenth-century practice, during a child's first few years issues of gender socialization were not a concern because all children were treated as girls. Both sexes wore long dresses that limited gross motor movement, and they were taught to be pliant and submissive. Differential treatment of boys and girls began, however, at the age of six, when boys were "breeched" during a ceremonial rite of passage. Freedom and autonomy withheld since birth, like the toy on the table, were now offered in a limited and controlled manner to boys, along with their first masculine clothing.[30]

For the sons of moderates in particular, their relative autonomy also became a source of tension as they approached manhood: "Moderates often liked to think of their piety as 'manly,' and the emphasis they placed on reason in religion was an oblique way of asserting the superiority of those qualities of temperament that were perceived as masculine over those associated with the passions, which were perceived as feminine."[31] Among the feminizing temptations that seduced young men were girls, guns, cards, flutes, and violins; men must keep to their books to practice manliness and industry and pursue fame.[32]

On the other hand, the gender socialization of girls begun at birth continued without a break; for girls this limited freedom was never offered, there was no ceremonial equivalent of breeching, and no change in behavior was allowed. They continued to be restricted in their movements by the same long dresses, they remained confined at home, they were given less food than their brothers to remain "slender and delicate," they were expected to avoid vigorous physical activity, and they were educated in domestic skills rather than in academic subjects.[33] Most important, they were expected to remain pious, self-abnegating, humble, and submissive.

One of the reasons moderates objected to Evangelical methods was concern that boys might not be able to grow into their expected roles after their wills were broken. Until the age of six, girls and boys were expected to have no wills of their own. Thereafter, although boys were still under parental discipline, in practice they had greater latitude: "While it was agreed that girls, like boys had sinful wills, in need of being 'broken' [or at least bent], it was implicitly and sometimes explicitly assumed that boys had stronger wills than girls, and passions that were more difficult to control [and that] the stronger wills of male children would in the end make them more manly men [with] a taste for ruling which is the germ of their future character."[34] Amy Cheney, a passionate and strong-willed child, demanded the more flexible treatment granted to boys; however, her very striving against limits may well have driven Clara Cheney to greater efforts to make the child conform to standards for girls.

When Amy was six, Clara Cheney finally agreed to teach her piano, but even then she limited her time at the instrument: "My mother devoted all her time to my education. I was being given piano lessons and other simple, regular instruction. I was not allowed to specialize on [sic] music. I was given an allotted time each day for practice. The piano was still, theoretically, in the top bureau drawer." Beach's statement suggests that being both mother and teacher left Clara Cheney little if any time for her own music making, that her musicality was in effect "erased" as it made room for the musical progress of the child.[35]

That progress was swift; within the year Clara Cheney reported that the child was playing "Heller's *Etudes*, Op. 47, Czerny's *Etudes de*

Velocité (Book 1), Handel's *Harmonious Blacksmith* [Variations], Mozart's *Andante and Variations* in G major, Mendelssohn's *Songs* arr[anged] by [Otto] Dresel, Chopin's *Valse,* Op. 18, and others in order, Beethoven's Sonatas, Op. 49, Nos. 1 and 2, Op. 2 No. 1, Op. 14 No. 2, with all his slow movements and Minuets of the Sonatas as far as Op. 49."[36]

At seven Amy Cheney was ready and eager "to give serious recital programs."[37] When opportunity arose at the First Congregational Church in Chelsea, where they lived at the time, it was her mother who bent. As in her first session at the piano, the child may have been aided by outside intervention. Beach explained that "I was allowed to play in a few concerts—I imagine the consent was unwilling—and for encores I used to play my own waltzes."

One of these recitals resulted in her first review. The press reported on a private recital where she played a Chopin waltz and one of her own waltzes "with an accuracy and style which surprised every listener." As a result, "the young pianist is exciting much surprise by the precocity of her musical talent."[38] Attracted by her talent and extreme youth, two or more concert managers offered contracts. Beach noted that she looked even younger than her seven years because she was "small for her age, fair, and slight." "It would have been merely play," she commented, "to enter upon the career of a travelling pianist, but my father and mother both agreed it would have been the worst possible thing for me mentally and physically."[39] Clara Cheney then announced that there were to be no more recitals, even at private Sunday-school events.

The child's unalloyed joy in performing for an audience may have been one reason that Clara Cheney was so opposed. The outcome, a press notice and offers from concert managers, was probably what she hoped to avoid, along with the "corrupting" power of such a heady experience. From then on it was public performance that was kept just out of reach.

Years later Beach made excuses for her parents' decision: "I shall always have the deepest gratitude for my inexperienced young parents that they did not allow me to be exploited by managers,"[40] an explanation that begs the question. Like every parent of a first child, they were by definition inexperienced; but perhaps Beach meant that they remained provincial in attitude, despite their move in 1875 to Boston, where Unitarians and Transcendentalists rejected the idea of infant depravity, and women's public activism as abolitionists and feminists suggested new ways of raising children, especially girls.[41]

Perhaps Beach was comparing her mother's mode with that of her maternal aunt Franc, whose masculine-sounding nickname matched a considerably more adventurous, perhaps even rebellious life. Marianne Hirsch has noted the typical distribution of roles between sisters: "One sister leads the more conventional life so that the other may be free to break away from it."[42] Of the Marcy sisters, Clara was the stay-at-home, who also gave her mother a home after her marriage, thus incorporating into the household an earlier and possibly stricter approach to child-rearing. Her older sister was the one who left home to live in Boston, where she taught music and met her future husband, Lyman Clement. They married in 1867 and moved to San Francisco in 1869, where she continued to teach voice, piano, and painting.

Franc Clement spent considerable time away from home after marriage. In addition to her trip to Boston for the Peace Jubilee, she traveled abroad as well. Her daughter Ethel (1874–1920) displayed artistic talent, and beginning in the 1890s she took Ethel to study in New York and then in Paris in 1898 and 1908. During their second stay Ethel's portrait of her mother was "hung on the line" at a Paris Salon.[43] Franc Clement's independent life-style and willingness to leave her husband and home to further a daughter's career could not have been more subversive of Clara Cheney's approach.

There were several transcontinental visits between the sisters and cousins. The first trip for Amy Cheney was at age ten, to spend what she described as a "delicious year" in San Francisco with the Clements.[44] Perhaps that delicious year gave her a taste of a freer and more relaxed—even indulgent—way of living than she had at home. One measure of the Clements' more affluent life-style was a boat they named "The Clara," for Amy's mother. A photo taken during her year in San Francisco shows Amy Cheney in an elaborate and fashionable dress of velvet, with a lace collar and cuffs and a bustle, the like of which is not seen in photos taken back East. Five years later, in 1883, Beach's devotion to her aunt was made public when she dedicated her first published song to "Mrs. Franc M. Clement."[45]

Four photographs in the Beach Collection at the University of New Hampshire, unidentified except for the addresses of the photographers, also suggest that the Marcy sisters had different personalities.[46] One face is austere to the point of coldness, the other warm and open, with large, dark eyes. It is tempting to assume that the latter is Aunt Franc.

With the important exception of music making, Clara Cheney comes alive in her daughter's words only as a mother, not as a daughter or wife or woman in her own right. As Marianne Hirsch points out, "It is the woman as *daughter* who occupies the center of the global reconstruction of subjectivity and subject-object relation. The woman as *mother* remains in the position of *other* and the emergence of feminine-daughterly subjectivity rests and depends on the continued and repeated process of *othering* the mother."[47]

There remains the barest outline of a life. In the most extensive retelling Clara Cheney is identified as "musician and botanist; [who] played and sang in New Hampshire concerts and continued teaching several years after marriage. In later years [she] took up botanical work, and presented to the Gray Herboriam [*sic*] of Harvard University a large collection of botanical specimens arranged by herself."[48] Otherwise, asides in a feature article about her daughter relate that she studied with Concord's leading music teacher, attended early music festivals, and was a "brilliant woman" and "a conscientious musician [who] was known all over the state both as a singer and a pianist."[49] Yet her name is missing from newspaper accounts of musical events in New Hampshire during the four years before her marriage to Charles Cheney, and no interviewer of Amy Beach ever mentioned hearing Clara Cheney play or sing. Lurking unannounced is the possibility of considerable competition for musical dominance, first between the two Marcy sisters and then between mother and daughter.

What were Clara Cheney's options before marriage? In the 1860s women who had professional careers in music usually were foreign-born and came from families of professional musicians. For a daughter of a middle-class family like the Marcys of Hillsboro, marriage was the only acceptable life plan, however. Did Clara Cheney ever dream of a career beyond New Hampshire? If so, what emotional price, if any, did she pay for giving up the dream? As the tradition-bound daughter who stayed at home, before and after marriage, she was conforming to societal norms. Was it done without regret? How did she feel about her older sister's freer definition of her role? Finally, how can we expect Clara Cheney to have the capacity for self-realization, applied either to herself or to her daughter, that only a handful of women were just beginning to envision for their own lives at a time when the country was struggling to recover from the Civil War and feminist thought was still a voice in the wilderness?

When Amy Cheney was just eight, Clara Cheney decided that her daughter had outgrown her as a piano teacher and sought advice about a new one. The child played for some of Boston's leading German-trained musicians, who were so impressed that they recommended study in Europe for Amy Cheney, confident that despite her extreme youth, any first-rate German conservatory would accept her on the spot. That was of course a compliment to both mother and child.

Attending such a conservatory would place her in the company of musical peers who planned to be professionals. These were the very experiences a gifted girl needed to imagine a public life for herself.[50] Predictably, the Cheneys decided against European study. Amy Cheney was to remain at home in Boston and study with German-trained Ernst Perabo, one of Boston's finest pianists and teachers. The auditions had an unintended side effect, however: they created a circle of Bostonians who were excited by her promise and would monitor her progress for the next eight years, until her debut.

That same year, 1875, Amy Cheney was allowed to attend concerts at night. One of the pianists she might have heard that year was American-born Amy Fay (1844–1928), fresh from six years in Germany and one of the earliest of the native-born women to study abroad. Her vivid epistolary account of her life as a music student in Germany, soon to be published, inspired hundreds of American girls and women to go and do likewise.[51] If Amy Cheney read Fay's very popular book, her sense of loss would have been acute.

While in 1875 American-born models were few indeed, there was a rich assortment of women from overseas who were first-rate role models, among them the violinist Teresa Liebe and the pianist Annette Essipoff. The most notable was the Venezuelan Teresa Carreño, to whom Beach later dedicated her piano concerto, op. 45. Carreño had blossomed after her New York debut in 1853 as a child prodigy and was a favorite in Boston. Her career was typical of virtuosi in that she also composed, mainly the expected display pieces for the piano, although later in life she wrote for string quartet and orchestra. Composition was thus a sideline for her.

If Carreño was a positive model for Amy Cheney, she was a negative model for those like Clara Cheney who objected to exploitation of prodigies—Carreño made her debut at age ten—and later for those who felt that the stage was no place for a lady—by the time Carreño was twenty-three, she was divorced and remarried. In the end she married four times and had a child out of wedlock—not the kind of life that middle-class Americans found acceptable.[52]

Despite the prohibition on public performance, Amy Cheney's reputation as a child prodigy grew, especially through playing in the drawing rooms of Boston's social and musical elite. In 1880 she and her teacher, Perabo, visited Henry Wadsworth Longfellow at his home in Cambridge to collect his autograph. While there she played for the poet. Afterward Longfellow sent her his autograph in a letter in which he also thanked her for playing so beautifully. In a letter to Perabo, Longfellow predicted a bright future for her and, most significantly,

discussed Perabo's plan to send her to Europe to study. To accomplish
this, he wrote, "all musical people should come to your aid."[53] Possibly
they discussed raising a fund to send her to Europe, similar to the fund
that Bostonians had raised earlier for Perabo himself.[54] Needless to
say, nothing came of Perabo's plan. Indeed, he was soon replaced by
another piano teacher.

   Others who heard her play during those years before her debut
included the famous pianist Raphael Joseffy and the singer, pianist,
and composer Clara Kathleen Rogers, who commented on her great
promise.[55] Louis C. Elson, critic and music historian, described another
such private audition when there was "a test of the fourteen-year-old
prodigy, made with Teresa Liebe, the violinist, wherein the young miss
not only played fugues from Bach's 'Well-tempered Clavichord,' but
transposed them into any required key. Her memory, her expression
in playing, her enthusiasm, her exhibitions of the sense of absolute
pitch, were wonderful. Her teachers considered her, at that time, the
greatest musical prodigy in America."[56] William Mason, a fellow Bos-
tonian who was this country's outstanding teacher of piano, listened
to her play in the home of her third and last piano teacher, Carl Baermann, and wrote her future husband that she had a fine technique
and was "musikalische," high praise from this German-trained musician.[57]

   One of Clara Cheney's justifications for deciding first to withhold
and then to limit music was concern for her daughter's intellectual
growth. She decided, quite rightly, that a one-sided emphasis on music
would shortchange the child. Yet that concern did not result in a solid
general education for Amy Cheney. She had limited formal schooling,
despite the variety of educational opportunities for Boston's girls—
including several private schools as well as the public Girls' Latin
School, which opened in 1878 to prepare students for college.[58] Although Harvard was closed to her, there were colleges in Boston that
admitted women, and just outside of Boston was Wellesley, which had
a fine music program developed by her theory teacher Junius Welch
Hill.[59]

   After she had spent several years at home under Clara Cheney's
tutelage, Amy Cheney's "school world enlarged" at age ten, when she
finally attended Professor William L. Whittemore's private day school
on Beacon Hill. During her two years as a full-time student she excelled
in all her subjects but was particularly fascinated with natural science.
Her daily routine, however, included three to four hours of practice,
allowing time for nothing but work.

There was one happy exception: while in school she joined the Attic Club, organized by a group of girls from Beacon Hill to pursue their literary interests. Along with other members she wrote stories and occasionally delighted the members by playing for them at the close of their weekly meetings.[60] Beach wrote that otherwise she worked very hard, with "little companionship or friends near my own age."[61] If Clara Cheney felt no need to provide companions for her daughter, she had considerable support in the practices of Evangelicals who considered playmates to be potentially corrupting and thus to be avoided.

Amy Cheney's formal schooling ended with her third year, when her mother finally agreed that a piano debut was inevitable. In preparation Amy limited her studies to French and German, both of which she learned at the piano while simultaneously practicing keyboard exercises. That sort of intense concentration may have alarmed her parents, who had earlier expressed concern for their daughter's health should she overwork.[62]

Such concern was widespread. Physicians warned that females were delicate and disease-prone, especially during puberty.[63] In nineteenth-century eyes, talent and intellectual interests in a girl were cause for alarm; no exertions should be allowed to divert essential energy from a girl's most important physical function, sexual maturation, which if disrupted could destabilize her entire life.[64] That being true for normal girls, what were the risks for a gifted child who was also intensely emotional? The Cheneys determined that in raising Amy "due regard must be paid to a judicious expenditure of health and energy."[65]

Why, after so many years of opposition, did Clara Cheney relent and allow her daughter to make her debut as a concert pianist? Perhaps there was considerable pressure not only from Amy Cheney but also from the child's teacher and others in the Boston community who had heard her play. Perhaps those Bostonians who knew of her remarkable talents believed they warranted a public career. This was the city where many believed music was "the language of heaven . . . of the Infinite" and valued those who practiced the "divine art."[66] But perhaps Clara Cheney agreed because she considered it important for Amy Cheney to have something to fall back on if she never married or, having married, needed to support herself. Or perhaps she hoped that her public appearances would attract a suitor.

"When I was sixteen," Beach wrote, "I was allowed to make my debut in Boston." "Allowed," not encouraged. The historian of the Attic Club remembers the evening of 24 October 1883: "About two years [after Amy Cheney joined the club] her master introduced her to her future public at the old Music Hall in Hamilton Place where the Boston Symphony Orchestra had recently been born. Of course we went to her debut and sat in an enchanted row as she, with two heavy plaits of hair hanging down her back, sat at the great piano, dealing with it already with a master's hand."[67]

It was a very rainy Wednesday night; nevertheless, the Music Hall was well filled. This was not the sort of solo debut recital that became the rule in the twentieth century. Rather, it was a variety program typical of the time, a much kinder way to introduce a debutante (see figure 6.1). On the program were five other soloists, with top billing going—quite rightly—to Clara Louise Kellogg (1842–1916), the woman with absolute pitch to whom Charles Cheney had referred. One of the first American-born and American-trained sopranos, Kellogg was esteemed as an opera singer in Europe as well as in the United States, and she was a favorite of the Handel and Haydn Society and Boston concert-goers.[68] Amy Cheney had illustrious company for a debut.

She performed Moscheles's G Minor Concerto, op. 58, for piano and orchestra. The reviews do not mention that she played from memory, but since this was a lifelong practice, she probably did so here as well.[69] The concerto, with its brilliant and extended octave runs and passages in thirds and sixths, was calculated to demonstrate her technical skills. She also played as a solo Chopin's Rondo in E-flat, op. 16, a piece that demands interpretive artistry as well as technical velocity. Her pleasure in the event was intense:

The presence of a throng of people was an inspiration. And as for the orchestra (it was my first experience with one), no words can tell the pleasure I felt performing with a band of instrumentalists, each member of it himself such a musician as to sense my wishes more quickly and surely than the greatest conductor could convey them. I can only compare my sensations with those of a driver who holds in his hands the reins that perfectly control a glorious, spirited pair of horses. One must live through such an experience to properly appreciate it.[70]

At least nine Boston papers, plus a monthly and the *New York Tribune*, reviewed the concert. All agreed that the chief event of the evening was Amy Cheney's debut. "Her success was immediate, and the young artist aroused an enthusiasm that was no less critically appreciative than it was fairly earned."[71] Her manner charmed the audience, while her total absence of nervousness in her opening phrases of the concerto allowed them to sit back and enjoy her playing: "scarcely had the first phrase, after the tumultuous tutti, been played, when all the audience became convinced that she was entirely adequate to the task, and it was no tremulous, nor even a colorless performance

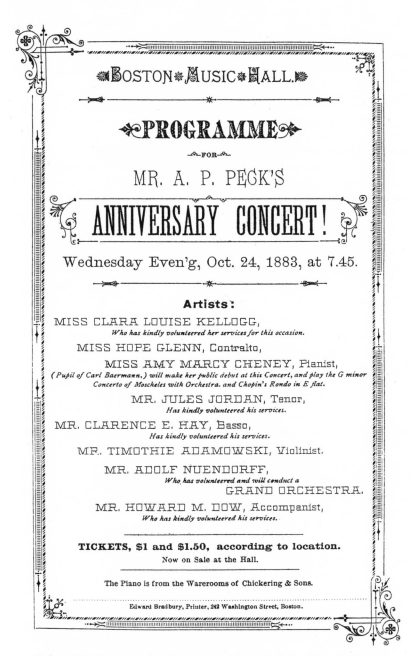

BOSTON ✳ MUSIC ✳ HALL.

PROGRAMME

⟶FOR⟵

MR. A. P. PECK'S

ANNIVERSARY CONCERT!

Wednesday Even'g, Oct. 24, 1883, at 7.45.

Artists:

MISS CLARA LOUISE KELLOGG,
Who has kindly volunteered her services for this occasion.

MISS HOPE GLENN, Contralto,

MISS AMY MARCY CHENEY, Pianist,
(Pupil of Carl Baermann,) will make her public debut at this Concert, and play the G minor Concerto of Moscheles with Orchestra. and Chopin's Rondo in E flat.

MR. JULES JORDAN, Tenor,
Has kindly volunteered his services.

MR. CLARENCE E. HAY, Basso,
Has kindly volunteered his services.

MR. TIMOTHIE ADAMOWSKI, Violinist,

MR. ADOLF NUENDORFF,
Who has volunteered and will conduct a
GRAND ORCHESTRA.

MR. HOWARD M. DOW, Accompanist,
Who has kindly volunteered his services.

TICKETS, $1 and $1.50, according to location.
Now on Sale at the Hall.

The Piano is from the Warerooms of Chickering & Sons.

Edward Bradbury, Printer, 242 Washington Street, Boston.

Figure 6.1. Program for the piano debut of Amy Marcy Cheney. (Scrapbook, Beach Collection, University of New Hampshire at Durham. Reprinted with the kind permission of the University of New Hampshire.)

which the audience was about to hear."[72] There was unanimous praise from critics. The review in the *Boston Gazette* summed it all up:

Her natural gifts and her innate artistic intelligence were made apparent in the very first phrases she played. Her manner is winningly modest, though it lacked nothing in easy self-possession. She has a brilliant and remarkably fluent technique, of which the grace and refinement are delightfully conspicuous. Her playing is wholly without affectation, and is surprising in the maturity of taste, the delicacy, warmth and propriety of expression, the largeness and beauty of phrasing, the thorough musicianly understanding, and the exquisite purity of style that characterize it throughout. A special charm was added to her performances by the freshness, the artless simplicity, and the thorough grasp of the composer's meaning that signalized them.[73]

It is hard to imagine a better review for a debut. The audience was "enthusiastic in the extreme, and flowers were heaped upon her in lavish profusion."[74] This was a coming-out party par excellence.

With her debut her life changed. Now she was out in the world, part of Boston's musical circle, a public figure who made strong contact with her audience. It was a sudden and important change from the isolation of the home and the relative anonymity of the student. Later she wrote of the debut, "Life was beginning."

For the next two years, she kept up a swift pace of performing, playing with orchestras and in recital programs. It is significant that all her performances took place in Boston or its environs. At this juncture, extended concert tours were needed to establish a national and an international reputation, something important to do while still considered a child prodigy. Clara Cheney was still in control, though; the life of a touring concert artist remained out of reach.

Amy Cheney described her life during that time: "I gave recitals and played a good deal of chamber music, in concerts, and in the intervals worked at my compositions. I had not then divided my enthusiasms; the work was complementary. It had not come to me there was a choice to be made; that where many people play music, few write music; that creation is higher than interpretation."

Although on the surface the mother's early decision that Amy was to be a musician, not a prodigy, was enigmatic—after all, even as a toddler it was apparent that she *was* a prodigy—its meaning became increasingly clear over the years of her childhood and youth: not only was she not to be exploited as a child prodigy but she was not to have a public career. Rather, she was to marry and to make music as a private person; like her mother, she was to place a man, not music, at the center of her life and take her place in the patriarchal succession.

Furthermore, she was to do this willingly and without rancor, for parents demanded that no anger against them be expressed.[75] That too was a lesson that Amy Cheney learned well. In her autobiography she apparently accepts her parents' decisions about her upbringing. Her objective reporting of incidents, however, allows the perceptive reader to glimpse contentious aspects of the intergenerational relationships.

Unlike her mother, Amy Beach had a talent that demanded music be the center of her life.[76] But would we have had this important and pioneering model of female compositional creativity if Mother Cheney had not had her way? Beach, with the energy and confidence of youth, believed she could manage both composition and performance and did not need to choose between them. Yet she accepted her mother's decision.

Very soon a new authority entered her life, and she accepted his decisions as well. Amy Cheney and Henry Harris Aubrey Beach, a widower twenty-five years older than his eighteen-year-old bride, were married on 2 December 1885 in Trinity Church, Boston. There is no record of their courtship; no diaries remain, only a newspaper article and a single letter suggesting that Henry Beach had earlier heard her play and was fascinated.[77] Nor is there direct evidence of an arranged marriage, something the discrepancy in the couple's ages would suggest. But Henry Beach as a suitor fit neatly into Clara Cheney's plan.

The marriage agreement specified that Amy Cheney abandon her concert career, playing only at annual recitals in Boston and to introduce her own works. In its stead she was to concentrate on composition, something she could do at home. Amy Beach was now "a musician, not a prodigy," and Clara Cheney had succeeded in getting the genie back in the bottle.

Henry Beach, through his support of her creative work, helped bring the genie back out, though. He had much to offer: a man of charm, he enjoyed the fine things of life and was gifted in music as well as in medicine. His adherence to Anglo-Catholicism simultaneously allowed for luxurious living and aesthetic pleasures as well as concern for ultimate values. For Beach this ambiance was highly conducive to creative work, even though she did not subscribe to her husband's religious beliefs at that time.

He had other attributes. As a self-made man, he offered a model of career-building for his wife to emulate. He also offered the money that allowed time for the big works, the emotional support to dare to write them, and access to musical and Brahmin circles that led to performances of those works. Her gifts as a composer and her steady production of works, almost without exception published and performed, built her reputation from a modest local one to a national and then an international one.

Nevertheless, the desire to pursue a concert career never left her. Following the deaths of her husband on 28 June 1910 and her mother on 18 February 1911, Amy Beach finally had the autonomy she had lacked for forty-three years. Alone and grieving, she soon chose the life of a touring concert artist, with emphasis on the promotion of her own works. The new life gave her much satisfaction. When asked in 1917 if she had plans for composing a new large-scale work, she replied that for this she needed a large block of time, unavailable because "she was too enthusiastic a traveler yet to settle down, too fond of [her] audiences to give them up."[78]

Yet she soon found the time and support she needed for composition in summer residencies at the MacDowell Colony. Although she produced somewhat fewer works in the last period of her life, among them were large-scale compositions that reflected greater freedom to experiment and resulted in a new musical synthesis. Examples of this musical maturity are found in her *Quartet for Strings in One Movement*, op. 89,[79] and the *Canticle of the Sun*, op. 123, the text by St. Francis of Assisi. Perhaps the two adult periods in her life—the years of her marriage from 1885 to 1910 and of her widowhood from 1910 to her death in 1944—were, like composition and performance, complementary.

* * *

Clara Cheney's plan at first seemed totally arbitrary; however, the figure under Clara Cheney's carpet that explained those actions was created out of the larger designs of society and the normative practices of both Victorian gender socialization and Protestant child-rearing. It must be pointed out that the methodological approach that views individual actions in the context of normative practices must be seen as suggestive rather than definitive, since socially sanctioned practices are subject to individual interpretation. The contrasting child-rearing practices of Clara Cheney and Franc Clement offer clear examples of the divergent paths that two individuals from the same family can take.

Clara's decisions might also have been unconsciously motivated or the product of conflicts inherent in mother-daughter relationships or of practices specific to the family rather than the family's social milieu.[80] For all these possibilities, however, data are lacking. The literature on Protestant child-rearing does provide powerful models of practices specific both to time and place that explain the mother's choices. Growing out of a value system that transcended the personal, these practices allowed her to weigh her child's musical gifts against eternal salvation and to find the latter, not the former, compelling. Consistent with the Victorian gender system, these practices provided for not only human submission to God but also woman's submission to man.

NOTES

Portions of this essay will appear in *Amy Beach (1867–1944), American Composer and Pianist,* to be published by Oxford University Press. I wish to thank Stuart Feder, M.D., Gabriel Moran of New York University, Nancy B. Reich of Bard College, Judith Tick of Northeastern University, and Elizabeth Wood of Sarah Lawrence College for their careful readings and helpful suggestions.

1. Pachter, *Telling Lives,* 16–34.
2. For this interpretation of her life, see Block, "Why Amy Beach Succeeded as a Composer." My earlier view is consistent with others' writings. See Epstein, "Amy Marcy Cheney Beach," who states that Beach led a charmed life. E. L. Merrill, "Mrs. H. H. A. Beach," 4, has no fault to find with the parent-child relationship and states that the reason for the parents' decision against European study was the child's "emotional nature and . . . sensitivity." Eden, "Huntington, Sculptor, and Beach, Composer," 52–53, indicates that her mother's restrictions were beneficial because they allowed the child's "talents to evolve naturally." Miles, "Solo Piano Works," 3, writes that Beach "was fortunate to have been born into a family who supported her musical efforts from the very beginning of her life" and that Beach was given "all possible advantages."
3. Beach, "Why I Chose My Profession." All quotations are from this article unless otherwise noted.
4. Greven, *Child-Rearing Concepts;* see also his *Protestant Temperament.* For a long historical view, see DeMause, *History of Childhood.*
5. Beach, Letter to Wiggers, [1].
6. Lee, *Lost Art of Reading,* 77.
7. Greven, *Protestant Temperament,* 35, 42.
8. Ibid., 164.
9. Portions of Bushnell's *Christian Nurture* are reprinted in Greven, *Child-Rearing Concepts,* 137–81.
10. Bushnell, *Christian Nurture,* 13.
11. Ibid., 57.
12. Ibid., 20.
13. In Greven, *Protestant Temperament,* 169.
14. DeMause, *History of Childhood,* 367.
15. In Greven, *Protestant Temperament,* 174.

16. Taylor, "Blessing the House," 444. Her source was Alcott, "Mother, Teach Your Child Submission," 16–18.

17. In Greven, *Child-Rearing Concepts*, 171–72.

18. Quoted in Kinscella, "Play No Piece in Public," 9.

19. Poem reprinted by permission of HarperCollins. See also Beach's "The Moon-path" (Katharine Adams), op. 99, no. 3 (Philadelphia, 1923).

20. Bremner, *Children and Youth in America*, 352.

21. Quoted in Greven, *Child-Rearing Concepts*, 133.

22. Quoted from Abbott, "On the Mother's Role in Education (1833)," in Greven, *Child-Rearing Concepts*, 129.

23. "Jubilee Sheet," 3.

24. Beach, Letter to Wiggers, [1].

25. Quoted in Kinscella, "Play No Piece in Public," 9.

26. Beach, Untitled biography, 2.

27. Greven, *Protestant Temperament*, 74.

28. Printed reports on this visit vary. Her grandfather's farm is variously located in "the country," in Maine, or in Henniker (most likely), where the 1870 census locates her grandfather. See, for example, her letter to Wiggers, in which she recalls this incident as happening in "the New Hampshire Hills with my grandfather." The year would have been 1872. Her age was given in some sources as three at the time, in others four; her stay ranges from six weeks to three months; and the number of waltzes she composed while there varies from one to four. To add to the confusion, two biographical sketches, both of which have handwritten additions by the composer, who could have but did not correct either one, disagree: the typescript biography at the Tucker Free Library in Henniker and the printed biography at the New Hampshire State Library, Concord, N.H.

29. Quoted in "How Mrs. Beach Did Her First Composing," 22.

30. Greven, *Protestant Temperament*, 282.

31. Ibid., 243–44.

32. Ibid., 246.

33. Gorham, *Victorian Girl*, 72–73.

34. Ibid., 77.

35. Hirsch, *Mother/Daughter Plot*, 39.

36. Beach, Untitled biography, 5. Although no author was given, the presence of the typescript, with additions in Beach's hand, suggests that Beach herself prepared it.

37. Beach, Letter to Wiggers, [2].

38. "Young Pianist," n.p. The reporter states the event was "a private musical entertainment." I wish to thank Leslie Petteys for bringing this article to my attention.

39. Beach, Letter to Wiggers, [2].

40. Ibid.

41. See M. D. Merrill, *Growing Up in Boston's Gilded Age*, for a very different kind of rearing of Alice Stone Blackwell by Lucy Stone and her hus-

band, Henry Blackwell, both feminists who encouraged their daughter's autonomy and self-concept as a writer. Alice Stone Blackwell wrote her diaries between the ages of fourteen and sixteen.

42. Hirsch, *Mother/Daughter Plot*, 64.

43. At Paris salons paintings were hung one above the other up to the ceiling. It was an honor to have a painting hung "on the line," that is, at eye level.

44. Beach, Letter to Fredricks.

45. "The Rainy Day" (Longfellow) (Boston: Oliver Ditson, 1883). Beach dedicated "Empress of Night," op. 2, no. 3 (Boston: Arthur P. Schmidt, 1891), to her mother; "The Thrush," op. 14, no. 4 (Boston: Arthur P. Schmidt, 1891), to "Mrs. L. M. Clement"; and "Shena Van," op. 56, no. 4 (Boston: Arthur P. Schmidt, 1904), to her cousin, Ethel Clement. About twenty songs are dedicated to her husband, identified as *"H."*

46. The photographs are identified by the photographers and their locations. Two views of the same person were taken by photographers in Concord, N.H., where Clara Cheney lived; W. G. C. Kimball took photos presumably of Clara Cheney, probably before marriage since her hair was well below her waist and women usually wore their hair up only after marriage (box 5, folder 91), and later took a picture of Amy Cheney when she was about two years old (box 5, folder 1). A second photo of the same woman, presumably Clara Cheney, was taken by J. P. Morgan of Concord, N.H. (box 5, folder 41).

A number of photographs were taken by Thors of San Francisco, including those tentatively identified as Franc Clement (box 5, folder 97); her husband, Lyman (box 5, folder 96); their daughter Ethel, born in 1874 (box 5, folder 78); and Amy Cheney (box 5, folders 81–83). The appearances of all four suggest that the photos were taken during Amy's stay in San Francisco in 1878–79. There also is a later photo done in San Francisco, probably of Franc Clement (box 5, folder 41a). All the above are in the Beach Collection.

47. Hirsch, *Mother/Daughter Plot*, 136.

48. Browne, *History of Hillsborough*, 2:406.

49. "In Musical Circles," unidentified clipping from Concord, N.H., 9 February 1892, scrapbook 1, 74; "Mrs. H. H. A. Beach," scrapbook 2, 55; A.M.B., "America's Chief Composer," *Sunday Times Herald* (Chicago), 28 November 1897, scrapbook 1, 118–19; "World's Fair Musician," *Chicago Record*, 3 May 1893, scrapbook 2, 12. All in the Beach Collection.

50. Heilbrun, *Writing a Woman's Life*, 97–98. For the very different life of a contemporary of Beach, see Schaffer and Greenwood, *Maud Powell*. Maud Powell, who was born the same year that Beach was, became America's first native-born concert violinist. She was chaperoned by her mother from the time she entered the Leipzig Conservatory at age fourteen, through her debut, and then on international tours until she was over thirty. Hers was a lustrous career, although won at the cost of a major disruption of family life.

51. See Fay, *Music Study in Germany*.

52. Milinowski, *Teresa Carreño*.

53. Letter from Longfellow to "Miss Amy," 15 November 1880, Cambridge, autograph album, 2; letter from Longfellow to Ernst Perabo, 20 November 1880, Beach correspondence. Both in the Beach Collection.

54. Scharfenberg, Letters to John Sullivan Dwight.

55. On Joseffy, see Kinscella, "Play No Piece in Public," 10. Rogers's statement is in the autograph album, 25, Beach Collection.

56. Elson, *History of American Music*, 298.

57. Letter from William Mason to Dr. Henry Harris Aubrey Beach, 3 October 1884, Orange, N.J., autograph album, 53, Beach Collection.

58. Cheney, "Women of Boston," 4:345–46.

59. Hill gave Amy Cheney private harmony and counterpoint lessons in 1881–82.

60. Talbot, "Attic Club," 3.

61. Beach, Letter to Edith [Brown].

62. Clara and Charles Cheney expressed concern for their child's health when she was seven and had offers to put her on the concert circuit ([Beach], "Mrs. H. H. A. Beach," [3]; Beach, Letter to Wiggers, [2]) and when she was eight and her parents decided against European study for her (Beach, Untitled biography, 6).

63. Wood, " 'Fashionable Diseases,' " 2.

64. According to Elaine and English Showalter, in 1873 Dr. Edward Clark of Harvard published *Sex in Education*. In this extremely influential volume he stated that "higher education was destroying the reproductive functions of American women, by overworking them at a critical time in their physiological development." Cited in their "Victorian Women and Menstruation," 87. See also Hellerstein, Hume, and Offen, *Victorian Women*, 69–70: "Any strain upon a girl's intellect is to be dreaded, and any attempt to bring women into competition with men can scarcely escape failure." Degler, *At Odds*, 311–12, also discusses this belief.

65. Beach, Untitled biography, 6; [Beach], "Mrs. H. H. A. Beach," 4.

66. Dwight, "Address," 1.

67. Talbot, "Attic Club," 3.

68. *The New Grove Dictionary of American Music*, s.v. "Kellogg, Clara Louise," 2:619; *History of the Handel and Haydn Society*, 1:373, 375–76, 383–84, 403, passim.

69. Mildred Aldrich, "Mrs. Amy Marcy Cheney Beach," scrapbook 1, 83–84, Beach Collection.

70. Quoted in Downes, "Mrs. Beach of Boston."

71. "Musical Notes," *Boston Gazette*, 27 October 1883, scrapbook 1, 3, Beach Collection.

72. "Mr. A. P. Peck's Concert," *Boston Courier*, 28 October 1883, scrapbook 1, 3, Beach Collection.

73. "Musical Notes," *Boston Gazette*, 27 October 1883, scrapbook 1, 3, Beach Collection.

74. "Mr. Peck's Anniversary Concert," *Boston Transcript*, 25 October 1883, scrapbook 1, 2, Beach Collection.

75. Greven, *Protestant Temperament*, 113.

76. Beach, Letter to Wiggers, [2].

77. Emily Constant, "Women Who Have Succeeded, I: Mrs. H. H. A. Beach," *New England Home Magazine* [a supplement of the *Boston Sunday Journal*], 5 March 1898, 408; Letter from William Mason to Dr. Henry Harris Aubrey Beach, 3 October 1884, Orange, N.J., autograph album, 53, Beach Collection.

78. Quoted in H.F.P., "Women Composers," 3.

79. This is one of the few works by Beach that was never published, despite its outstanding quality and modernizing tendencies. I am preparing an edition of the string quartet, to be published as vol. 3 of Music of the United States of America by the American Musicological Society.

80. See, for example, the girlhood of Alice Stone Blackwell as described in her diaries: M. D. Merrill, *Growing Up in Boston*.

REFERENCES

Alcott, William A. "Mother, Teach Your Child Submission." *The Mother's Magazine*, 1864, 16–18.

Beach, Amy. Letter to Edith [Brown], 6 November 1940. Attic Club Papers, Boston Athenaeum.

———. Letter to Jessica Fredricks, 6 February 1939, New York (353 West 57th Street). Music Collection, San Francisco Public Library.

———. Letter to Mrs. Edwin H. Wiggers, 25 August 1935, Centerville, Mass. National Archives of the PEO, New York.

———. "Why I Chose My Profession: The Autobiography of a Woman Composer." An interview written by Ednah Aiken in *The Mother's Magazine*, February 1914, 7–8.

[Beach, Amy]. "Mrs. H. H. A. Beach." Printed biography (circa 1928) with additions in Beach's hand, unpaginated. New Hampshire State Library, Concord, N.H.

———. Untitled biography of Amy Beach [typescript], with hand-written additions by Amy Beach, [1903–circa 1924]. Tucker Free Library, Henniker, N.H.

Beach Collection. Special Collections, Dimond Library, University of New Hampshire, Durham, N.H.

Block, Adrienne Fried. "Why Amy Beach Succeeded as a Composer: The Early Years." *Current Musicology* 36 (1983): 41–59.

Bremner, Robert Hamlet, comp. *Children and Youth in America: A Documentary History*. Vol. 1, *1600–1865*. Cambridge, Mass.: Harvard University Press, 1970.

Browne, George Waldo. *The History of Hillsborough, New Hampshire, 1735–1921*. 2 vols. Manchester, N.H.: Town of Hillsborough, 1921–22.

Bushnell, Horace. *Christian Nurture*. New York: Charles Scribner, 1863.

Cheney, Ednah D. "The Women of Boston." In *The Memorial History of Boston, 1630–1880*, vol. 4, edited by Justin Winsor. Boston: James R. Osgood, 1881.

Degler, Carl N. *At Odds: Women and the Family in America from the Revolution to the Present*. Oxford: Oxford University Press, 1980.

DeMause, Lloyd, ed. *The History of Childhood*. New York: Psychohistory Press, 1974.

Dickens, Charles. *A Child's Dream of a Star*. Illustrated by Hammett Billings. Boston: Fields, Osgood, 1871.

Downes, Olin. "Mrs. H. H. A. Beach of Boston, Now Noted as Composer," 1907. Unidentified clipping in scrapbook. Fuller Public Library, Hillsboro, N.H.; now on deposit at the University of New Hampshire, Durham, N.H.

Dwight, John Sullivan. "Address Delivered before the Harvard Musical Association," 25 August 1841. New York Public Library.

Eden, Myrna Garvey. "Anna Hyatt Huntington, Sculptor, and Mrs. H. H. A. Beach, Composer: A Comparative Study of Two Women Representatives of the Cultivated Tradition in the Arts." Ph.D. diss., Syracuse University, 1977.

Elson, Louis C. *The History of American Music*. 1925. Reprint. New York: Burt Franklin, 1971.

Epstein, Dena J. "Amy Marcy Cheney Beach." In *Notable American Women, 1607–1950: A Biographical Dictionary*, vol. 1, edited by Edward T. James, Janet Wilson James, and Paul S. Boyer. Cambridge, Mass.: Belknap Press, 1971.

Fay, Amy. *Music Study in Germany*. A new introduction by Edward O. Downes. 1896. Reprint. New York: Da Capo Press, 1979.

Gorham, Deborah. *The Victorian Girl and the Feminine Ideal*. London: Croon Helm, 1982.

Greven, Philip J. *Child-Rearing Concepts, 1626–1861: Historical Sources*. Itasca, Ill.: F. E. Peacock, 1973.

———. *The Protestant Temperament: Patterns of Child-Rearing, Religious Experience, and the Self in Early America*. New York: Alfred A. Knopf, 1977.

Heilbrun, Carolyn G. *Writing a Woman's Life*. New York: W. W. Norton, 1988.

Hellerstein, Erna Olafsen, Leslie Parker Hume, and Karen M. Offen, eds. *Victorian Women: A Documentary Account of Women's Lives in Nineteenth-Century England, France, and the United States*. Stanford, Calif.: Stanford University Press, 1981.

H.F.P. "Believes Women Composers Will Rise to Greater Heights in World Democracy." *Musical America*, 21 April 1917, 3.

Hirsch, Marianne. *The Mother/Daughter Plot: Narrative, Psychoanalysis, Feminism*. Bloomington: Indiana University Press, 1989.

History of the Handel and Haydn Society of Boston, Massachusetts. 2 vols. Reprint. New York: Da Capo Press, 1977.

"How Mrs. Beach Did Her First Composing." *Musical America,* 8 August 1914, 22. Also in Beach Clipping File, New York Public Library.

"Jubilee Sheet." *Boston Daily Evening Transcript,* 17 June 1872, 13.

Kinscella, Hazel Gertrude. "Play No Piece in Public When First Learned, Says Mrs. Beach." *Musical America,* 7 September 1918, 9–10.

Lee, Gerald Stanley. *The Lost Art of Reading.* New York: G. P. Putnam, 1903.

Merrill, E. Lindsey. "Mrs. H. H. A. Beach: Her Life and Music." Ph.D. diss., Eastman School of Music, 1963.

Merrill, Marlene Deahl, ed. *Growing Up in Boston's Gilded Age: The Journal of Alice Stone Blackwell, 1872–74.* New Haven, Conn.: Yale University Press, 1990.

Miles, Maramaduke Sidney. "The Solo Piano Works of Mrs. H. H. A. Beach." D.M.A. diss., Peabody Conservatory, 1985.

Milinowski, Marta. *Teresa Carreño: "By the Grace of God."* New Haven, Conn.: Yale University Press, 1940.

The New Grove Dictionary of American Music, s.v. "Kellogg, Clara Louise." 4 vols. Edited by H. Wiley Hitchcock and Stanley Sadie. London: Macmillan, 1986.

Pachter, Marc, ed. *Telling Lives: The Biographer's Art.* Philadelphia: University of Pennsylvania Press, 1981.

Schaffer, Karen A., and Neva Garner Greenwood. *Maud Powell: Pioneer American Violinist.* Ames: Iowa State University Press, 1988.

Scharfenberg, William. Letters to John Sullivan Dwight. Rare Book and Manuscript Division, Boston Public Library.

Showalter, Elaine, and English Showalter. "Victorian Women and Menstruation." *Victorian Studies* 14 (September 1970): 83–89.

Talbot, M. Eloise. "A Brief Resumé of the History of the Attic Club." Typescript. Attic Club Papers, Boston Athenaeum.

Taylor, Karen. "Blessing the House: Moral Motherhood and the Suppression of Physical Punishment." *Journal of Psychohistory* 15 (Summer 1987): 431–54.

Wood, Ann Douglas. " 'The Fashionable Diseases': Women's Complaints and Their Treatment in Nineteenth-Century America." In *Clio's Consciousness Raised: New Perspectives on the History of Women,* edited by Mary Hartman and Lois M. Banner. New York: Harper and Row, 1974.

"A Young Pianist." *Folio* 12 (April 1875): n.p.

7

Anna Maria della Pietà: The Woman Musician of Venice Personified

Jane L. Baldauf-Berdes

The eighteenth-century Venetian musician Anna Maria della Pietà (circa 1689–sometime after 1750) began life by entering history through humanity's backdoor, as one of many thousand "Figlie della casa, Scaffetta Numero———" in the *Ospedale di Santa Maria della Visitazione o della Pietà*, the centuries-old home for abandoned children of uncertain paternity, that is, those born *au naturel*.[1] The Pietà, the name by which the asylum has always been popularly known, was founded by patrician and middle-class women by 1336; it figured in the history of the early Franciscan religious movement and exists today on the Riva degli Schiavoni, near the Basilica di San Marco, as a child care and adoption agency. It is the only one of the four major welfare foundations, the *ospedali grandi*, about which much is known even today.[2]

Anna Maria's musical virtuosity and versatility, her indelible celebrity effected through the published works of leading contemporary European writers, and the musical tributes to her that were commissioned by benefactors and composed by composers of international stature, including Antonio Vivaldi (1678–1741), are all reasons Anna Maria della Pietà may be considered one of the central figures in the musical life of sacral Venice during the last third of three hundred years of musical activity inside the historically unique Venetian musical foundations. More important, she personifies ten generations of women who were educated over a decade for the music profession in the *cori*, which existed as institutions-within-institutions in the *ospedali grandi* from 1525 to 1855.[3]

At the Pietà, where about one-fourth of the over 840 currently identifiable women musicians of Venice resided, Anna Maria was pronounced the leading violinist of Europe by an early practitioner of the literary genre of travel writing, Joachim Christoph Nemeitz. Nemeitz, a north German court counsellor, heard Anna Maria perform while he was in Venice in 1721. He found the "orchestras," which were composed exclusively of *figlie del coro* (daughters of the choir of the church of the *ospedale*), at Venice's unique welfare institutions to be "as grand as any at the courts of Europe."[4] Nemeitz named Anna Maria and described her as a brilliant soloist in concertos. Johann Joachim Quantz (1697–1773), German flutist, composer, theorist, and author, singled out Anna Maria, concert mistress of the Pietà's orchestra, for his praise, without naming her.[5] In the next decade, Anna Maria was included in Johann G. Walther's paradigmatic reference for musicians, *Musikalisches Lexicon.*[6] In 1734 Baron Karl Ludwig von Pöllnitz declared Anna Maria was "the premier violinist in Europe."[7] In 1739 an astonished Charles de Brosses, first president of the Parliament of Dijon, France, wrote, "The *ospedale* that I frequent most and where I enjoy myself the most is the Pietà; it is also the first for the perfection of its symphonies. What strictness of execution! Only there can one hear that first stroke of the bow so falsely vaunted by the Paris Opera." For de Brosses, Anna Maria was "unsurpassed" as a violin virtuosa.[8]

In 1743, toward the close of several decades of Anna Maria's artistic dominance at the Pietà, Jean-Jacques Rousseau, secretary to the French ambassador to Venice, the Comte de Montaigu, confronted the performance practices of the *cori,* which were hidden behind wrought-iron *grilles* in multiple elevated choir lofts so listeners could hear but not see the singers and instrumentalists. Admitted into the hermetic inner sanctum of the *coro,* Rousseau recorded an epiphany that now refutes misguided vulgar perspectives on the *figlie del coro* as a group in their uniquely Venetian context:

What vexed me was the iron grate, which suffered nothing to escape but sounds and concealed from me the angels of which they were worthy. I talked of nothing else. One day I spoke of it at [M.] le Blond's: if you are so desirous, said he, to see those little girls [*sic*], it will be an easy matter to satisfy your wishes. I am one of the administrators of the house, I will give you a collation with them. I did not let him rest until he had fulfilled his promise. In entering the saloon, which contained these beauties I so much sighed to see, I felt a trembling of love which I had never before experienced. M. le Blond presented to me one after the other, these celebrated female singers, of whom the names and voices were all with which I was acquainted. Come, Sophia,—she was horrid. Come, Cattina,—she had but one eye. Come Bettina,—the smallpox had completely disfigured her. Scarcely one of them was without some striking defect. Le Blond laughed at my surprise; however, two or three of them appeared tolerable; these never sung but in the choruses; I was almost in despair. During the collation, we endeavoured to excite them, and they soon became enlivened; ugliness does not exclude the graces, and I found they possessed them. I said to myself, they cannot sing in this manner without intelligence and sensibility, they must have both; in fine, my manner of seeing them changed to such a degree, that I left the house almost in love with each of these ugly faces. I had scarcely courage enough to return to Vespers. But after having seen the girls, the danger was lessened. I still found their singing delightful; and their voices so much embellished their persons, that, in spite of my eyes, I obstinately continued to think them beautiful.[9]

In March 1740 the Prince of Saxony-Poland, Frederic Christian, was awestruck to discover that "Vivaldi's orchestra" contained only female instrumentalists: "what makes the Pietà so famous is not just that all of the instrumentalists are truly excellent musicians, but an even rarer fact, which is that all of the instruments are being played by females without any males in the ensemble at all."[10]

Maestra or Signora Anna Maria, as she was titled, is immortalized in the anonymous poem "Concerning the *Putte* in the *Coro* at the Pietà," which dates from approximately 1740. Six of the poem's seventy-one verses concern her:

> First to be presented to you
> Is the concertmistress Anna Maria.
> Ugly she may be, but she's due
> Credit. She's the ideal *figlia.*

> When she plays her violin suchwise,
> Countless angels dare to hover near.
> All who hear her fly to Paradise.
> Her sounds create a most heav'nly atmosphere.

> Equally skilled with fingerboard and bow
> Vainly do men try to find her peer
> Anywhere in all the Veneto.
> Music in her lovely hands need not fear.

> Rather, in all the world, I should say,
> Can't be found her match, woman or man.
> It's the truth; and I want to gainsay
> Your suspicion I'm just being partisan.

> Where would you find a musician like her?
> Violinist, she plays the cembalo, too.

> Not cello, nor viola d'amore can deter,
> Nor lute, theorbo, nor mandolin new.
>
> Hers are truly skills and virtues
> To immortalize her who owns them.
> Far more has she from which I choose,
> Witness how I bow to kiss her hem.[11]

* * *

In 1985 Marie-Thérèse Bouquet-Boyer asserted that Anna Maria remains forever linked to the history of the concerto in music history because of her association with Antonio Vivaldi at the Pietà and because of the patrician benefactors they shared. According to Bouquet-Boyer, the evolution of the concerto form in music history was guaranteed when a Maecenas-like patronage system, as it existed in the Venetian *ospedali*, was joined by an artist like Anna Maria to enflame the energies and inspire the genius of a composer like Vivaldi.[12] Bouquet-Boyer's conclusions were based on the existence of only two concertos by Vivaldi (Concerto in F Major, RV 286, and Concerto in A Major, RV 762 [=763a]) recognized at the time as having been composed for Anna Maria.

Since then, archival research has focused deservedly, if belatedly, on the solo partbook of not one but twenty-eight violin concertos composed by Vivaldi for Anna Maria, now in the *Fondo Esposti* of the Conservatorio di Musica "Benedetto Marcello" in Venice.[13] There is nothing in the collection to compare with this elegant book of seventy-eight folios of ten-staved, prebound paper measuring 29 x 22 cm., bound in fine leather, dyed Venetian red to match the color of the uniform worn by wards of the Pietà, and adorned with gold-leaf calligraphy, including Anna Maria's name. The item also contains violin concertos composed for her by Giuseppe Tartini (1692–1770), Giovanni Brusa (circa 1700–circa 1768), Andrea Bernasconi (circa 1706–95), Carlo Tessarini (circa 1690–1766), and Mauro d'Alaij.[14] The thirty-one principal violin parts are all in the same hand, possibly Anna Maria's. The partbook is a pristine example of the custom-composed soloists' repertory for the idolized *virtuose* in the star system that was fostered on behalf of females in the institutions and, more to the point, for the commonweal and greater glory of Venice. The existence of one more concerto, not in the collection but composed for Anna Maria by Lorenzo (Reggiano) Morini, who worked at the Pietà from 1750 to his death in 1765, supports the thesis that she continued to perform in public into mid-century, past the age of sixty.[15]

Of the thirty-one violin parts in Anna Maria's partbook, twenty-two are new sources for Vivaldi's concertos authenticated by Peter Ryom.[16] Most of the works were missing from the original edition of the Ryom catalog, published in 1974. Vivaldi's solo display works for Anna Maria are three times as many as the well-known concertos he composed for Johann Georg Pisendel (1687–1755) of Dresden. Indeed, Pisendel is shown to have copied five of the concertos Vivaldi composed for Anna Maria, and Johann Joachim Quantz, the historian and court musician at Berlin and Potsdam, copied two.

Three of Anna Maria's concertos by Vivaldi—RV 179a, 581, and 582—were composed for celebrations of the Feast of the Assumption of the Virgin Mary. For a long time scholars have assumed that the Feast of the Assumption was the patronal Marian feast at the Pietà, an error disproved in the Pietà's name.[17] The event that called forth Concerto in E Major, RV 270a, bearing the title *Il riposo* (Rest) or *Per il Santo Natale*, was the Feast of the Nativity during the night hours when the Pietà was one of only three locations in Venice permitted to stage a "midnight Mass" for the vigil of Christmas.[18] The feast of the canonized Venetian noble and patriarch San Lorenzo Giustiniani, a feast not known to have been observed at the Pietà, prompted the writing of the Concerto in F Major, RV 286.

Only three of Anna Maria's concertos from Vivaldi were published during the composer's and her lifetime. Two, RV 207 and 308, appeared in print from La Cène in Amsterdam in 1729 as op. 11, nos. 1 and 4. The Concerto in C, RV 582, a version of Concerto in C, RV 179a, was published in about 1736 as Vivaldi's Concerto 3 in Witvogel's *VI Concerti a Cinque Stromenti*. The Concerto in F, RV 286, was no. 4 in the autograph set of twelve concertos in *La cetra*, presented by Vivaldi to the Holy Roman Emperor Charles VI in 1728 and published by La Cène as op. 9. Four concertos in Anna Maria's collection have been recorded, including the two from Vivaldi's op. 11: RV 207 in D, 270a in E, 308 in G, and 581 in C.

One-third of Vivaldi's original, flamboyant, and technically demanding concertos for Anna Maria remains unperformed and unpublished today. When they were performed by Anna Maria, accompanied by the orchestra of her *coro*, it was common to find royalty, grandees of Europe, and members of their entourage among the listeners, including King Frederic IV of Denmark and Norway in 1709; Ferdinand III of Tuscany in 1711, the dedicatee of Vivaldi's op. 3; Emperor Charles VI in 1728, dedicatee of the twelve concertos in *La cetra;* Count Wenzel von Morzin, dedicatee of his op. 8; Count Johann Joseph Wrtby, governor royal of Prague in 1730; Marquis Bentivoglio d'Aragona of Ferrara in 1737; Ferdinand of Bavaria; and Prince Frederic Christian of Poland and Saxony in 1740.

* * *

A myriad of questions arises about Anna Maria, who personifies baby girls left in the *scaffetta* and educated for the music profession. From where did she come—musically and sociologically—and why or how? What were her privileges, legal rights, and duties? Why is she representative of the women musicians in Venetian society? How did the Pietà and its wards fit into Venice's social policy? Curiosity extends to the Venetian civilization. What factors enabled females to prepare for and join the musical culture as apprentices, teachers, performers, copyists, administrators, composers, tuition-paying boarders from abroad, and local scholarship students? How were the *figlie del coro* able to be liturgical musicians when females were traditionally barred from participation in religious celebrations by papal decrees that have not yet been wholly rescinded?[19] What role did the *cori* play in Venice's urban economy and its political system? What was the role of the *figlie del coro* as Venetian subjects and as producers of culture? Finally, how valid is the belief that the career of the "famous violin virtuosa Anna Maria was sacrificed because of the customs of the age which did not yet permit a female to perform professionally in public?"[20]

* * *

The search for answers to these questions begins with Anna Maria's arrival at the Pietà. Studies of infanticide in the Republic of Venice show that most foundlings were born to poor young women who came to the city from the Veneto. Without dowries, these women were not marriageable and were led unwittingly into prostitution. As a female foundling, Anna Maria was even more devalued than the males, as is still the case of females throughout the world today.

Anna Maria's mother, who may have been a prostitute, deposited Anna Maria in the revolving drawer, or *scaffetta*, which had been built centuries earlier in the Pietà's east wall.[21] Her mother's final departing gesture was to ring the bell attached to the *scaffetta* to announce her arrival to the staff on duty inside the home. Anna Maria was bathed, named, baptized, outfitted with clothing, and assigned to a nursing female.[22] A file, identifying her by her assigned *scaffetta* number, was begun for her. Any items on or near her at the time of her arrival may be found, along with documents pertaining to her life.[23] At this time,

she was branded with the letter *P,* designating the Pietà, either on her
arm or on the sole of a foot. The procedure, gruesome by our standard
and abandoned in the eighteenth century, was considered a legitimate
means of controlling the widespread practice of foster parents' sub-
stituting live children for the state's wards who died.[24] When she was
still a toddler, she was taken before the administrators and musical
staff for evaluation of her talents, which led to her thorough education
in music for the next ten years.

Venice's only native music historian, Francesco Caffi, reminiscing
about the phenomena of the *cori,* provides a context for Anna Maria's
life and a basis for understanding her artistic prowess:

Education . . . was given to many maidens in the four Ospedali of the Incurabili, the Mendicanti, the Derelitti [Ospedaletto], and the Pietà in playing instruments and in singing not only in the ecclesiastical style for the Divine
Office which was observed in their churches, but also in the theatrical style
for those delightful oratorios which were written metrically in Latin and then
set to music by the most renowned musicians and accompanied by a very full
orchestra during the afternoon of every feastday. The female musicians performed in competition with each other, each hidden in their own raised and
enclosed choir lofts in churches [adjoined to the *ospedali*] from which, because
they were crowded to capacity with listeners who came from all over, the
Eucharist had been removed beforehand. Oh! what a wondrous and indeed
unique memory which now is fading away.[25]

In addition to being born in Venice, where centuries earlier sensitivity to women's condition had led Venetians to an awareness of the
inhumane treatment of infants like her and to the establishment of
the Pietà, it was also Anna Maria's good fortune to arrive when she
did. An emphasis placed on violin teaching, begun with the defrocked
Leipziger priest-composer Johann Rösenmuller (circa 1618–94) during
his quarter-century as the Pietà's *maestro di coro,* or music director,
from 1658 to 1682, was continued by the priest-violinist Bonaventura
Spada (circa 1645–circa 1701), who served as its violin instructor until
1701. Next onto the external staff came the priest-composer Antonio
Vivaldi, whose first association with the Pietà was as a newly ordained
twenty-five-year-old priest in the Church of Venice, beginning in 1703,
just when Anna Maria needed a master teacher. His employment as a
musician falls into six periods: (1) as a violin teacher, from 1 September
1703 to 1709; (2) as teacher of *viole inglesi,* from 17 August 1704 to
1709; (3) as *maestro de' concerti* (i.e., in charge of instrumental music),
from 27 September 1711 to 29 March 1716 and from 24 May 1716
to 1717; (4) as an external supplier of instrumental music, from 2 July
1723 to 1729; (5) again as *maestro de' concerti,* from 5 August 1735

to 1738; and (6) as an external supplier of compositions. His last works for the Pietà are three violin concertos, for which Anna Maria was the soloist, and a sinfonia to the cantata *Il Coro della Muse*, commissioned in honor of Prince Frederic Christian of Poland and Saxony in 1740.[26] Vivaldi transferred from Venice to Vienna in 1740, but his post was not filled until 1744 when the governors named Lorenzo Carminati their *maestro di violino*.

Soon after Vivaldi joined the music faculty, a legacy, distributed by name to 398 young female wards of the Pietà, lists Anna Maria among 111 recipients in the *figliole grandi* (the adult group).[27] As a student musician, she was among the group from the *coro* whose visit to the Opera in Carnival 1704 was sponsored by the nobleman and Pietà governor Tommaso Soranzo.[28] She was still a student musician in 1707, when "full-fledged" *coro* musicians were licensed to teach and accept private students from the city.[29] By 1712 she had become one of the solo violinists, if not yet one of the fourteen *privilegiate*, or leaders, of the *coro*. She performed Vivaldi's *Concerto per la Solennità di San Lorenzo* during vespers to mark the annual observance on 8 January in the Venetian liturgical calendar of the semidouble Feast of St. Lawrence Giustiniani, bishop, confessor, and first patriarch of Venice who died in 1455. Typically, this feast also served the purpose of commemorating Venice's liberation from the Plague of 1631.[30] It was an unusual event in that the governors allowed Anna Maria to perform outside the Pietà, in the Basilica di San Marco or, perhaps, in the Church of the Benedictine Convent of San Lorenzo. The following December, she was one of three performers who performed outside the institution when Marietta Corner, a noblewoman and *visitatrice* (female volunteer elected by the governing board), arranged the program for a meeting of Franciscan Tertiaries.[31] In 1714 she had a singing role in Vivaldi's oratorio *Moyses Deus Pharaonis*, performed by the *coro*.[32] She was the principal violin teacher on the internal teaching staff by 1737.[33] In this capacity she would have led the orchestra in the concert given that year in the ducal palace to honor the doge, Alvise Pisani (1735–42), and the patriarch.[34]

Membership in the Pietà's *coro* was supposedly limited to the symbolic number 40, but the *coro* ranged from 42 to 187 during Anna Maria's decades. In 1745, for example, the *coro* included thirty-two *attive* (active members): eighteen singers, eight string players, two organists, two soloists, and two *maestre*. There were also fourteen *iniziate* (apprentices), the youngest of whom was nine years old.[35] The percentage of the population represented by members of the *coro* varied radically, from less than 10 percent to 33 percent.

References to Anna Maria in archives testify to her prowess as the "complete instrumentalist": *figlia del coro*, meaning "performing member"; later *figlia di coro*, meaning a "leader," with rank; and, ultimately, *maestra di concerti*.[36] She became by stages Anna Maria *del violino*, Anna Maria *del theorbo*, Anna Maria *del cembalo*, Anna Maria *del violoncello*, Anna Maria *del luta*, Anna Maria *della viola d'amore*, and Anna Maria *del mandolin*. In addition, she was a teacher, copyist, concertmistress, and conductor of the Pietà's prototypical orchestra. The only posts she does not appear to have held were *maestra di coro* (one of two internal *coro* directors) and prioress, the highest promotion reserved for a woman musician at the institutions.

* * *

Devotion, modesty, good behavior, avoidance of idleness, silence, and obedience, the basic requirements for survival at the Pietà, characterized Anna's Maria's daily life. No one could enter without written permission from the governors. The prioress, responsible for a professional staff of seventeen, a domestic staff of two hundred, and multiple self-supporting small industries comparable to the *coro*, could not leave without permission. Segregation according to age and gender was enforced. In emergencies, two governors accompanied a priest into the female sector. Religious duties involved attendance at daily Mass, observance of the Office, and frequent confession. Correspondence was censored, first, by the prioress, then by the governors, none of whom was obligated to deliver the letters or to make known their contents to intended recipients. Casual talk was forbidden. Visits from close relatives were nonexistent for foundlings. Infractions of rules were monitored; offenders would be severely punished in the manner of monastic imprisonment practices. The *horarium*, the most enduring and conspicuous feature of monastic existence, decreed the pace of life. Upon waking, each person was to pray aloud while dressing, participate in Matins, and then attend Mass before breakfast. Activity in the intervals between the Hours was partitioned into study for children, work assignments, prayers, special duties, and recreation. Females had one holiday annually that involved monasticlike trips into the country. The Pietà's wards were not permitted to attend free urban schools. Schoolroom classes and religious services were held in common for boys and girls until the age of ten, when children boarded out to foster families were to be returned to the Pietà, if they were going to be. Until then, children were taught reading, grammar, arithmetic, and catechism, all of which were framed to instill the fear of

God. Writing skills were included less often, though vocational arts and crafts were introduced.

The levels through which a student musician at the Pietà moved en route to the ranks of the *coro* began in earnest with the class of *educande*, which lasted from ages thirteen to twenty-four. At the age of twenty-four, Anna Maria was promoted to *sottomaestra* (assistant *maestra*). Appointments as *maestra* (teachers and supervisors) were limited to those over the age of thirty. If a woman had not married by the time she reached the age of forty, she automatically advanced to the class of nonperforming retirees, called the *giubilate*, and was eligible for election by the governors to the *privilegiate*. Upon reaching retirement, a member advanced to the class of *discrete*, older women who were responsible for directing the details in the life of a child assigned to them.

Coro musicians ranked among the elite of the Pietà, along with administrators, teachers, and members of the staff of professionals. Their privileges included special food and quarters, social status, exemption from nonmusical duties, opportunities to earn extra income by taking private pupils, the title Signora, and personal income. The manner of allocating contributions from performances allowed three-fourths to be divided equally among *maestre*, singers, and instrumentalists. The remaining one-fourth was divided into thirds, with two-thirds allocated to the apprentices and one-third to copyists and soloists in equal shares.

Figlie del coro were not free to marry without permission from their superiors; if they attempted to do so, they lost accrued income, including the dowry, and perhaps spent time in solitary confinement. On the other hand, governors arranged marital contracts and even encouraged foundlings to rise socially into the ranks of the citizen and patrician classes.[37] Wards of the Pietà received one of the largest dowries awarded by any of the *ospedali:* 200 ducats and 50 more for housekeeping needs. This sum compares favorably with the equal amount given at the Derelitti at the turn of the eighteenth century and far better than the 137 ducats given as dowries to wards of the Mendicanti in 1767.

Three vows were required of the musicians who chose not to remain in permanent service: to dedicate themselves to service in the *coro* for ten years after completing ten years of musical training; to train two successors as potential replacements; and to withdraw from performing in public.[38] If they chose to continue their celibate life—as the majority of them did—by rejecting late marriage bids from suitors, especially from the music professionals who came in search of well-dowered wives, retirement benefits were forthcoming, and they spent their old age inside the Pietà. If they chose to end their days as nun-musicians, they had to leave Venice, where choir nuns were exclusively noblewomen. Notably, *figlie del coro* had three life options, not the traditional two—marriage or the convent—from which to choose.

Workers—and every Pietà resident, including very young children, was a worker—were paid in money rather than in goods; they in turn paid sums to the Pietà for allotments of food, oil, and clothes. The custom gave wards practical experience in handling their own finances. Females who were not destined for the *coro, figlie della comune,* were educated to assume specific posts at all levels, for instance, as pharmacists and surgeons, to eliminate as much as possible the need to hire outsiders. Whether working, studying, or performing, wards received remuneration. Amounts were on a graded scale that rewarded the acquisition of new skills. Premiums were also given semiannually to children who advanced most in developing skills. The deposits of *figlie del coro* in the Pietà's credit bank earned a higher interest rate—8 percent—than those of other depositors. Archival data demonstrate that poor health, such as convulsions and hysterics, and premature death were endemic among the musicians.

In addition to fixed voice, instrumental, and theory classes, group and private lessons, and individual practice schedules, the duties of *coro* members encompassed attendance at all rehearsals and performances, whether they were actively involved or not. Days when the *cori* performed complemented the calendar of feasts observed in Venice. Mass and vespers were sung on the Saturdays and after the noon meal on the Sundays of Lent. Compline was sung during Lent; Holy Week called for a full accompaniment to the rituals; *versetti* were performed between the verses of the Marian antiphons, and *sonate da chiesa* were played after the reading of the Epistle. Liturgical dramas and oratorios were added on special occasions until the *ospedali* became "temples of Euterpe" and "*teatri di divozione.*"

The known facts of Anna Maria's life fit her for the role of representative of the women musicians in Venetian society because they allow us to see the importance of the role assigned to musical activity in the welfare system and to begin to understand the achievements of women in Venetian music history long after Andrea and Giovanni Gabrieli's and Claudio Monteverdi's times. They also suggest that she typifies the sort of celebrity psychologists have determined is a special craving of the orphaned.[39] Studies showing religious women to be characteristically sensitive, self-effacing, and in search of ways to prove their own worth are helpful in attempting to appreciate an essential condition of the *cori*.[40]

The Pietà and its wards fit into Venice's social policy in several important ways. In addition to heavy, well-publicized public performance schedules throughout the year, the *coro* fulfilled commitments to benefactors' legacies, such as singing anniversary masses and litanies, in a spiritual insurance system by which the state relied on its women musicians to pay for its social policies. Testaments of Venetians frequently designated legacies of fifty, a hundred, or two hundred ducats for individual women. Gifts extracted from visiting dignitaries were equally important revenue sources, since, as the antiquarian and scientist Martin Folkes noted after visiting Venice in 1733, few local people contributed when a purse for charitable donations was passed through the congregation/audience during the concerts at the Pietà.[41]

The Venetian state's acceptance of responsibility for foundlings and fatherless children was historic, and the *cori* became a key to its success. Private self-interest and public equilibrium were persuasive forces over the centuries and prompted adoption of paradigmatic social policies. Adoption of Poor Laws in the sixteenth century led to the rescue and legally enforced confinement of those unable to help themselves; however, relegating the poor inside institutions resulted in their being "distanced" from essential potential benefactors.[42] The remedy was to integrate institutional life with liturgical, musical, and related activities. This occurred with increasing intensity at the Pietà, until the *ospedale* became mistakenly identified with its *coro* and remains so.

Collectively, the *coro* was recast in the image of the *cori* of ancient Greece, while individual *figlie del coro* took on the image of Rome's vestal virgins, chaste females chosen and trained to conduct religious ceremonies for the purpose of securing for the state the goodwill of the gods. Venice's *inservienti della musica agl'ospedali* became "*vergines choristae*" and then vestal virgins. At the same time they were praised for having attributes of Polyhymnia, the young, beautiful, and modest virgin, the muse of sacred music and harmony in Greek mythology. Cast as the angelic musicians of Christian symbolism, the chaste women musicians enhanced Venice's own methodically self-made mythology by serving as representatives of the chaste city of Venice. In the popular imagination they evoked the angelic choirs and orchestras that dominated medieval and Renaissance art. In 1716, when Venice's war with the Turks at Corfu took on grievous dimensions, the Senate ordained that their *cori* must intensify their work of placating the divine anger so that God would be moved to forgive the Venetians for their sins and give his blessing to the armies of the

Republic. Anna Maria would have had to assume this added duty. When one *maestro di coro* wanted adult women who were already finished performers admitted into his *coro*, as had been done at the Pietà since 1705, he reassured his governors that the step would not damage the carefully honed image of "angelic messengers" that had been cultivated for *figlie del coro* as part of the self-dramatization of a nation that dared to boast it had been born on the Day of the Assumption.

How were Anna Maria and other women musicians of Venice empowered to become church musicians when females were barred from active participation in liturgical celebration by papal decrees that have yet to be rescinded? Venetians' legitimization of women as musicians in the churches belonging to the *ospedali*, places of public worship, constituted a radical departure from established practice as dictated by the Code of Canon Law and promulgated by the Vatican for centuries, up to the twentieth century. Ecclesiastical independence from the Holy See of "sacral" Venice, where church and state were as one in the manner adopted from Eastern Christianity, explains this little-understood phenomenon.

Many factors enabled females to prepare for and join the musical profession as apprentices, teachers, performers, copyists, administrators, composers, tuition-paying boarders, and local scholarship students. Through negotiation Venetians eliminated the unnatural servitude of secular serfdom during the centuries of medieval feudalism, yet they embraced the supernatural servitude prescribed as a musical accompaniment to the Christian liturgy. In keeping with a consistently utilitarian attitude toward its arts and artists that is characteristic of the Venetian aesthetic, the role of the *cori* was balanced between the mounting needs and satisfactions of Venetians' spiritual welfare and Venice's welfare system. Historically, declining population was an enduring concern in Venice. Making musical activity a female monopoly at the *ospedali* provided a solution, because it allowed adult females to be economically productive while at the same time it provided a ready resource of womanpower for work that, if not almost cost-free, at least need not involve male inmates or external *salariati* (salaried employees) on a full-time basis.

The *figlie del coro* played a significant role in the urban economy and in the political system.[43] First of all, the *cori* presented Venetians with a model for solving the perennial problem of how to banish idleness, the bane of leisured societies and a peculiar challenge to inhabitants of a tiny, water-locked city like Venice. Moreover, they were agents of cultural transmission and important in the spread of musical activity. Local and foreign commentators referred to *coro* muscians as angels, nymphs, muses, sirens, swans, and "ornaments for the city." They were more than ornaments, however; they were of economic, political, and cultural significance to the state. Their musical activity in the *ospedali* developed into an essential element in the life of Venice.

A concinnity of historic forces resulted in the *ospedali*'s becoming "the birthplace of the Italian church musical idiom."[44] Faced with a recurring onslaught of hungry and possibly diseased in-migrants during the plague- and famine-ridden fifteenth and sixteenth centuries, Venice developed social welfare policies that extended traditional almsgiving and tended to justify its publicists' claims that Venice was an exemplary environment.[45]

The state's acceptance of responsibility for foundlings and fatherless children was unprecedented in history. The purposes of the *ospedali* were to help those unable to help themselves and at the same time to complement Venetians' religious zeal. The mandate of the *ospedali* was to nurture and educate foundlings and orphan children, to give shelter to travelers and free medical care to the poor, to control disease, to prepare members of the working class for economic independence, to provide work for the unemployed, and to give a home to needy old people. The purpose of the *cori* was to so enhance the liturgies celebrated in public churches and private chapels attached to the foundations that contributions and legacies would finance welfare and guarantee social stability.

The *figlie del coro* played multiple roles as Venetian subjects and as producers of culture. The music schools were managed by leaders of the *cori* independently of their governing boards. They evolved as models for tripartite organizational plans of modern performing arts organizations that consist of lay administrators, part- and full-time professional artistic directors, teachers, and staff.

Income from the *cori* went toward salaries for musicians, bonuses and stipends, dowries, and costs accruing from performances, including publication of librettos that were distributed free of charge, costumes, instrumental purchases and repairs, refreshments, and the commissioning and copying of the repertory. Among countless legacies for the Pietà is one from Procuratore di San Marco Pietro Foscarini, written in 1735 and activitated in 1745, which stipulated annual scholarship awards for apprentices to the *coro* between the ages of thirteen and twenty-four. The legacy also financed salaries, like Anna Maria's, and commissions for new musical compositions until the disappearance of the *coro* after 1855.[46]

How valid are observations, such as that of Marie-Thérèse Bouquet-Boyer in 1985, that the "famous violin virtuosa Anna Maria was sacrificed because of the customs of the age which did not yet permit a female to perform professionally in public"? By the sixteenth century the Venetians were building on an exploitation of music. Music, *ancilla religionis*, became the chosen handmaiden of the Venetian state-church. All Venetians, but musicians in particular, had parts to play. Over time, administrators became aware of a relationship between the quality of the liturgical music performed in their churches and the quantity of their endowments. The improved quality of the musicianship of their cloistered musicians increased the size and prestige of their audience-congregations, as well as treasuries. The more popular the *cori* became, the more governors were willing to do to keep members content. What was basically an economic drive led, first, to searches for organists and *cantrices* (female cantors). These women either had lived in convents or were affiliated with religious orders for women and acted as music leaders.[47] In the role of a *cantrix* they were experienced in the performance of chant, rehearsal techniques, the problems of performing chant, and, perhaps, the rendition of polyphony. Education and apprenticeship in the work of music were added to the routine of the female sectors of the *ospedali;* female teachers were introduced, at first on a barter basis, then hired from outside; musical instruments were acquired; and new repertory was commissioned. Next came male composers and voice and instrumental teachers who were familiar with the best of what was available in musicianship—stylistically, instrumentally, and in performance practice. Ultimately, music schools for external students became another means for the *cori* to become self-supporting, self-governing subsidiaries of the *ospedali.* For Giovanni Morelli and Elvidio Surian, the foundlings of the Pietà, to whom the Venetians traditionally turned in a type of ritual collective exorcism, were sacrificial victims, who dedicated their lives as musicians to prayers of praise, thanksgiving, penance, and petition in the hope of improving the floundering fortunes of the Republic and its people.[48]

If the achievements of the *figlie del coro* are so exceptional, why has musicological scholarship been reluctant to investigate their story until now?[49] Elizabeth Wood provides a partial explanation: "The new scholarship on exceptional, successful women in art music provides repeated evidence for their historical devaluation as cultural creators, for the trivialization of both their ambitions and the genres in which the majority of them produced, and for societal attitudes and conditions which have prescribed or confined women's musical activity—

factors which have undergone significant changes in the past ten years."[50]

Another explanation is that despite the pioneering work of a few scholars in adopting interdisciplinary approaches to studies of Venetian history and of the *ospedali*, the field of research remains virgin territory, literally and figuratively. Perhaps the most lasting achievement of Anna Maria and her sisters—Apollonia, Geltruda, Julia, Ambmrosina, Barbara, Annetta, Antonia, Lucieta, Pelegrina, Angelica, Michielina, Susanna, Chiaretta, Santina, Candida, Samaritana, Prudenza, and so many others—will be that they succeed in luring feminist scholars into investigating the patronage system peopled by Venetian women and men, in both the aristocracy and the citizen class, who helped found, endow, and administer their musical organizations.

Focus on Anna Maria as an exemplar leading to the recovery of the history of women musicians' role in Venetian society reminds us that in Venice's patriarchal society there were two traditions that were passed on from generation to generation of women church musicians. The first was that women excelled as bearers of a music-centered cultural tradition unique to the Venetian civilization. The second was that no matter how a woman was born into life, no matter if her family was too poor or "dishonored" to claim her, no matter if she was crippled, disfigured, or disabled, she had dignity. She was valued as an individual worthy of being given the best education available according to her talents at public and private expense. She was appreciated, rewarded for her work, and acclaimed. She might rise socially through marriage. She was needed and nurtured for economic independence in adulthood. She was valued enough that the facts about her life were preserved so we could one day remember.

This investigation supports what feminist scholars hold true: challenges to the assumptions, stereotypes, and perceptions implicit in the literature surrounding the *figlie del coro* are in order. Such challenges hold the implicit promise that what has been could, with certain exceptions, occur again.

NOTES

This essay is a greatly expanded version of a paper read at the American Musicological Society Midwest Chapter meeting held at the University of Wisconsin–Milwaukee in April 1991. All translations have been provided by the author.

1. In 1978, during the renovation of the Pietà as part of the observances of the tercentenary of the birth of Antonio Vivaldi, the Venice Committee of

the International Fund for Monuments discovered a massive collection of documents relating to wards of the Pietà. The archive, in a chaotic state, was long believed to have been destroyed at the time of Napoléon's invasion in 1797. Since its discovery, Gabriella Cecchetto of the Venetian State Archive has been in charge of rescuing it for scholars' use. Unfortunately, this work was halted recently for financial reasons. When the archive is accessible, data, such as Anna Maria's *scaffetta* number and the full details of her life, will become available. For more on this motherlode of data awaiting investigation, see Kaley, *Church of the Pietà;* and Cecchetto, "L'Archivio di Santa Maria," 28–41.

2. Even the most recent Venetian studies continue to perpetuate misperceptions about the musical life at Venice's *ospedali.* See Hibbert, *Venice,* 138, 156–58, 169, 180; Landon and Norwich, *Five Centuries,* 109–38; Norwich, *Venice,* 341–52, 380–81; and Marqusee, *Venice,* 107–15. All four *ospedali* included male and female orphans among their welfare clientele, but foundlings were the exclusive mission of the Pietà, where care could be for a lifetime. Venetian law recognized orphans as children without fathers in the home. It was the duty of the doge to act as foster father to such children, who were wards of the state. This duty, first promulgated in the tenth-century inscription in the Clemente chapel of the Basilica di San Marco, formed part of the doge's annual oath of office. See Pullan, *Rich and Poor.*

3. Essential terms for studying the Venetian welfare institutions—*coro, ospedale, figlia del coro, maestra/o, collegio,* and *seminario* (with their plurals)— are not readily translatable. *Coro,* for instance, has multiple historical, liturgical, architectural, and theological definitions. Morelli and Surian, "Musica strumentale e sacra," 1:403, describe the slow, almost imperceptible, emergence of the new musical tradition in the *cori* of the *ospedali,* in which spectacle and drama are replaced by psychologically rich, emotion-provoking works of a tasteful yet melancholy nature that leave listeners in a mood of romantic mysticism. The *cori* represent a new and different concept in music history, making attempts at translation not only inappropriate but counterproductive.

4. Nemeitz, *Nachlese,* 61. Nemeitz was surprised to see women playing the violin, violoncello, organ, theorbo, oboe, transverse flute, and bassoon. He reported that the orchestra at the Pietà had twenty violins, several cellos and theorbos, and one organ.

5. Quantz visited Venice in 1726. Quantz, *Selbstbiographie,* 60–62, reported, "The best music in Venice is at performances by female musicians in the churches of the *ospedali,* especially at the Pietà where there is a violinist who plays extremely well."

6. Walther, *Musikalisches Lexicon,* 37.

7. *Lettres,* 4:113.

8. De Brosses, Letter to M. de Blancey, 29 August 1739, in his *Lettres historiques;* also in Norwich, *Venice,* 241–43.

9. Rousseau, *Confessions,* 275. No evidence has been found to indicate that the artifically cloistered milieu created for the women musicians of Venice

had been intended to assign otherworldly powers derived from physical ab-
normalities, as was suggested in myths, fables, and witches' tales in medieval
European culture. Rather, the objective was to create and perpetuate an image
for them as Dantesque, ascetic "angel musicians."

10. Frederic Christian, "Journal," 2:263.

11. Anon., "Putte in the Coro," stanzas 46–51. The poem was first published in Degrada, Testimonianza sull'Ospedale della Pietà; reprinted in Giazotto, Antonio Vivaldi, appendix A, 389–96.

12. Bouquet-Boyer, Vivaldi et le concerto, 14, 17, 50, 116.

13. Vivaldi, [Violin Concertos]. First mention of Anna Maria's partbook
is in Hansell's review of Giazotto's Antonio Vivaldi. The Fondo Esposti contains about fifteen hundred manuscripts from the music library of the Pietà.

14. Of these, only Bernasconi held a teaching post at the Pietà; he directed
the coro from 1744 to 1753. Tartini gave free lessons to pupils at all four
ospedali from approximately 1730 to 1766 without holding an appointment;
Tessarini taught violin at the Derelitti from around 1727 to 1733; and Brusa
was music director for the Incurabili from 1765 to 1768. Alaij was working
in Venice around 1735 but is not known to have been affiliated with any of
the cori.

15. Baldauf-Berdes, Women Musicians of Venice.

16. Ryom, Verzeichnis, includes the following concertos for Anna Maria:
RV 72 in D, RV 74 in A, RV 75 in B-flat, RV 76 in C, 179a in C, RV 207 in
D, RV 213a in D, RV 229 in D, RV 248 in d, RV 260 in E-flat, RV 261 in E-
flat, RV 267 in E, RV 270a in E, RV 286 in F, RV 308 in G, RV 343 in A, RV
349 in A, RV 363 in B-flat, RV 366 in B-flat, RV 387 in B, RV 581 in C,
RV 582 in C, RV 763 in A, RV 772 in D, RV 773 in F, RV 774 in C, and RV
775 in F. Another concerto, without opus number or Ryom identification, is
in C.

17. An example is Pincherle, Vivaldi.

18. According to a witness in 1714, the French archeologist Count Anne-
Claude Philippe de Caylus. The other two were the Basilica di San Marco and
Franciscan Church of the Frari.

19. See Drinker, Music and Women; Hayburn, Digest of Regulations; and
Baer, Chorische Gesang.

20. Bouquet-Boyer, Vivaldi et le concerto, 14: "celebre Anna Maria, vio-
loniste virtuose a la carriere sacrifiée par les usages de l'époque qui ne per-
mettaient pas encore à une femme de se produire en public."

21. Much is made of the fact that from the seventeenth century Venice
was well-populated with prostitutes, but use of the term Frauenzimmer to
refer to figlie del coro by writers then and now, including J. W. von Goethe,
constitutes a flagrant injustice. In 1988 a British academician stated in a lecture
at the University of Leicester, later broadcast over the British Broadcasting
Corporation, that figlie del coro "would sometimes take their turns in the
local brothels." A tax levied on prostitutes and fines were traditionally directed
toward helping finance the Pietà.

22. Clark, "Nurse Children," reveals the harsh survival rates for such children. The rates were even lower in the financially pressed Pietà, where one nursing female could be assigned as many as five infants simultaneously. Payments to wet nurses was the Pietà's leading expenditure.

23. To date the Venetian State Archives has indexed the collections containing documents for the Pietà *ospedale e luoghi* and *provveditori sopra ospedali,* containing 1,031 and 170 *buste,* respectively. Few of the *buste* have been analyzed or systematically investigated by scholars.

24. A stone inscription, now on the Campo Sant'Angelo in Venice near the theater where Vivaldi produced many of his operas, promised excommunication to anyone abandoning their children to the Pietà without good reason.

25. Caffi, "Materiale della musica teatrale di Venezia," fol. 125: "educazione che davasi a molte fanciulle ne' quattro Spedali Incurabili, Mendicanti, Spedaletto, e Pietà al suono di stromenti ed al canto non solo nello stile Ecclesiastico per la regolare ufficiatura nelle lor Chiese, ma anche nello stil teatrale per guegl'Oratorii deliziosissima che scritti in lingua latina metricamente, posti in musica dai più rinomati musurgi ed accompagnati da pienissima orchestra esse nel dopo pranzo d'ogni giornata festiva esse dall'alto de' chiusi lor Cori eseguivano a gara nelle stesse lor Chiese dalle quali, perchè zeppe d'uditori che vi accorrean da ogni lato, l'adorato pane prima toglievarsi. Oh! veramente deliziosa ed affatto unica oggi estinta memoria!"

26. See Talbot, *Antonio Vivaldi.*

27. *Ospedale e luoghi, busta* 688, *notatorio* 7/G, fol. 131r. In addition to adult women, the list includes thirty young girls (*figliole piccole*), 106 middle-aged women (*figliole mezane*), and 151 girls whose expenses were paid by the state (*figliole dalla Zuecca*). The Pietà's resident population in 1733 was about five hundred, with about fifteen hundred additional infants and children up to the age of ten placed in foster care either temporarily or permanently.

28. Ibid., *busta* 689, *notatorio* I, fol. 51.

29. Ibid., fols. 181r-182v.

30. The feast is observed on 5 September in the Roman rite.

31. *Ospedale e luoghi, busta* 689, *notatorio* I, fol. 51.

32. Arnold and Arnold, *Oratorio in Venice,* 97. Her name is found on the source for the work preserved at the Casa Goldoni, Venice.

33. *Ospedale e luoghi, busta* 691, *notatorio* O, fol. 196v, 30 August 1737.

34. "Consultori in jure," fol. 163, 3 September 1737.

35. *Provveditori, busta* 48, "Del Coro," articles 45–99.

36. For example, *Ospedale e luoghi, buste* 690 (1720) and 691 (1722).

37. Quantz expressed suprise at discovering a member of the Pietà's *coro,* Angioletta della Pietà, "a fine singer and cembalist," had been pledged in marriage to a Venetian banker (Quantz, *Selbstbiographie,* 100).

38. *Derelitti* [*Ospedaletto*], *busta* 14, *pergamena* 93.

39. Gilligan, *Different Voice,* 169–74.

40. Higgins, Review of *Red Virgin.* See Hampl's forthcoming *Virgin Time,* an exploration of Catholic spirituality; and Kraemer, "Conversion of Women."

41. Folkes, "Journal."
42. Pullan, "Nuova filantropia," 19–34, especially 28.
43. Other composers and teachers employed by the governors of the charities for their *cori* include the greater and lesser figures of seventeenth- and eighteenth-century music history. Although only a minority of over three hundred male professional musicians are remembered for having worked at the *ospedali*, their number includes Pasquale Anfossi, Ferdinando Bertoni, Vincenzo Ciampi, Domenico Cimarosa, Bonaventura Furlanetto, Baldassare Galuppi, Johann Adolf Hasse, Niccolò Jommelli, Gaetano Latilla, Giovanni Legrenzi, Antonio Lotti, Giovanni Battista Martini, Carlo Pallavicino, Gaetano Pampani, Carlo Francesco Pollarolo, Antonio Pollarolo, Nicola Porpora, Giovanni Porta, Antonoio Rigatti, Johann Rosenmüller, Giovanni Rovetta, Giuseppe Tartini, Tommaso Traetta, Antonio Sacchini, Giuseppe Scarlatti, Giovanni Benedetto Vinaccesi, Giuseppe Sarti, Marc'Antonio Ziani, and Pietro Andrea Ziani.
44. Arnold, "Vivaldi's Church Music," 66.
45. Slack, *Impact of Plague*, 317–18, 329, 393.
46. "Testamento."
47. Yardley, " 'Ful weel,' " 16.
48. Morelli and Surian, "Musica strumentale e sacra," 403.
49. Ellero, "Origini nel quattro grandi ospedali."
50. Wood, "Review Essay," 290.

REFERENCES

Anon. "Sonetto: Concerning the *Putte* in the *Coro* at the Pietà." Codice Cicogna 1178, fol. 206r-212r. Biblioteca del Museo Correr, Venice, Italy.

Arnold, Denis. "Vivaldi's Church Music: An Introduction." *Early Music* 1 (April 1973): 66–75.

Arnold, Denis, and Elsie Arnold. *The Oratorio in Venice*. London: Royal Musical Association, 1986.

Baer, Käthi Meyer. *Der chorische Gesang der Frauen*. Mittenwald: Arthur Nemayer, 1917.

Baldauf-Berdes, Jane L. *The Women Musicians of Venice: Musical Foundations, 1525–1855*. Oxford: Oxford University Press, 1993.

Bouquet-Boyer, Marie-Thérèse. *Vivaldi et le concerto*. Paris: Presses Universitaires de France, 1985.

Caffi, Francesco. "Materiale e carteggi per la ctoria della musica teatrale di Venezia." Codice Italiana, Classe IV-748 [=10466]. Biblioteca Nazionale Marciana, Venice, Italy.

Cecchetto, G. "L'Archivio di Santa Maria della Pietà a Venezia: Risultanze della prima fase dell'ordinamento." In *Economia e società nella storia dell'Italia contemporanea: Fonti e metodi di ricerca*. Rome: Edizioni di Storia e Letteratura, 1983.

Clark, Gillian. "Nurse Children in Berkshire." *Journal of the Berkshire Local History Association* (1985): 25–33.

"Consultori in jure." *Regole* 559 *(Ceremoniale)*. Archivio di Stato, Venice, Italy.

De Brosses, Charles. *Lettres historiques et critiques sur l'Italie*. 2d ed. Edited by Yvonne Bezard. Paris: Firmin-Didot, 1931.

Degrada, Francesco. *Un'inedita testimonianza settecentesca sull'Ospedale della Pietà*. Turin: Edizioni del Convegno, 1965.

Derelitti [Ospedaletto]. Busta 14. Archivio, Istitutioni Ricovero e di Educazione, Venice, Italy.

Drinker, Sophie. *Music and Women: The Story of Women in Their Relationship to Music*. New York: Coward-McCann, 1948.

Ellero, Giuseppe. "Origini e sviluppo storico della musica nel quattro grandi ospedali di Venezia." *Nuova rivista musicale italiana* 1 (January-March 1979): 160–67.

Folkes, Martin. "Journal." Ms. English misc. d 444. Bodleian Library, Oxford, England.

Frederic Christian, Prince of Saxony. "Journal der Reise des Kurprinzen Friedrich Christian von Rom nach Wien." Loc. 355. Staatsarchiv, Dresden, Germany.

Giazotto, Remo. *Antonio Vivaldi*. Turin: Edizioni Radio Television Italiano, 1973.

Gilligan, Carol. *In a Different Voice: Psychological Theory and Women's Development*. Cambridge, Mass.: Harvard University Press, 1982.

Hampl, Patricia. *Virgin Time*. Forthcoming.

Hansell, Sven H. Review of *Antonio Vivaldi*, by Remo Giazotto. *Musical Quarterly* 61 (Winter 1975): 600–607.

Hayburn, Robert R. *Digest of Regulations and Rubrics of Catholic Church Music*. Boston: Laughlin and Reilly, 1960.

Hibbert, Christopher. *Venice: The Biography of a City*. New York: W. W. Norton, 1989.

Higgins, Lynn A. Review of *The Red Virgin: Memoirs of Louise Michel*, edited and translated by Bullitt Lowry and Elizabeth E. Gunter. *Tulsa Studies of Women's Literature* 1 (Summer 1982): 214–16.

Kaley, Diana. *The Church of the Pietà*. Washington, D.C.: International Fund for Monuments, 1978.

Kraemer, Ross S. "The Conversion of Women to Ascetic Forms of Christianity." *Signs* 6 (Summer 1980): 298–307.

Landon, H. C. Robbins, and John Julius Norwich. *Five Centuries of Music in Venice*. New York: Schirmer Books, 1991.

Lettres: Nouveaux mémoires contenant l'histoire de sa vie et la relation de ses premières voyages. 4 vols. Liège, 1734. Translated by Stephen Whatley. London: D. Brown, 1737–38.

Marqusee, Michael, comp. *Venice: An Illustrated Anthology*. Topsfield, Mass.: Salem House, 1989.

Morelli, Giovanni, and Elvidio Surian. "La musica strumentale e sacra e le sue istituzioni a Venezia." In *Storia della cultua veneta: Il settecento*, vol. 1, edited by Girolamo Arnaldi and Manlio Pastore Stocchi. Vicenza: Neri Pozza, 1986.

Nemeitz, Joachim Christoph. *Nachlese besonderer Nachrichten von Italien.* Leipzig: J. F. Gleditschens Sohn, 1726.

Norwich, John Julius, comp. *Venice: A Travellers' Companion.* London: Constable, 1990.

Ospedale e luoghi pii diversi. Archivio di Stato, Venice, Italy.

Pincherle, Marc. *Vivaldi: Genius of the Baroque.* New York: W. W. Norton, 1957.

Provveditori sopra ospedali e luoghi pii. Archivio di Stato, Venice, Italy.

Pullan, Brian. "La nuova filantropia nella Venezia cinquecentesca." In *Nel regno dei poveri,* edited by Bernard Aikema and Dulcia Meijers. Venice: Istituzioni di Ricovero e di Educazione, 1989.

———. *Rich and Poor in Renaissance Venice: The Social Institutions of a Catholic State to 1620.* Oxford: Basil Blackwell, 1971.

Quantz, Johann Joachim. *Selbstbiographie.* In *Selbstbiographie deutscher Musiker der XVIII Jahrhunderts,* edited by Willi Kahl. Cologne: Staufen, 1948.

Rousseau, Jean-Jacques. *Les confessions.* Paris: n.p., 1874.

Roym, Peter. *Verzeichnis der Werke Antonio Vivaldis: Kleine Ausgabe.* 2d ed. Leipzig: Deutscher Verlag für Musik, 1979.

Slack, Paul. *The Impact of Plague in Tudor and Stuart England.* London: Routledge and Kegan Paul, 1985, 1990.

Talbot, Michael. *Antonio Vivaldi: A Guide to Research.* London: Garland, 1988.

"Testamento." Codex Italiana, Classe VII-1780. Biblioteca Nazionale Marciana, Venice, Italy.

Vivaldi, Antonio. [Twenty-eight Violin Concertos.] Anna Maria Partbook, busta 55. *Fondo Esposti,* Conservatorio di Musica Benedetto Marcello, Venice, Italy.

Walther, Johann G. *Musikalisches Lexicon.* Facsimile ed. Edited by Richard Schaal. Kassel: Bärenreiter, 1953.

Wood, Elizabeth. "Review Essay: *Women in Music.*" *Signs* 6 (Summer 1980): 283–97.

Yardley, Anne Bagnall. " 'Ful weel she soong the service dyvyne': The Cloistered Musician in the Middle Ages." In *Women Making Music: The Western Art Tradition, 1150–1950,* edited by Jane M. Bowers and Judith Tick. Urbana: University of Illinois Press, 1986.

8

Ladies' Companion, Ladies' Canon? Women Composers in American Magazines from *Godey's* to the *Ladies' Home Journal*

Bonny H. Miller

The idea of a magazine—literally, a storehouse of information and entertainment published at some regular interval—originated in France in the mid-seventeenth century. As early as 1678 chansons and airs for performance and entertainment in the home appeared in the *Mercure Galant*, or *Mercure de France* (1672–1965), including music by a woman, Mlle. Sicard. The pages of American household magazines are likewise a rich but little-known storehouse of nineteenth-century songs and piano pieces for the home, containing many works by women composers. Out of a total of approximately thirty-five hundred songs and piano pieces found in fifteen selected American periodicals from 1830 to 1930, more than three hundred, or almost 10 percent, of the musical works are by women.[1] Although limited to house music genres (i.e., musical entertainment at home), magazines provided a forum where women faced less gender prejudice than in most other public fields of concert or stage music. Music by more than 150 women composers includes works by celebrated performers and widely published composers of the day as well as many forgotten teachers and unknown amateurs. A study of this musical treasure trove reveals yet again the power of gender ideology in musical culture, confirms the popularity of certain women composers from the last century, and brings a host of new composers to our attention.[2]

As with much research on women's musical contributions, the evidence documents considerable musical activity by women in the nineteenth-century home; however, the music in magazines, whether by men or by women, reflects the gender construction that pervaded virtually all periodicals aimed at the household, which mainly meant the women's market. Then, just as now, women's magazines presented paradigms of acceptable female behavior, activities, and appearance through instruction, fiction, and illustration in keeping with the conception and construction of femininity as centered in the household, as "assigned to [women] by nature and required by society."[3] The genres of music that appeared in magazines confirm the consistent gender construction of songs and simple piano pieces as house music genres that were acceptable for women to perform, and thus to compose, for their "natural" world—the private sphere of the home. The lack of any thoughtful history of the music published in three centuries of household magazines is consistent with the valuation of house music genres as insignificant because of their forms (small), function (home entertainment), and sphere (private).[4]

Magazines aimed at upper-class female readers sprang up in imitation of men's journals in eighteenth-century Britain, after a French Protestant refugee, Pierre Anthony Motteaux, established the first English magazine, the *Gentleman's Journal* (London, 1692–94), which included songs by Henry Purcell and others. Alongside social news, letters, stories, and poetry, popular new airs from the London stage appeared in the *Lady's Magazine* (London, 1770–1837), *Ladies' Monthly Museum* (London, 1798–1832), and *La Belle Assemblée* (London, 1806–32), just as they did in the *Gentleman's Magazine* (London, 1731–1907), the *London Magazine* (London, 1732–85), and the *Universal Magazine* (London, 1747–1815).[5] All household magazines were based on the desire to entertain, instruct, and provide interchange between readers. Men's journals contained more accounts of battles, while women's magazines contained more household advice, but a continuum of content existed. The distinction was in tone rather than in content; the tone in women's magazines was characterized by a patriarchal ideology that while men enjoyed widening their world through education, women needed instruction to fulfill their proper duties in the home.[6] Some of the magazines aimed at the women's market were edited or written largely by women, but the tone and content were consistent with other household magazines. Except for newspapers and periodicals devoted to specialized topics, by 1800 most magazines for the home consisted of serialized novels, short stories, poetry, reviews, and letters. Despite a wonderful array of descriptive titles used interchangeably (e.g., magazine, journal, review, gazette, paper, museum, cabinet, emporium, casket, treasury, miscellany, repository, companion, and visitor), household journals in Europe, the

United States, Canada, and South America were strikingly similar throughout the nineteenth century.

The range of materials in these magazines was directed not just at white middle-class women. The serialized novels offered entertainment to generations of American readers, male and female, young and old. Although the fashion illustrations show clothing for wealthy women who could afford luxurious materials and seamstresses, much advice appeared on household maintenance, cooking, and child care for the lower-income mother. Self-instruction was offered to those readers who worked in textile mills or in homes as domestic help, often without the benefit of formal schooling. Specialty features, such as fashion engravings, dress and needlework patterns, and music, provided a selling edge in the competitive magazine market. The projected audience for these periodicals was thus quite broad, although just how widely read they were or by whom is difficult to ascertain.[7] The year 1830 marked a watershed for American publishing, as publishers refined the combination of content, audience, and marketing that resulted in lasting success for many household periodicals, exemplified by *Godey's Lady's Book.*

Godey's Lady's Book had the widest circulation of any magazine before the Civil War and was undoubtedly read by many men as well as by women and children. *Godey's Lady's Book* resulted from the 1837 purchase of Sarah Hale's *Lady's Magazine* by the astute merchandiser Louis Godey. For forty years, Hale continued to edit the magazine and maintained a high literary standard with such contributors as Ralph Waldo Emerson, Henry Wadsworth Longfellow, Nathaniel Hawthorne, Edgar Allan Poe, and Harriet Beecher Stowe. Godey added the beautiful, hand-tinted fashion plates in every issue, for which the magazine was famous. Women pored over the latest fashion plates, clothing patterns, and handiwork designs included in each issue. In the *Little House* books Laura Ingalls Wilder recounts how the magazine was eagerly awaited and passed from household to household on the frontier as late as the 1880s.[8] Music was a part of most monthly issues for more than half a century and grew scarce only when the magazine entered a general decline in the 1890s.[9] Of the fifteen journals selected for this survey, six were direct competitors (*Graham's Monthly Magazine, Ladies' Companion, Peterson's Magazine, Christian Parlor Magazine, Sartain's Union Magazine,* and *Arthur's Home Magazine*) that closely imitated *Godey's* style and content.

The *Ladies' Home Journal* represents the style of women's magazines that became popular at the turn of the century, and it carried on the tradition of magazine music just when *Godey's* declined in popularity. From a back-page column in an obscure farmers' magazine, the *Ladies' Home Journal* had by 1903 become America's most widely read magazine—in fact, the first periodical ever to reach a million subscribers. In its pre–World War I heyday, the *Ladies' Home Journal* was a unique periodical that combined mass marketing with public service and entertainment. This vision was the work of Edward Bok, who edited and shaped the *Journal* for thirty years. Bok was a penniless Dutch immigrant, who became a millionaire and philanthropist. He believed that a periodical could be both altruistic and profitable, and he sought to direct the American middle class toward progressive reforms in many areas, including health, civic life, and culture. The magazine contents during the Bok years constituted a "who's who" of leaders in American public life and the arts.

Together, *Godey's* and the *Ladies' Home Journal* provide a kaleidoscope of American popular music from 1830 to 1930. They were not unique in including music for their readers, but they were outstanding in the quality of music they included. Both periodicals made an effort to commission some of their musical works from well-known composers of the day specifically for publication in the magazine.[10] Both journals also made a point of presenting songs and dances submitted by readers alongside works from popular composers of the day supplied by music publishing houses.

Making music at home had long provided a source of entertainment for family and friends, and music was included without explanation or comment in eighteenth- and nineteenth-century magazines. Only a handful of eighteenth-century American journals and newspapers contained music, but after 1800 there was an explosion of music in weekly papers and monthly household journals from New York, Philadelphia, Baltimore, and Richmond. For the aspiring middle class in the United States, a musical instrument in the home was a measure of social standing, and performance on it was a measure of a young woman's accomplishment and desirability.[11] Music was considered a useful and valuable aspect of education for women and was included at most schools for girls.[12] Magazine music provided a constantly updated supply of suitable music for amateurs to learn and perform at home, a service that must have been especially valued at locations far from cities and music stores.[13]

The periodicals show that musical entertainment at home included songs and duets with piano, guitar, or harp accompaniment; two- to four-voice devotional settings; short instrumental solos for piano, flute, guitar, or violin; and instrumental dances. By at least twenty to one, songs with piano accompaniment, or occasionally with guitar or harp accompaniment, constituted the favorite genre of magazine music, with piano dances as the second most popular genre. Both songs and dances were written in homophonic texture, featuring strongly tonal melodies with simple accompaniments. Anonymous melodies labeled as folk songs (e.g., "Irish Air") appeared frequently. Ensemble pieces for two, three, or four voices, both a capella and with piano accompaniment, were also included.

The majority of selections had few technical difficulties. As Judith Tick has discussed, the accepted musical niche for nineteenth-century women was to play and compose pleasantly in acceptable forms and formulas but not to attempt elaborate or difficult works.[14] House music genres lay midway between the vernacular style of music hall songs and the academic difficulties of concert music. Magazine music supplied this repertory perfectly: the music is graceful and genteel but never showy, a reflection of how women were expected to conduct themselves. Although skillfully written melodies abound, the learned areas of counterpoint, instrumentation, and complex forms—areas considered unfeminine because they displayed musical erudition—were avoided. The same melodious, homophonic style was used by male composers of house music intended for the predominantly female readership. The house music in magazines thus demonstrated the acceptable styles and forms in which women could exercise their performance and compositional skills. Because household magazines presented paradigms of acceptable female behavior, these forms and genres also defined the limits that women "should" observe in their compositional efforts. In short, magazine music canonized what kind of music women could and should compose and the limits they ought not exceed.

The selections in these periodicals were rarely longer than two or three pages. Strophic and da capo forms, which combined maximum poetic length with minimum space and music typesetting cost, were favored. Because poetry was an important component of household journals, songs were often listed in the poetry section in magazine indexes or listed according to author of the text rather than by composer. Songs and piano dances were alternatively listed as "embellishments," along with fashion engravings and illustrations. Inclusion of the latest popular songs was indeed an element of fashion, but the perennial reprinting in many periodicals of favorites, such as George Webb's "Last Rose of Summer" or Johann Strauss's "Coronation Waltz" (composed for the accession of Queen Victoria), had little to do with current style. Although household magazines presented a valuable means for composers and publishers to bring new music to a broad spectrum of society, music editors also cultivated and supplied a repertory of standard music for the home.

After 1850 an abundance of dance music appeared in the household monthlies. Polkas, mazurkas, quicksteps, galops, marches, and, above all, waltzes appeared by the hundreds before the turn of the century. Since dance instructions and diagrams sometimes appeared alongside the music, these pieces might well have been intended for actual dancing at home. The phrase lengths were square, the rhythms mechanical, the melodies simple, and the harmonies most rudimentary. Although they lacked the asymmetry, rubato, melodic finesse, and harmonic complexity of the stylized waltzes or mazurkas by such composers as Frédéric Chopin and Peter Tchaikovsky, these dances featured fresh, natural melodies and infectious rhythmic spirit.

Despite the presence of the names of such accepted masters as Wolfgang Amadeus Mozart, Ludwig van Beethoven, and Carl Maria von Weber, most of the music in magazines came from now-forgotten figures who once enjoyed local renown or from eager amateurs. Some examples were simply stolen from music journals, such as the *Harmonicon* (London, 1823–33), although selections for household magazines were more limited in length and genre, in keeping with works intended for home entertainment instead of being a music specialty. A few selections were included after being popularized by a famous theater production or by a famous concert artist, such as Maria Malibran or Jenny Lind.[15] In other cases a fixed musical editor or publisher supplied examples to a magazine on a regular basis.[16]

Many examples, however, were clearly submitted by readers and were unmistakably labeled as such, with such inscriptions as "Composed expressly for *Godey's Lady's Book*." Reader contributions, such as letters, poems, and prose, were a vital part of household magazines. As Kathryn Shevelow notes, these amateur contributions were "one of the most characteristic features of the genre."[17] Such works by women or by men were welcomed by magazine publishers—they cost nothing, filled the pages, fostered reader identification with the magazine, and helped develop a loyal following. It was good business for American magazines to nurture women amateurs and musicians, and it gave women composers a chance to publish, which regular music companies might not have given them. The magazines thus contain many compositions by amateurs and obscure musicians that exist in no other location. More than twenty works by thirteen women were composed expressly for *Godey's Lady's Book*. The *Ladies' Home Journal* even sponsored contests for musical works by amateurs, rewarding the winners with sizable prizes as well as publication in the *Journal*.

During the 1890s alone, contests were held for the best original ballad, anthem, piano solo, and children's song. Among the prize winners between 1893 and 1906 were Kate Llewellyn-Fitch, Frances J. Moore (or Hatton-Moore), Edna Randolph Worrell, Mrs. A. Wedmore Jones, and Isidora Martinez.

Typically, any piece by a well-known composer was published elsewhere as sheet music, unless it was a commissioned work or a reader's contribution. Almost one hundred numbers by women from the selected magazines were listed in the Board of Music Trade's *Complete Catalogue of Sheet Music and Musical Works, 1870,* and some other pieces were published by firms not included.[18] Even during the 1880s *Godey's* and *Peterson's* included many old hits that had been listed in the 1870 catalog. Of the magazines surveyed, only the *Ladies' Home Journal* was established too late to have music included in the 1870 catalog. Of the approximately 285 works by women in nineteenth-century magazines, excluding the *Ladies' Home Journal,* more than one-third were published separately as sheet music. Allowing for obscure sheet music publications, this figure suggests that perhaps half of the 327 works by women in this study were unique to the magazines and never published elsewhere.

Godey's published the largest number of works by women: seventy-eight works by fifty women, of whom forty were listed with complete surnames (see appendix 8.1 for a summary of contributions by women composers in each of the fifteen selected periodicals). *Godey's* also had the longest publication run of any nineteenth-century household magazine and contained the most music, a total of some seven hundred pieces.[19] The women composers in *Godey's* cover the gamut from the most famous (e.g., Amy Beach, Maria Malibran, Claribel [Charlotte Allington Barnard]) to the obscure (e.g., Mrs. Croxall, Cordelia C. Crozet, Wilse Reitmeyer).

The *Columbian Lady's and Gentleman's Magazine* had the second largest number of works by women—forty-six pieces by six women—out of a total of sixty published works. Of the fifteen selected journals, the *Columbian* was unique in having the majority (over 75 percent) of its music by women, although the contributors were limited to a small circle of professional female musicians, notably the prolific composers Augusta Browne (1821–82) and Anne Sloman (fl. 1840–50). No information is readily available for the other women—Mrs. C. L. Hull, Anna Blackwell, Elizabeth Anne White, and Gertrude Grey, although Hull and Blackwell published in other magazines as well.

Many works by women also appeared in the *Ladies' Home Journal* (forty pieces by twenty-six women) and *Peterson's Magazine* (thirty-eight works by twenty women, eighteen listed by name). Between 10 and 15 percent of the music published by these magazines, as well as *Godey's*, was written by women. Similar percentages were achieved in the *Boston Miscellany*, *Christian Parlor Magazine*, *Ladies' Companion*, and *Sartain's Union Magazine*. The remaining periodicals contained less than 10 percent works by women, but they published a variety of women, whose work appeared in other journals as well.

The names, locations, dates, genres, and titles of compositions for more than 150 composers who can be identified as women by their name (Christian or surname), title (Miss, Mrs., Lady, etc.), female pseudonym (e.g., "Adela"), or anonymous attribution (e.g., "A Lady of Virginia") appear in appendix 8.2. More than 130 women composers are listed with surnames in this textual study.[20] The woman's full Christian name, or husband's full Christian name, appears for only about one hundred of the composers, and biographical information is currently available for scarcely more than fifty.[21] Many of these composers were English or English-born; fewer than twenty are known to have been born in the United States. A few contributors are identified by a Christian name that might be for either a man or a woman (e.g., Valentine, Enna, and Wilse).[22] Dozens of composers are identified by initials plus a surname, and some of these might have been women, but they have not been included in this survey unless they were identified elsewhere as women composers. Men sometimes took female pseudonyms, as in the case of Septimus Winner's publishing under his mother's name, Alice Hawthorne, but it was probably more common for a woman to disguise her sex in hopes of publication.

Songs by the same composers often turn up in journals that were similar in style, such as *Godey's* and *Peterson's*. More than twenty women had works in at least two journals, yet they are hardly celebrated composers. Mrs. Philip Millard (fl. circa 1840), for example, had works in five journals. She was British and composed several hit songs, such as "Alice Grey," which was included between 1829 and 1832 in the *Albion, Godey's*, the *Boston Pearl*, and the *New York Mirror*. The English music journal *Harmonicon* published several of her songs and listed her Christian name as Virtue. Her works were obviously popular successes in her own time, yet little is known of her now.

Better known today are Maria Garcia Malibran (1808–36), the brilliant soprano operatic star of the 1820s and 1830s who had works in four U.S. journals, and Mrs. Thomas Haynes Bayly (fl. 1830–40), wife of a famous English songster and poet who also had works in four journals. Harriet Mary Browne Hughes (fl. 1830–40), sister of the popular poet Felicia Browne Hemans (1793–1835), had songs in four American journals, as did famous British musicians Maria Billington Hawes (1816–86) and Mrs. Price Blackwood (Lady Helen Dufferin, 1807–67). A more shadowy figure is Miss Penelope Smith (fl. 1830–40), who had one hit song, "A Place in Thy Memory, Dearest," included in an 1836 *Albion*, an 1837 *Godey's*, and an 1838 *New-Yorker.* She probably was the same person with songs in the *New York Mirror.* A Miss Smith also had a song in the 1831 *Harmonicon*, suggesting an English origin.

Several hit songs appeared in three or more journals in this study. Mrs. Thomas Haynes Bayly's "I Cannot Dance Tonight" was published in the *New York Mirror, Graham's*, and *Godey's* between 1839 and 1843. The "Evening Song of the Tyrolese Peasants," or "Come to the Sunset Tree," with words by Felicia Browne Hemans and music by her sister, Harriet Mary Browne Hughes, appeared four times in three journals between 1829 and 1839—twice in *Graham's*, once in the *New-Yorker*, and once in the *Boston Weekly Magazine.* Later in the century the ballad "Far Away," by the British composer Mary Lindsay (Mrs. J. Worthington Bliss, fl. 1860–80), was published between 1874 and 1879 in *Arthur's, Peterson's*, and *Godey's*. At least a dozen other songs were popular enough to be published in more than one journal, including songs by Claribel, Malibran, Lady Dufferin, and Mrs. Caroline Norton.[23] A few songs were reprinted more than once in the same journal, probably owing to readers' requests. The many instances of multiple magazine printings indicate a healthy demand by readers for familiar favorites and for more works by popular women composers.

Anne Sloman had more works than any other woman in these journals—a total of twenty-eight in four journals—followed by Claribel (1830–69) with twenty songs and Augusta Browne with seventeen in three magazines each.[24] Numerous publications in the *Columbian Lady's and Gentleman's Magazine* produced the high totals for both Sloman and Browne. Composers with works in three journals also included Mrs. J. Worthington Bliss and Mrs. C. L. Hull (fl. 1840–50). Other famous English composers with works in more than one journal were Annie Fortescue Harrison (Lady Arthur Hill, 1851–1944), Felicia Browne Hemans (1793–1835), and Mrs. Cornwall Baron Wilson (1797?–1846). Boston composer Charlotte Saunders Cushman (1816–76) is probably the "Miss C.S.C." and possibly the "C.S.C." found in journals other than the *Ladies' Companion.* Forgotten nineteenth-century women who were active enough to have works in more than one journal were Mrs. Mary A. Asay, Mrs. Sarah R. Burtis, Miss A. (probably Augusta) Cowell, Miss E. L. Deacon, and Annette Marriott. Other than their musical works, we know nothing of these women. Less information is currently available about the women with music in the *Ladies' Home Journal* than those in *Godey's Lady's Book*, but information is no doubt waiting to be uncovered in contemporary newspapers and magazines for such figures as Edna Randolph Worrell, Leila A. De Vere, and Frances J. Moore (or Hatton-Moore), all of whom published several songs or piano pieces in the *Ladies' Home Journal.*

For women and men alike, nineteenth-century magazines "provided the means to make authorship a viable profession in the United States."[25] Magazines provided a nurturing milieu for female writers, artists, and editors, as well as for women composers. Publication in magazines presented a unique means of national exposure for women who composed and performed strictly in the private home, or sphere, according to the accepted mores of modesty for Victorian ladies. While it is unlikely that magazines could support musicians as successfully as they could support writers, a clever composer could use magazines to supplement her earnings and expose her musical style to a wide audience of potential buyers.[26] Even though 90 percent of the music in periodicals was still composed by men and many magazines included no music by women, at least a few journals—notably the *Columbian Lady's and Gentleman's Magazine, Godey's,* and the *Ladies' Home Journal*—offered a public forum for women composers. Successful women professionals who composed works just for particular magazines, presumably with commissions, included Anne Sloman (twenty-one times in the *Columbian Lady's and Gentleman's Magazine*), Augusta Browne (ten times in the *Columbian Lady's and Gentleman's Magazine*), and Cécile Chaminade (twice in the *Ladies' Home Journal*).[27]

Magazine music was a means of publication that allowed women to achieve national exposure without violating the privacy and mores of the home. Although magazine music is limited to genres for the home—songs, ballads, duets, hymns, and piano dances—this repertory provides an abundant source of music by long-forgotten women, as well as by their famous sisters. The sheer volume of songs and dances published in magazines, numbering in the thousands, confirms that women created a lively and rich musical experience, even within the strict confines of Victorian expectations for women. After World War 1, when radio and phonograph replaced music making as home entertainment, music disappeared from the magazines as well. Today, as concert audiences shrink and passive video consumption replaces musical literacy, we can better appreciate the level of technical and musical sophistication of nineteenth-century amateurs, many of them women, who performed, enjoyed, and composed music for their own pleasure at home. Household periodicals present a precious mirror of women's music making in nineteenth-century America, even though these contributions were severely limited by gender practice to music for the private sphere and therefore have been regarded as of little value as art music in terms of form, technique, abstract thought, or creativity. The triumph of these musical foremothers was to achieve so extensive a contribution within such a circumscribed sphere; their presence as active musical agents demands a reassessment of this kind of musical activity and an acknowledgment of how other musical activities similarly influenced by gender practice came to be privileged over it in our historical examinations. The contribution of these women cannot be written out of the history of music, because, like a snapshot, the evidence is permanently preserved in the pages of household journals.

APPENDIX 8.1: Summary of Women Composers in Selected Magazines

1. *The Albion: Or, British, Colonial, and Foreign Weekly Gazette.* New York: 1822–76.
   17 compositions (15 songs and 2 piano solos) by 13 women:

Bayly, Mrs. (Thomas) Haynes	Marshall, Mrs. William
"A Canadian Lady"	Maywood, Mary
F., Miss Adelia	Millard, Mrs. Philip (Virtue)
Horn, Mrs. Charles E.	Smith, Miss (Penelope)
Linwood, Miss Mary	Wilson, Mrs. Cornwall Baron
Malibran, Madame (Maria Garcia)	(Margaret)
or Garcia, Signorina	Wood, Mrs. Mary Ann
Marriott, Annette	

2. *Arthur's Home Magazine (Home Magazine; Lady's Home Magazine; Arthur's Lady's Home Magazine; Arthur's Illustrated Home Magazine).* Philadelphia: 1852–98.
   11 compositions (7 songs and 4 piano pieces) by 7 women:

B., Mrs. S. G.	Lowthian, Caroline
Bliss, Mrs. J. W.	Wentworth, Eveleen W.
Claribel	Young, Ella V.
Hodges, Faustina Hasse	

3. *Boston Miscellany of Literature and Fashion (Boston Miscellany and Lady's Monthly Magazine).* Boston and New York: 1842–43.
   2 compositions (2 songs) by 2 women:

Malibran, (Maria Garcia)	Mendelssohn, Mademoiselle (Fanny)

4. *Boston Pearl (Bouquet: Flowers of Polite Literature; Pearl and Literary Gazette; Hartford Pearl and Literary Gazette; Boston Pearl and Literary Gazette)—A Gazette of Polite Literature*. Hartford, then Boston: 1831–36.
5 compositions (5 songs) by 5 women:

C., Miss C. S. [Charlotte Saunders	McClellan, Miss A. J.
Cushman?]	Millard, Mrs. P(hilip) (Virtue)
Collier, Susannah	Robinson, Mrs. Alfred

5. *Boston Weekly Magazine*. Boston: 1838–41.
11 compositions (10 songs and 1 duet) by 9 women:

Arkwright, Mrs. Robert (Fanny)	Hawes, Maria B(illington)
Blackwood, Mrs. Price (Lady	[Hemans, Mrs. Felicia Browne—
Dufferin)	erroneous]
Clarkson, Miss	Hughes, Harriet Mary Browne (Mrs.
Cowell, Miss A[ugusta?]	Hemans's sister)
Deacon, Miss E. L.	Scrooby, Miss

6. *Christian Parlor Magazine*. New York: 1844–55. *Happy Home and Parlor Magazine*. Boston: 1855–60.
10 compositions (10 songs) by 9 women:

Blackwell, Anna	Sloman, Anne
Browne, Cornelia Gould	Smith, Lydia B.
Burnham, Georgiana N.	Taylor, Gussie E.
Burr, Mrs. H. A.	Tillinghast, Mrs. [William?]
Shipman, Miss Mary E.	

7. *Columbian Lady's and Gentleman's Magazine*. New York: 1844–49.
46 compositions (43 songs, 1 vocal duet, and 2 piano solos) by 6 women:

Blackwell, Miss Anna	Hull, Mrs. C. L. [Mrs. William?]
Browne, Miss Augusta	Sloman, Miss Anne
Grey, Gertrude	White, Miss Elizabeth Anne

8. *Godey's Magazine (Lady's Book; Godey's Lady's Book, and Ladies' American Magazine; Godey's Magazine and Lady's Book; Godey's Book and Magazine)*. New York: 1830–98.
78 compositions (45 songs, 27 piano works, and 2 vocal duets, with 4 additional complete works included in articles) by 53 women:

Aarup, Caia	Bowers, Mrs. Lizzie
"Adela"	Bright, Mrs. S. B.
Asay, Mary A.	Browne, Augusta
B., Miss J.	Browne, Harriet Mary
Baker, Mrs.	(Mrs. Hughes)
Bayly, Mrs. T(homas) Haynes	Burtis, Mrs. Sarah R.
Beach, Amy Marcy Cheney	C., Miss C. M., of Baltimore
Beckett, Mrs. Gilbert À	C., Mrs. J. M., of Virginia
Bell, Coralie	C., Miss Mary
Bergenshold, Erika	Claribel

Croxall, Mrs.
Crozet, Cordelia C.
Dana, Mrs. Mary S. B.
  (Mrs. Schindler)
Dance, Miss
Dixon, Miss F.
Dufferin, Lady (Helen)
Gaynor, Jessie Love
Harrison, Annie Fortescue
Haughton, Mrs. S. B.
Hemans, Felicia Browne
Henry, Miss F.
Hull, Mrs. C. L.
Hunsicker, Mrs. F. H.
"A Lady of Georgia"
"A Lady of Virginia"
Lang, Margaret Ruthven
Leslie, Miss [E.?]
"Leura"

Lind, Jenny
Lindsay, Mary
  (Mrs. J. Worthington Bliss)
"Little Maud"
Malibran, Maria Garcia
Miles, Mrs. [Jane Mary?]
Millard, Mrs. Philip Millard (Virtue)
Palmer, Mrs. H. W. T.
Reitmeyer, Wilse
Rogers, Clara Kathleen
Smith, Miss (Penelope)
Smith, Rosalie E.
Stith, Mrs. Townsend or Townshend
Sullivan, Marion Dix
Walsh, Mary E.
Welsh, Mary Ann Wilson
  (Mrs. Thomas Welsh)
"A Young Lady"

9. *Graham's American Monthly Magazine of Literature, Art, and Fashion* (*Atkinson's Casket; Casket; Graham's Lady's and Gentleman's Magazine; Graham's Magazine of Literature and Art; Graham's Magazine*). Philadelphia: 1826–58.
16 compositions (15 songs and 1 piano solo) by 14 women:

Bayly, Mrs. Thomas Haynes
Beauharnais, Hortense
Bellchambers, Juliet
Blackwood, Mrs. Price
  (Lady Dufferin)
Dister, Valentine
Duval, Enna
Hawes, Maria B.

Hemans, Mrs. [Felicia Browne]—
  erroneous
Hughes, Harriet Mary Browne
Jones, Miss Agnes H.
M'Cord, Miss E.
Norton, Mrs. (Caroline)
Sloman, Miss [Anne?]
"A Young Lady"

10. *Ladies' Companion, and Literary Expositor.* New York: 1834–44.
11 compositions (10 songs and 1 piano solo) by 8 women:

Bayly, Mrs. (Thomas) H(aynes)
Clenell, Miss
Cushman, Charlotte Saunders
Dufferin, Lady

Gibbs, Mrs.
Hawes, Maria Billington
Waylett, Mrs. (Harriet)
Yates, Mrs. M.

11. *Ladies' Home Journal.* Philadelphia, then New York: 1883-present.
40 compositions (27 songs, 10 piano pieces, 3 children's songs or plays with music) by 26 women:

Abbott, Jane Bingham
Arden-Cartland, Blanche

Barbour, Florence Newell
Bodde, Margaret Peddle

Booth, Evangeline Cory
Burr, Katherine Rose
Chaminade, Cécile
Craven, Katherine Tabb
De Vere, Leila A.
Evans, Frances Billings
Farrell, Jessie Hilton
Graham, Miriam
Howard, Hattie Sterling
Jones, Mrs. A. Wedmore
Llewellyn-Fitch, Kate

Martinez, Isidora
Moore (Hatton-Moore), Frances J.
Paterson, Mrs. J. A.
Robinson, Frances C.
Rowland, Ethel
Sheldon, Lillian Tait
Stanley, Alma
Terhune, Anice
Wisman, Julia Marie
Wood, Ada Gertrude
Worrell, Edna Randolph

12. *New York Mirror.* New York: 1823–42.
15 compositions (14 songs and 1 song or duet) by 13 women:
Andrae, Miss Nathalia
Bartholomew, Mrs. Hullmandel
Bayly, Mrs. Thomas Haynes
Beckett, Mrs. A.
Deacon, Miss E. L.
Fitzgerald, Mrs. Edward
Martyn, Eliza

Millard, Mrs. Philip (Virtue)
Orme, Mrs.
Smith, Miss [Penelope?]
Turnbull, Mrs. Walter [Anne?]
Wallack, Mrs. Henry
Wilson, Mrs. Cornwall Baron
(Margaret)

13. *The New-Yorker.* New York: 1836–41.
11 compositions (11 songs) by 9 women:
Browne, Miss (Harriet Mary)
Cowell, Miss A[ugusta?]
Fitzgerald, Mrs. Edward
Hawes, Maria B(illington)
Malibran, Madame (Maria Garcia)

Marriott, Annette
Millard, Mrs. Philip (Virtue)
Mounsey, Miss (Ann)
Smith, Miss (Penelope)

14. *Peterson's Magazine (Lady's World; The Artist and Lady's World; Ladies National Magazine; Peterson's Ladies National Magazine; New Peterson Magazine).* Philadelphia: 1842–98.
38 compositions (24 songs and 14 piano solos) by 20 women:
Alexander, Miss
Asay, M. A. (Mrs. Mary A.)
Bliss, Mrs. J. Worthington (Mary
   Lindsay)
Bolton, Ada
Brewster, Miss
Burtis, Mrs. S(arah) R.
Campbell, Miss Jane F.
Claribel (Charlotte Allington
   Barnard)
Dufferin, Lady
Escher, Amelia M.

Fricker, Anne
Gabriel, Virginia
Harrison, Anne Fortescue (Lady
   Arthur Hill)
Heron, Miss Fanny
"A Lady"
Morrison, Mrs. Mary
"Nita"
Norton, Mrs. (Caroline)
Scott, Lady John Douglas
Whilldin, Mrs. H. C.

15. *Sartain's Union Magazine of Literature and Art (Union Magazine of Literature and Art).* New York: 1847–48; Philadelphia: 1849–52.
11 compositions (10 songs and 1 solo for harp or piano) by 4 women:

Browne, Miss Augusta   Hull, Mrs. C. L.
Cubell, Mrs. Julia Mays   Sloman, Miss Anne

APPENDIX 8.2: Catalog of Women Composers in Selected American Magazines

Magazine abbreviations: *Al* = *Albion, Ar* = *Arthur's, BM* = *Boston Miscellany, BP* = *Bosto Pearl, BW* = *Boston Weekly, Cr* = *Christian Parlor, Co* = *Columbian Lady's, Go* = *Godey Gr* = *Graham's, LC* = *Ladies' Companion, LH* = *Ladies' Home Journal, NM* = *New York Mirr NY* = *New-Yorker, Pe* = *Peterson's, Sa* = *Sartain's*

Compositions are listed in chronological order of publication, unless attribution is doubtful based on circumstantial evidence (e.g., Mary A. Asay precedes M. A. Asay).

Symbols under Genre: S = Song, D = Duet, P = Piano solo, H = Harp solo, C = Childrer song or play with songs

Name	Magazine/Date/ Genre	Title
Aarup, Caia	*Go* Aug. 1893/S	"A Serenade"
Abbott, Jane Bingham	*LH* May 1912/S	"Just for Today"
"Adela"	*Go* Feb. 1852/P	"The Mocking Bird"
Alexander, Miss	*Pe* May 1868/P	"Regiment Quickstep"
Allington, Charlotte. See Claribel		
Andrae, Clara Nathalia	*NM* July 25, 1840/S	"I'll Twine Thee a Chaplet"
Anonymous:		
"A Canadian Lady"	*Al* Jan. 1, 1842/P	"The Canadian Union Waltz"
"A Lady"	*Pe* Sept. 1861/P	"The Fascination Schottisch"
"A Lady of Georgia"	*Go* Jan. 1852/P	"Gondola Waltz"
"A Lady of Virginia"	*Go* Dec. 1847/S	"New Song"
"A Lady of Virginia"	*Go* June 1848/P	"Magpie Waltz"
"A Lady of Virginia"	*Go* Nov. 1849/S	"Temperance Song"
"A Lady of Virginia"	*Go* Aug. 1850/S	"Song for the Spanish Guitar"
"A Young Lady"	*Gr* May 1830/S	"Pretty Marian the Oyster Girl"
"A Young Lady"	*Go* Jan. 1840/S	"No More"
Arden-Cartland, Blanche	*LH* Apr. 1912/S	"In April"
Arkwright, Mrs. Robert (Fanny)	*BW* May 9, 1840/S	"Xarifa, or the Bride of Andallo"
Asay, Mrs. Mary A.	*Go* Aug. 1869/P	"Minia Waltz"
[Asay, M. A.]	*Pe* Mar. 1869/P	"Marriott Polka"
B., Miss J.	*Go* May 1860/S	"The Golden Ringlet"
B., Mrs. S. G.	*Ar* Mar. 1871/S	"Winsome Winnie"
Baker, Mrs.	*Go* Sept. 1837/S	"The Golden Dream"
Barbour, Florence Newell	*LH* Jan. 1905/P	"Invitation to the Dance"
Barnard, Mrs. Charles. See Claribel		

Barnett, Clara Kathleen. See
Rogers, Clara Kathleen
Bartholomew, Ann Sheppard.
See Mounsey, Ann or
Elizabeth
Bartholomew, Mrs.   *NM* Mar. 27, 1841/S   "Summer Is Breathing"
  Hullmandel   or D
Bayly (or Bayley), Mrs.   *Al* Dec. 12, 1835/S   "The Fair Puritan"
  Thomas Haynes
                             LC Apr. 1836/S   "The Fair Puritan"
                             NM Aug. 17, 1839/S   "I Cannot Dance Tonight"
                             Gr Nov. 1839/S   "I Cannot Dance Tonight"
                             Go Apr. 1843/S   "I Cannot Dance Tonight"
Beach, Mrs. H. H. A.   *Go* Jan. 1896/P   "Phantoms"
Beauharnais, Hortense   *Gr* July, 1855/S   "Partant pour la Syrie: New
                                                     National Air of France"
Beckett, Mrs. A.   *NM* May 27, 1837/S   "When Day is Going"
Beckett, Mrs. Gilbert À   *Go* May 1847/S   "One Kindly Word before We
                                                     Part"
Bell, Coralie   *Go* July 1870/S   "I Love You"
                             Go Aug. 1872/S   "Nell and I"
                             Go Feb. 1873/S   "Night Comes Creeping Slowly
                                                     o'er Me"
                             Go Mar. 1874/S   "Helen to Claude"
                             Go July 1877/P   "Sunny Days"
Bellchambers, Juliet   *Gr* Apr. 1846/S   "The Spell Is Broken"
Bergenshold, Erika   *Go* Nov. 1847/S   "Soft Wind that Sigheth"
Beriot, Mme. de. See
  Malibran, Marie Garcia
Billington, Maria. See Hawes,
  Maria Billington
Blackwell, Miss Anna   *Co* Jan. 1846/S   "Fairy Kandore"
                             Co Apr. 1846/S   "By the Flowing Arno"
                             Co Dec. 1846/S   "The Persian Wife to Her Hus-
                                                     band"
                             Co Nov. 1848/S   "The Song of the Zephyrs"
                             Cr Vol. 8, [1852]/S   "Song of the Zephyrs"
Blackwood, Mrs. Price. See
  Dufferin, Lady (Helen)
Bliss, Mrs. J. Worthington   *Ar* Oct. 1874/S   "Far Away"
                             Pe June 1876/S   "Far Away"
  [Mary Lindsay]   *Go* Dec. 1878/S   "Tired"
                             Go Oct. 1879/S   "Far Away"
Bodde, Margaret Peddle   *LH* Nov. 1908/C   "Good Night"
                             LH Nov. 1908/C   "Shadow March"
                             LH Nov. 1908/C   "In Port"
                             LH Nov. 1909/C   "Bed in Summer"
                             LH Nov. 1909/C   "Windy Nights"
Bolton, Ada   *Pe* Sept. 1858/P   "Rose of the Prairie Waltz"
Booth, Evageline Cory   *LH* Sept. 1905/S   "Commander Booth's New Song: Me"

Bowers, Mrs. Lizzie	Go Feb. 1866/P	"Titania Mazourka"
	Go Apr. 1867/P	"Pine Bluff Quickstep"
	Go Feb. 1868/P	"Twilight Mazourka"
	Go Mar. 1870/P	"Clinton Mazourka"
	Go Jan. 1877/P	"New-Year Waltz"
Brewster, Miss	Pe Dec. 1855/S	"The Truant Lover"
Bright, Mrs. S. B.	Go June 1869/P	"Camille Waltz"
Browne, Augusta	Go Jan. 1841/D	"The Stranger's Heart"
	Go Dec. 1841/S	"Bird of the Gentle Wing"
	Co Mar. 1844/S	"New England Churches"
	Co Sept. 1844/S	"I Watch for Thee!"
	Co Dec. 1844/P	"The Columbian Quick-Step"
	Co Sept. 1845/S	"Wake, Lady Mine: Serenade"
	Co Nov. 1845/P	"German Air, with Variations"
	Co July 1846/S	"Pleasure! Naught but Pleasure!"
	Co June 1847/S	"The Persian Lover's Song"
	Sa Oct. 1847/S	"The Soldier's Departure"
	Co Jan. 1848/S	"Where Quair Runs Sweet amang the Flowers"
	Sa Feb. 1848/S	"The Merry Sleigh Bell"
	Co Apr. 1848/S	"The Courier Dove"
	Sa Apr. 1848/S	"Speed, Gallant Bark!"
	Co June 1848/S	"Vive le Republique! America to France"
	Sa July 1848/S	"Wake, Poland, Awake!"
	Sa Aug. 1850/D	"The Youth's Parting Song"
Browne, Cornelia Gould	Cr Vol. 10, [1854]/S	"They Grew in Beauty"
Browne, Felicia. See Hemans, Felicia Browne		
Browne, Harriet Mary	Gr Jan. 1829/S	"Come to the Sunset Tree!"[a]
[Mrs. Hemans's sister]	Go Sept. 1830/S	"The Captive Knight"
[Mrs. Hemans's sister]	Go Dec. 1832/S	"The Last Wish"
	Gr Mar. 1833/S	"Come to the Sunset Tree"[a]
[Mrs. Hemans's sister]	Gr Aug. 1835/S	"The Recall"
	NY Nov. 19, 1836/S	"Come, Come to the Sunset Tree"
	BW July 13, 1839/S	"Come to the Sunset Tree!"
	BW Mar. 14, 1840/D	"Evening Song to the Virgin"
	BW April 3, 1841/D	"The Messenger Bird"
Burnham, Georgiana N.	Cr Vol. 7, [1851]/S	"O Worship Not the Beautiful"
Burr, Mrs. H. A.	Cr Vol. 10, [1854]/S	"Westward Ho!"
Burr, Katherine Rose	LH July 1908/S	"I Wish"
Burtis, Mrs. Sarah R.	Go Apr. 1853/P	"Lady's Book Polka"
	Go Apr. 1855/P	"Meade Polka"
	Pe Nov. 1855/P	"Morning Star Polka"
	Go Dec. 1855/P	"Evening Star Polka"
C., Miss C. M., "of Baltimore"	Go Sept. 1854/S	"Summer Wind, Summer Wind"
C[ushman?], C[harlotte] S.	BP Nov. 29, 1834/S	"Fly to the Desert"
C., Mrs. J. M., "of Virginia"	Go Feb. 1856/P	"Weyanoke Waltz"
	Go Mar. 1856/P	"Powhattan Waltz"
	Go Apr. 1856/P	"Richmond Waltz"

C., Miss Mary	*Go* Jan. 1842/S	"An Original Serenade"
Campbell, Miss Jane F.	*Pe* May 1862/P	"Inverary Waltz"
	Pe June 1862/P	"Jura Polka"
Chaminade, Cécile	*LH* Feb. 1906/P	"New Debutante Waltz"
	LH Nov. 1908/P	"Rosemary: A Pastel"
Claribel	*Ar* Feb. 1867/S	"I Cannot Sing the Old Songs"
	Ar Mar. 1867/S	"Five O'Clock in the Morning"
	Ar June 1867/S	"Only a Lock of Hair"
	Pe Oct. 1867/S	"Maggie's Secret"
	Pe Nov. 1867/S	"Five O'Clock in the Morning"
	Ar May 1868/S	"All along the Valley"
	Pe Apr. 1869/S	"I Cannot Sing the Old Songs"
	Pe June 1869/S	"Something to Love"
	Pe Apr. 1871/S	"Won't You Tell Me Why, Robin?"
	Pe Mar. 1872/S	"We'd Better Bide a Wee"
	Pe Aug. 1872/S	"Take Back the Heart"
	Ar Aug. 1872/S	"Faithful to You I Ever Will Be"
	Pe Aug. 1873/S	"We Sat by the River, You and I"
	Go July 1878/S	"We'd Better Bide a Wee"
	Go Aug. 1878/S	"Janet's Choice"
	Go Nov. 1878/S	"You and I"
	Pe July 1880/S	"Maggie's Welcome"
	Pe Aug. 1882/S	"Strangers Yet"
	Pe Sept. 1884/S	"Oh Mother! Take the Wheel Away!"
	Pe Oct. 1885/S	"Open the Pearly Gate"
	Pe June 1886/S	"Silver Chimes"
	Pe Sept. 1887/S	"Drifting"
Clarkson, Miss	*BW* June 5, 1841/S	"The Bridal Morn"
Clennell, Miss	*LC* Nov. 1840/S	"You Pretty, Little, Giddy Flirt"
Collier, Susannah	*BP* Mar. 28, 1835/S	"Swiss Shepherd's Song"
Cowell, Miss A[ugusta?]	*BW* Jan. 26, 1839/S	"We Have Been Friends Together"
	NY Nov. 23, 1839/S	"The Lonely Harp"
[(Augusta?) Cowell]	*Gr* Jan. 1842/S	"Thy Name Was Once a Magic Spell" [b]
Craven, Katherine Tabb	*LH* Dec. 1904/S	"At the Manger"
Croxall, Mrs.	*Go* May 1843/S	"Oh Ask Me Not to Love Again"
Crozet, Cordelia C.	*Go* July 1844/S	"Oh! Lady, Sing Again that Song"
Cubell, Mrs. Julia Mays	*Sa* Dec. 1847/P or H	"La Vera Cruz Quadrille"
Cushman, Charlotte Saunders	*LC* Aug. 1837/P	"A Waltz"
	LC Feb. 1838/S	"The Flying Brigand"
	LC Dec. 1838/S	"Ask Not Why It Is I Love Thee"
Dana, Mrs. Mary S. B.	*Go* May 1880/S	"Flee as a Bird"
Dance, Miss	*Go* Nov. 1831/S	"I Love Thee"
Deacon, Miss E. L.	*BW* April 17, 1841/S	"The Sailor's Farewell to Home"
	NM Nov. 8, 1834/S	"The Sailor's Farewell to Home"
DeVere, Leila A.	*LH* Dec. 1903/S	"Christmas Love Song"
	LH June 1904/S	"Red and White Roses"
Dister, Valentine	*Gr* Dec. 1848/S	"Voices from the Spirit Land"
Dixon, Miss F.	*Go* Aug. 1834/S	"The Forsaken"

Doria, Clara. See Rogers,
Clara Kathleen
Dufferin, Lady (Helen)
  [Mrs. Norton's sister]   *LC* May 1837/S   "The Fairy Bells"
  [Mrs. Price Blackwood]   *BW* Feb. 27, 1841/S "By-Gone Hours"
                      Gr Oct. 1841/S   "Bye-Gone Hours"
                      Pe Oct. 1870/S   "Katey's Letter"
                      Go Sept. 1878/S   "Katey's Letter"
Duval, Enna   *Gr* Aug. 1850/S   "Chant of the Néreides from . . .
                                              Goethe's *Faust*"
Escher, Amelia M.   *Pe* June 1861/P   "The Triumphant Polka"
Evans, Frances Billings *LH* Dec. 1902/S   "Hark, 'Tis the Bells"
F., Miss Adelia   *Al* July 14, 1838/P "Zurich Waltz"
Farrell, Jessie Hilton   *LH* Mar. 1895/S   "Come unto Me"
                      LH Oct. 1905/S   "Come unto Me"
Fitzgerald, Mrs. Edward *NM* Oct. 22, 1836/S "The Dying Girl to Her Lover"
                      NM June 16, 1838/S "The Dying Girl to Her Lover"
                      NY April 20, 1839/S "I Remember How My Childhood
                                              Fleeted By"
Fortescue, Annie. See
Harrison, Annie Fortescue
Fricker, Anne   *Pe* July 1885/S   "I Built a Bridge of Fancies"
Gabriel, Virginia   *Pe* Aug. 1876/S   "Only"
                      Pe Aug. 1887/S   "A Mother's Song"
Garcia, Signorina (Maria). See
Malibran, Maria Garcia
Garrett, Augusta Browne. See
Browne, Augusta
Gaynor, Jessie Love   *Go* July 1897/S   "Nocturne"
Gibbs, Mrs.   *LC* Jan. 1839/S   "The Mountain Sylph: A Romance"
                      LC Sept. 1839/S   "The Castle Hall"
Goldschmidt, Mrs. Otto. See
Lind, Jenny
Graham, Miriam   *LH* Oct. 1, 1910/S "The Life-Road: A Marriage Song"
Grey, Gertrude   *Co* Apr. 1847/S   "The Fetter 'neath the Flowers"
Harries, Margaret. See
Wilson, Mrs. Cornwall
Baron
Harrison, Annie Fortescue *Go* July 1881/S   "In the Gloaming"
                      Pe Oct. 1882/S   "In the Gloaming"
  [Lady Arthur Hill]   *Pe* Feb. 1886/S   "Sing to Me"
Hatton-Moore, F. J. See
Moore, Frances J.
Haughton, Mrs. S. B.   *Go* Apr. 1872/S   "Indian Maiden's Song"
Hawes, Maria Billington *BW* Dec. 28, 1839/S "I'll Speak of Thee"
                      NY Feb. 22, 1840/S "'Tis Very Sweet to Love Thee,
                                              Maiden"
                      LC Jan. 1842/S   "I'll Speak of Thee, I'll Love Thee,
                                            Too!"
                      Gr Mar. 1850/S   "Thou Art Lovlier"
Hayes, Miss. See Bayly, Mrs.
Thomas Haynes

Hemans, Felicia Browne	*Gr* Jan. 1829/S	Come to the Sunset Tree!" [a]
	Gr Mar. 1833/S	Come to the Sunset Tree!" [a]
	BW Jan. 25, 1840/S	"The Bride of the Greek Isle" [c]
	Go Sept. 1843/S	"Bring Flowers"
Henry, Miss F.	*Go* Mar. 1849/P	"Oakland Gallopade"
	Go Jan. 1850/P	"Ella Waltz"
Hensel, Fanny Mendelssohn.		
See Mendelssohn, Fanny		
Heron, Miss Fanny	*Pe* July 1856/P	"Myrtle Waltz"
Hill, Lady Arthur. See		
Harrison, Annie Fortescue		
Hodges, Faustina Hasse	*Ar* Aug. 1870/P	"Mazurka"
Horn, Mrs. Charles E.	*Al* Sept. 8, 1838/S	"The Early Tomb"
(Maria)		
Hortense, Queen of Holland.		
See Beauharnais, Hortense		
Horton, Maria. See Horn,		
Mrs. Charles E.		
Howard, Hattie Sterling	*LH* Mar. 1901/S	"Eugene Field's Armenian
		Lullaby"
Hughes, Mrs. See Browne,		
Harriet Mary		
Hull, Mrs. C. L. [Mrs.	*Co* May 1844/S	"I've Won Thee to Love Me"
William?]		
	Co July 1844/S	"Come to Me, Love"
	Co Oct. 1844/S	"Love's First Step Is upon the
		Rose"
	Go Nov. 1844/S	"My Own Marie"
	Co Jan. 1845/S	"The Lover's Farewell"
	Sa Aug. 1847/S	"Life's Music"
	Sa Jan. 1848/S	"Love's Memories"
Hunsicker, Mrs. F. H.	*Go* Aug. 1868/S	"A Mother's Tribute: Baby Ella"
Inverarity, Eliza. See Martyn,		
Eliza		
Jones, Mrs. A. Wedmore	*LH* June 1906/P	"Prelude"
Jones, Miss Agnes H.	*Gr* Oct. 1848/S	"The Ocean-Buried"
Kemble, Frances Crawford.		
See Arkwright, Mrs. Robert		
Lang, Margaret Ruthven	*Go* Jan. 1896/S	"Ghosts"
Lennox, Lady William. See		
Wood, Mrs. Mary Ann		
Leslie, Miss [E.?]	*Go* Feb. 1844/S	"The Parlours, Both, Are Occupied"
"Leura"	*Go* Oct. 1849/D	"Helmsman's Song"
Lind, Jenny	*Go* Oct. 1847/S	"Hear Me Maiden, while I Sue"
Lindsay, Miss Mary. See		
Bliss, Mrs. J. Worthington		
Linwood, Miss Mary	*Al* Jan. 3, 1829/S	"Pretty Fairy: A Canzonet"
Llewellyn-Fitch, Kate	*LH* Aug. 1893/S	"My Star"
Lowthian, Caroline	*Ar* May 1886/P	"Venetia Waltz"
MacFarren, Mrs. See Andrae,		
Clara Nathalia		

Malibran, Maria Garcia	Al Nov. 17, 1827/S	"Away o'er the Blue Waves of the Ocean"
	Al Jan. 26, 1830/S	"I Saw Thee Weep"
	Go Mar. 1839/S	"There Is No Home like My Own"
	NY Sept. 21, 1839/S	"There Is No Home like My Own"
	BM Mar. 1842/S	"The Return of the Tyrolese"
March, Mrs. George E. See Gabriel, Virginia		
Marriott, Annette	Al Aug. 13, 1836/S	"Proudly Will I Meet Thee"
	NY Aug. 20, 1836/S	"Proudly Will I Meet Thee"
	NY July 15, 1837/S	"We'll Go No More a Roving"
	NY July 22, 1837/S	"We'll Go No More a Roving"
Marshall, Mrs. William	Al Sept. 1, 1832/S	"The Banished Pole"
Martinez, Isadora	LH June 1906/P	"At Twilight"
Martyn, Eliza (Mrs. Charles)	NM Oct. 17, 1840/S	"The Evergreen"
"Maud," "Little"	Go Aug. 1871/S	"The Broken Lily"
Maywood, Mary	Al May 2, 1840/S	"Ever Still Must I Adore Thee"
McClellan, Miss A. J.	BP Nov. 8, 1834/S	"The Sea Boy to His Barque"
M'Cord, Miss E.	Gr July 1853/P	"May-Flower Mazurka"
Mendelssohn, Fanny	BM Dec. 1842/S	"Ave Maria"
Miles, Mrs. [Jane Mary?]	Go Jan. 1835/S	"The Bonnie Wee Wife"
Millard, Mrs. Philip (Virtue)	Al Aug. 29, 1829/S	"Alice Gray"
	Al May 8, 1830/S	"The Soldier's Return"
	Go Feb. 1831/S	"Alice Gray"
	NM Aug. 20, 1831/S	"Alice Gray"
	BP Mar. 10, 1832/S	"Alice Gray"
	Al Jan. 26, 1833/S	"Forget Thee, My Susie"
	NY Dec. 9, 1837/S	"Ellen of Lindale"
Mogford, Mrs. See Fricker, Anne		
Moore, Frances J.	LH Feb. 1894/P	"Aberdeen Waltzes"
	LH July 1896/P	"Lyndon Polka"
[F. J. Hatton-Moore]	LH Nov. 1898/C	"The Message of the Bells"
Morrison, Mrs. Mary	Pe June 1866/P	"Grand March Victorious"
	Pe Oct. 1866/P	"The Silvery Sparkling Polka"
Mounsey, Miss [Ann]	NY Apr. 29, 1837/S	"The Merry, Merry Spring"
"Nita"	Pe Mar. 1861/P	"The Heath Polka"
Norton, Mrs. Caroline	Gr Jan. 1842/S	"Thy Name Was Once a Magic Spell" b
	Pe Aug. 1862/S	"Juanita"
	Pe Aug. 1877/S	"Juanita"
Orme, Mrs., "of Edinburgh"	NM Feb. 4, 1832/S	"I'm Far Away from Thee, Mary"
Palmer, Mrs. H. W. T.	Go June 1862/P	"Carrie Polka"
Paterson, Mrs. J. A.	LH May 1904/P	"Panamanikin Two-Step"
Paton, Mary Ann. See Wood, Mrs. Mary Ann		
Reitmeyer, Wilse	Go May 1875/P	"Lyda Polka"
	Go Dec. 1876/P	"Merry Christmas Quickstep"
Robinson, Mrs. Alfred	BP Feb. 21, 1835/S	"The Last Link"
Robinson, Frances C.	LH June 1898/S	"First Summer Days"
Rogers, Mrs. Clara Kathleen	Go Jan. 1896/P	"Allegro giojoso"

Rowland, Ethel	LH Dec. 1912/C	"The Garden of the Christmas Fairy"
Scott, Lady John Douglas	Pe Mar. 1878/S	"Douglas, Tender and True"
Scrooby, Miss	BW Nov. 23, 1839/S	"To Reason's Isle a Bark There Came"
Sheldon, Lillian Tait or Traitt	LH Jan. 1897/S	"Rock-a-by-baby Lullaby"
Shindler, Mrs. See Dana, Mrs. Mary S. B.		
Shipman, Miss Mary E.	Cr Vol. 10, [1854]/S	"The Parting of Summer"
	Cr Vol. 10, [1854]/S	"Come Home!"
Sloman, Anne (or Ann)	Co Jan. 1844/S	"Let Me Perish in the Early Spring"
	Co Feb. 1844/S	"The Chain that Links My Heart to Thine"
	Co Apr. 1844/S	"The Willow by the Well"
	Co June 1844/S	"The Braid of Sunny Hair"
	Co Aug. 1844/S	"The Days that Are Past"
	Co Nov. 1844/S	"Go and Forget"
	Co Feb. 1845/S	"The Parting"
	Co Apr. 1845/S	"Wo's Me, Wo's Me"
	Co June 1845/S	"Sometimes Remember Me"
[Miss Sloman]	Gr July 1845/S	"Song of the Spring"
[Miss Sloman]	Gr Aug. 1845/S	"The Star"
	Co Aug. 1845/S	"When through the Toilsome Roads of Life"
[Miss Sloman]	Gr Sept. 1845/S	"The Appeal"
	Co Oct. 1845/S	"The Gondolier"
	Co Dec. 1845/S	"Good Night! Good Night!"
	Co Mar. 1846/S	"The Midnight Wind"
	Co May 1846/S	"A Dreamer's Song"
	Co Sept. 1846/S	"Recall Me Not"
	Co Oct. 1846/S	"Memory"
	Co Feb. 1847/S	"Ever Away on the Stormy Sea"
	Co Aug. 1847/S	"Thou Shalt Sing to Me"
	Sa Sept. 1847/S	"Summer Days"
	Co Oct. 1847/S	"The Moonbeam"
	Sa Nov. 1847/S	"The Emigrant Maiden"
	Co Nov. 1847/S	"The Heart that's True"
	Co Dec. 1847/S	"The Bridal Wreath"
	Sa June 1848/S	"Song of a Greek Islander in Exile"
	Cr Vol. 10, [1854]/S	"Ever Away on the Stormy Sea"
Smith, Jessie Love. See Gaynor, Jessie Love		
Smith, Lydia B.	Cr Vol. 8, [1852]/S	"The Lily Bells"
Smith, Miss	NM Apr. 17, 1831/S	"Spirit of Music"
	NM June 21, 1834/S	"The False One"
[Penelope Smith]	Al June 18, 1836/S	"A Place in Thy Memory, Dearest"
[Penelope Smith]	Go Jan. 1837/S	"A Place in Thy Memory, Dearest"
[Penelope Smith]	NY Jan. 6, 1838/S	"A Place in Thy Memory, Dearest"
Smith, Rosalie E.	Go Sept. 1861/P	"Bonnie Jeanie Polka"
	Go Apr. 1862/P	"Prince Alfred Waltz"
	Go Oct. 1862/P	"Bermuda Galop"

Spottiswoode, Alicia Anne.
  See Scott, Lady John
  Douglas
Stanley, Alma   LH Feb. 1921/S   "The Lincoln Who Lives"
Stirling-Maxwell, Lady W.
  See Norton, Mrs. Caroline
Stith, Mrs. Townsend (or   Go Nov. 1830/S   "Our Friendship"
  Townshend)
Stockton, Morris. See   Go Mar. 1834/S   "Good Night"
  Terhune, Anice
Sullivan, Mrs. Marion Dix   Go Apr. 1850/S   "The Bridal"
Taylor, Gussie E.   Cr Vol. 3 [1856]/S   "I Am Not Changed"
Terhune, Anice   LH Nov. 1920/S   "The Turkey and the Pilgrim"
                                 LH Dec. 1920/S   "Christmas Waits"
                                 LH Apr. 1922/S   "Easter Morning"
Tillinghast, Mrs [William?]   Cr Vol. 10, [1854]/S "The Blind Boy's Been at Play,
                                                        Mother"
Turnbull, Mrs. Walter   NM Mar. 1, 1834/S   "Our Village Home"
  [Anne?]
Turpin, Miss. See Wallack,
  Mrs. Henry
Wallack, Mrs. Henry   NM July 21, 1838/S   "Oh! When Wilt Thou Return"
Walsh, Mary E.   Go Sept. 1880/P   "Black Hawk Waltz"
Waylett, Mrs. [Harriet?]   LC June 1840/S   "My Own Green Isle: Irish
                                                        Maiden's Song"
Welsh, Mrs. T[homas]   Go June 1834/S   "Sweet Lavender"
Wentworth, Eveleen W.   Ar Mar. 1895/P   "Dreamland Waltz"
Whilldin, Mrs. H. C.   Pe Dec. 1873/P   "Minnehaha March"
White, Elizabeth Anne   Co June 1846/S   "A Sister's Grave"
                                 Co Mar. 1847/S   "The Voice of Sorrow"
                                 Co May 1847/S   "Lament on the Death of Maj.
                                                        Ringgold"
                                 Co Sept. 1847/S   "The Lonely Bird"
                                 Co Feb. 1848/S   "Midnight Musings"
                                 Co May 1848/S   "Mother, I Die! Farewell!"
Wilson, Mrs. Cornwall Baron   Al July 23, 1831/S   "My Early Love"
  (Margaret)
                                 Al Feb. 20, 1836/S   "Our Auld Roof Tree"
                                 NM Apr. 9, 1836/S   "Hame Is No Longer a Hame
                                                        for Me"
Wilson, Mary Ann. See
  Welsh, Mrs. T.
Wisman, Julia Marie   LH June 1907/P   "Machigonne Waltz"
Wood, Mrs. Mary Ann   Al Sept. 21, 1833/S   "Return, Return Again"
Wood, Ada Gertrude   LH June 1903/P   "American Girl Two-Step"
Worrell, Edna Randolph   LH Dec. 1902/C   "The Toys' Rebellion"
                                 LH Jan. 1909/S   "Don't Stop Praying"
                                 LH Dec. 1914/S   "For the Christ-Child's Sake"
                                 LH May 1915/C   "Flag Makers"
                                 LH Oct. 1920/S   "Little Orphant Annie"

| Yates, Mrs. M. | LC Oct. 1835/S | "Fly Pretty Butterfly" |
| Young, Ella V. | Ar June 1869/P | "President Grant's Polka" |

a. "Come to the Sunset Tree" or "Evening Song of the Tyrolese," is often listed as the work of Mrs. Hemans, who wrote the words, but the music is by her sister, Harriet Mary Browne Hughes.
b. The song had words by Mrs. Norton but is listed in the 1870 *Catalog* with music by either Norton or Cowell. Miss A. Cowell's other songs all have words by Mrs. Norton, so it is likely that she also composed the music for "Thy Name Was Once a Magic Spell."
c. This work is actually by Paul Schmidt, with words by Mrs. Hemans. The attributions are backward in the magazine.

NOTES

1. The fifteen journals were selected for their influence and literary quality, the presence of works by more than one woman, and their availability on microfilm. For specific reel locations and excellent background information, consult Hoornstra and Heath, *American Periodicals.*

2. Appendix 8.1 presents a summary of music by women in each of the fifteen selected magazines; appendix 8.2 lists the titles and location of works for each woman.

3. Shevelow, *Women and Print Culture*, 187.

4. Fatout, "Threnodies," exemplifies this attitude of disdain.

5. The history of women's magazines is traced in several studies, including Adburgham's *Women in Print*, Foster's "Earliest Precursor," White's *Women's Magazines*, and Woodward's *Lady Persuaders.*

6. The emergence of the gender construction in women's magazines from the eighteenth century to the present has been based on the notion that "women's duties, although based in nature, require the intervention of culture," whereas "periodical publishers do not seem to think that men need the same kind of instruction in being men that women need in being women" (Shevelow, *Women and Print Culture*, 191, 196). Shevelow concludes, "Unlike men's magazines, which tend to specialize around certain pastimes or interests rather than gender in itself, the women's magazines first and foremost address their readers as women" (196).

7. Kribbs estimates the numbers of subscribers and readers of American household journals in *American Literary Periodicals.* The titles of many periodicals changed frequently, probably in an effort to market periodicals to the widest possible audience. The *Columbian Lady's and Gentleman's Magazine* appears to have been aimed at both sexes, yet this magazine contained the highest proportion of music by women of any of the selected periodicals. *Graham's Magazine* absorbed *Burton's Gentleman's Magazine* and was known variously through the years as *Graham's Lady's and Gentleman's Magazine* and *Graham's American Monthly Magazine.* The best discussion and history of American magazines remains Mott's *History of American Magazines.*

8. Wilder, *Little Town on the Prairie*, 91.

9. Despite the decline of music in *Godey's*, a memorable series of twenty-

four articles by Rupert Hughes discussed outstanding American composers, including twenty-two women. In "Music in America IX" Hughes mentions composers Faustina Hasse Hodges, Amy Beach, Clara Kathleen Rogers, Margaret Ruthven Lang, Patty Stair, Fanny M. Spencer, Harriet P. Sawyer, Laura Sedgwick Collins, Mary Knight Wood, Helen Hood, Constance Maud, Jenny Prince Black, Gertrude Griswold, Georgina Schuyler, Alice L. Pitman, Marie S. Hammer, Rose Mansfield Eversole, Ella C. Howard, Josephine Rand, Julie Rivé-King, and Josephine Gro. "Music in America XXIII" includes discussion of Jessie Love Gaynor.

10. *Godey's* commissioned works from such composers as Julian Cramer, J. Starr Holloway, Edward Ambuhl, B. S. Barrett, and Charles Neilson. The *Ladies' Home Journal* commissioned works from such figures as Cécile Chaminade, Moritz Moszkowski, Richard Strauss, Edvard Grieg, Eduard Strauss, and Ignace Paderewski.

11. The cultivation of music by accomplished young ladies in nineteenth-century England was satirized by Jane Austen in *Pride and Prejudice*, 142–46, and by Charlotte Brontë in *Jane Eyre*, 133–34.

12. Tick, *American Women Composers*, 33–56.

13. A case in point is offered by *Graham's American Magazine*, which offered music regularly from 1829 through 1853, then omitted music entirely in 1854. Apparently due to readers' demands, the magazine not only restored music in 1855 but included two pieces per month, instead of the one selection that had been customary in prior years.

14. Tick, *American Women Composers*, 73–143.

15. Excerpts from contemporary operas by Giacchino Rossini, Vincenzo Bellini, and Michael Balfe appeared in weekly or bimonthly literary papers published in New York and Boston during the 1830s (*Albion, New York Mirror, New-Yorker, Boston Pearl, Boston Weekly Magazine*, and *Boston Miscellany*). The excerpts reveal that even technically difficult selections from the theater and concert stage were acceptable as home entertainment.

16. For example, the Philadelphia firm of Lee and Walker supplied *Graham's Magazine* with most of its music from 1850 to 1856, and the Philadelphia firms of Edward L. Walker and Septimus Winner supplied several magazines, including *Graham's, Arthur's*, and *Peterson's*. Musical editors at the magazines included James G. Osbourn, who was active with *Godey's* in the 1830s and at *Graham's* in the 1840s, and J. A. Getze, who selected music for *Arthur's Home Magazine* from 1866 until 1872.

17. Shevelow, *Women and Print Culture*, 190.

18. Board of Music Trade, *Complete Catalogue of Sheet Music*.

19. Koza presents a detailed study of music up to 1877 in *Godey's* by analyzing musical examples, illustrations, articles about music, and references in articles and stories in her recent article "Music and the Feminine Sphere," taken from material in her dissertation, "Music and References to Music in Godey's Book, 1830–1877."

20. Not included in the survey are women who rearranged the work of

another composer (e.g., Kate Douglas Wiggin, who supplied new words and adapted works by Franz Abt and Anton Rubinstein for the *Ladies' Home Journal*). Such *contrafacta* were common throughout the century.

21. Biographical sources include Cohen's *International Encyclopedia*, Skowronski's *Women in American Music*, Stern's *Women Composers*, Ammer's *Unsung*, and Hixon and Hennessee's *Women in Music*.

22. Clare W. Beames, who published songs in the *Columbian Magazine* and *New-Yorker*, is a case in point. Beames was included in this list until advertisements for "Mr. Clare W. Beames, organist, etc." were found in the 1858 *New York Musical World*.

23. Could there be a connection between Claribel and Coralie Bell, who published in *Godey's* at roughly the same time, such as Coralie Bell being an earlier pseudonym for Charlotte Barnard? Further evidence is lacking, but the similarity of names is intriguing.

24. In the case of young Augusta Browne, a review in the *New York Mirror* ("New Music") indicates that she submitted her work to the paper in hopes of publication: " 'I would I were a Fairy,' written by R. F. Houseman, composed and dedicated to Miss Euphemia Patton, of Philadelphia, by her friend Miss Augusta Browne. The music is pretty and fairy-like, and gives us a good opinion of the talents and accomplishments of the young lady to whom we are indebted for the copy upon our desk. The words are well worth the honour of being transferred to the columns of the Mirror." Although the poem by Houseman was printed, Browne's music never appeared in the *New York Mirror* (compare Tick, *American Women Composers*, 151 and n. 28).

25. Cyganowski, *Magazine Editors*, 312.

26. Men also found that magazines presented a valuable opportunity for publication of their compositions. Male composers whose works appeared frequently in household magazines included Charles E. Horn, Henry Russell, Henry Bishop, George Herbert Rodwell, Michael Balfe, G. A. Hodson, John Augustine Wade, George Alexander Lee, John Barnett, Joseph Phillip Knight, Samuel Lover, Charles W. Glover, Septimus Winner, George Root, Franz Abt, J. Starr Holloway, George Linley, James G. Maeder, Arthur Sullivan, Alfred Scott Gatty, and Hart Pease Danks.

27. Only the *Ladies' Home Journal* contains confirmation of commissions. In the November 1893 issue Bok wrote that the cost of including a new work of music was more than $8,500, including the "author's work, the composition, electrotyping plates, paper, printing, etc." (13).

REFERENCES

Adburgham, Alison. *Women in Print: Writing Women and Women's Magazines from the Restoration to the Accession of Victoria*. London: George Allen and Unwin, 1972.
Ammer, Christine. *Unsung: A History of Women in American Music*. Westport, Conn.: Greenwood Press, 1980.
Austen, Jane. *Pride and Prejudice*. London: Folio Society, 1975.

Board of Music Trade of the United States of America. *Complete Catalogue of Sheet Music and Musical Works, 1870.* New York: Da Capo Press, 1973.

Brontë, Charlotte. *Jane Eyre.* New York: Random House, 1943.

Cohen, Aaron. *International Encyclopedia of Women Composers.* 2d ed. New York: Books and Music, 1987.

Cyganowski, Carol Klimick. *Magazine Editors and Professional Authors in Nineteenth-Century America: The Genteel Tradition and the American Dream.* New York: Garland, 1988.

Fatout, Paul. "Threnodies of the Ladies' Books." *Musical Quarterly* 31 (October 1945): 464–78.

Foster, Dorothy. "The Earliest Precursor of Our Present Day Monthly Miscellanies." *Publications of the Modern Language Association of America* 32, no. 1 (1917): 22–58.

Hixon, Don L., and Hennessee, Don. *Women in Music: A Biobibliography.* Metuchen, N.J.: Scarecrow Press, 1975.

Hoornstra, Jean, and Trudy Heath, eds. *American Periodicals 1741–1900: An Index to the Microfilm Collections.* Ann Arbor, Mich.: University Microfilms International, 1979.

Hughes, Rupert. "Music in America IX—The Women Composers." *Godey's Magazine,* January 1896, 30–40.

———. "Music in America XXIII—The Chicago Colony." *Godey's Magazine,* July 1897, 80–87.

Koza, Julia Eklund. "Music and References to Music in Godey's Lady's Book, 1830–1877." 4 vols. Ph.D. diss., University of Minnesota, 1988.

———. "Music and the Feminine Sphere: Images of Women as Musicians in Godey's Lady's Book, 1830–1877." *Musical Quarterly* 75 (Summer 1991): 103–29.

Kribbs, Jayne K. *An Annotated Bibliography of American Literary Periodicals, 1741–1850.* Boston: G. K. Hall, 1977.

Mott, Frank Luther. *A History of American Magazines.* 5 vols. Cambridge, Mass.: Belknap Press, 1930–68.

"New Music." *New York Mirror,* 25 September 1841, 311.

Shevelow, Kathryn. *Women and Print Culture: Constructing Femininity in the Early Periodical.* London: Routledge, Chapman, and Hall, 1989.

Skowronski, JoAnn. *Women in American Music: A Bibliography.* Metuchen, N.J.: Scarecrow Press, 1978.

Stern, Susan. *Women Composers: A Handbook.* Metuchen, N.J.: Scarecrow Press, 1978.

Tick, Judith. *American Women Composers before 1870.* Studies in Musicology, no. 57. Ann Arbor, Mich.: UMI Research Press, 1983.

White, Cynthia L. *Women's Magazines: 1693–1968.* London: Michael Joseph, 1976.

Wilder, Laura Ingalls. *Little Town on the Prairie.* New York: Harper and Row, 1941.

Woodward, Helen. *The Lady Persuaders.* New York: Ivan Obolensky, 1960.

9

Feminine or Masculine:
The Conflicting Nature of Female Images
in Rap Music

Venise T. Berry

We all have a certain picture to paint.
Sisters are just evening the scales;
setting things straight.
                    —Queen Latifah, 1990

The feminist movement for black women has evolved into a powerful
and necessary cultural dynamic in recent years. Critics within this
discourse have found a significant difference between feminist theory
and black feminist theory. According to bell hooks in *Talking Back:
Thinking Feminist—Thinking Black*, both movements grew out of the
need for women to speak for themselves, yet the message of black
women is different from that of white women because their circumstances are different.[1]

While the white middle-class woman in U.S. history was cared for
and catered to in her silence, the black woman was often the caretaker
and caterer. Female oppression for black females was heightened because their rejection involved being both female and black.[2] The personal independence and equality that white women fight for is not the
same for black women. The black woman has maintained an unsoli-
cited independent work status since the days of slavery, an independence that is inextricably linked to the black social and political movement as well as the black man, who remains an integral part of her
struggle. Because of these differences, bell hooks calls for varied strategies for participation in the feminist movement: "Because each individual starts the process of engagement in feminist struggle at a
unique level of awareness, very real differences in experience, per-

spective and knowledge make developing varied strategies for partic-ipation and transformation a necessary agenda."[3]

The major connection, then, between the black feminist and fem-inist movements is the finding of voice, ultimately public voice. The major difference is the direction and meaning of the message that voice will carry. Valerie Smith says many black feminist theorists argue that the meaning of blackness in the United States profoundly shapes the experience of gender, and, in the same vein, the conditions of wom-anhood specifically affect the experience of race.[4] Speaking out in either venue has been difficult for black women, if not impossible. Yet, ac-cording to hooks, speaking out is essential: "Speaking becomes both a way to engage in active self-transformation and a rite of passage where one moves from being object to being subject. Only as subjects can we speak. As objects, we remain voiceless—our beings defined and interpreted by others."[5]

As both feminist movements grew into popular social and political operations, they developed a public voice, and their issues remained separate yet connected. As a result, questions of gender roles, per-spectives, and images have led to a rethinking of traditional ideology, particularly in music. The internal struggle for black feminine identity in music is ongoing, and today in rap music the positive images and messages of black female rappers are loud and clear. This essay explores the unique contributions of the black female experience through the conscious development of a black feminist voice in the popular music genre of rap. It examines the need for rethinking popular assumptions and perspectives about stereotypical roles of feminine and masculine in relation to today's rap music phenomenon.

Female Images and Roles in Music

One result of this evolutionary consciousness among feminists, black and white, has been the much talked about negative, stereotypical female roles in music. Music is a business. It is the business of mar-keting a product for profit, and research has shown that sex can sell.[6] A study by Larry Lance and Christina Berry found a significant increase between 1968 and 1977 in the number of popular songs with impli-cations of sexual intercourse and in the number of females initiating those sexual encounters.[7]

Negative sexual images of females in the male-dominated music industry is a prominent topic of criticism. Men dominate the pop music arena, defining sex role standards from a patriarchal perspective.[8] Research indicates that in country music a woman's role and status is usually related to her ability to get and hold a man.[9] Colleen Hyden and N. Jane McCandless have found that women are typically portrayed as youthful, passive, and childlike in contemporary popular music.[10] Susan Butruille and Anita Taylor have identified three prominent female images in popular music: the ideal women or saint; the evil/fickle witch, sinner, or whore; and the victim (usually dead). In the same study women were most often shown as sex objects, possessions, or providers in black music culture.[11]

Rock music and music videos have come under intense scrutiny. Barry Sherman and Joseph Dominick examined 366 rock music videos and found a significant amount of violence, sex, and other aggressive acts directed at women.[12] Women were also portrayed in a condescending manner in an overwhelming number of music videos examined by Richard Vincent, Dennis Davis, and Lilly Boruszkowski.[13] Christine Hansen and Ronald Hansen found in their studies that images in rock music videos suggest women are considered more nonthreatening, submissive, sexual, and sympathetic when they return the man's advances.[14] Finally, Jane Brown and Kenneth Campbell report that females, both black and white, are rarely portrayed on MTV or Video Soul as professionals; however, black women in their study were least likely to be found in roles projecting antisocial behavior or victimization.[15]

Research on the acceptance and perpetuation of stereotypical images of women in American culture is prominent and has shown that the application of gender labels and other stereotypical attributes are learned as early as the age of three.[16] Sex role stereotypes are linked to specific gender-related activities and domains, such as girls playing inside with dolls and boys outside playing with guns.[17] Many studies have illustrated the importance of gender relations and appropriate activity selection in the United States, suggesting that children are taught these roles through peer interaction, socialization, and cultural experience.[18]

Many critics have acknowledged that other music, such as the blues, reflects the sexual exploitation of women. Themes that emerged in a 1988 book about the blues by Daphne Harrison included infidelity, sexual exploitation, and mistreatment. Harrison argued that women in blues usually do not joke about lost love but instead sing of grief, while men brag about their conquests and exploits with women.[19] Mary Ellison, in her book *Lyrical Protests: Black Music's Struggle against Discrimination*, agreed. She discussed such female blues singers as Ma Rainey, Bessie Smith, and Victoria Spivey, who often sang about inadequate men, but she also found the music of female blues reflects black women's strong determination to lead their own lives.[20] Hazel Carby's analysis of the sexual politics of women's blues explained how important "classic blues" were for women: "What has been called 'Classic Blues,' is the women's blues of the twenties and early thirties. It is a discourse that articulates a cultural and political struggle over sexual relations; a struggle that is directed against the objectification of female sexuality within a patriarchal order, but which also tries to reclaim women's bodies as the sexual and sensual subjects of women's songs."[21]

The struggle for independence, equality, and freedom among black women, Ellison also pointed out, has been a part of black music styles from slavery to the present: "There is an explosive dynamism coursing through the songs that black women write specifically about themselves—a tension that springs from the determination to free themselves from male domination and misuse, conflicting with a strong resolution to stand with black men in the fight for the liberation of all black people."[22]

This spirit of rebellion and independence was a major part of music in the 1960s. Ellison observed that Aretha Franklin's popular hit "Respect," insisting that respect be given to black women and men, became a banner for the civil rights movement.[23] She also discussed other contemporary black women, like Millie Jackson and Grace Jones, who sang of independence and individuality through female role reversals.[24]

Evolving Rap Music Style

The negative images and messages concerning women in rap music have spawned tremendous publicity. As Reebee Garofalo explained, it is the frankness of rap that creates many of its problems. While making no excuses for rap stars, he suggests that the sexism in rap is a product of all genres of popular music and life in the United States.[25] Music has long been a powerful form of expression in black culture, with rap music stretching and redefining previous boundaries. Born in the New York streets of Harlem and the South Bronx, rap evolved as part of the privileged black male urban street culture, popularizing black dialect, street fashion, style, attitude, and mannerisms.

David Toop in *The Rap Attack* related the evolution of rap music to the griot in West Africa, who was a great singing storyteller and served as a living history book. He went on to link this oral genre to other powerful black traditions, like oral preaching, rhyming stories called toasts, and verbal rhyming word games, such as the "dozens" and "signifying," all popular in urban black neighborhoods and resembling the rhythmic talking style of rap. These cultural legacies were specifically black male traditions. They were a prominent part of the black male experience carried out wherever black men gathered—on street corners or in bars, the armed forces, and prisons.[26]

Male-privileged space is a primary issue for Lisa Lewis in her evaluation of female images on MTV. She explains that the street is traditionally a place for males to explore freedom, rebellious practice, male bonding, and female pursuit. For women, however, the streets are dangerous, feared, and inappropriate. Women on the street are considered prostitutes, or whores, objects of male desire and dominance.[27]

Rap music, a product of black male tradition and experience, has defined the images of women from that limited perspective. Many male rap groups tend to view women with a common lack of respect, but controversial groups like the 2 Live Crew, The Ghetto Boys, Easy E, and Too Short perpetuate extreme negatives. In many male rap videos, the female body is presented as a product of male sexual pleasure; candid shots of breasts, crotches, and buttocks are the norm. Women in these raps are called "skeezers," "hoes," "sluts," "whores," and "bitches." They are described as objects to be sexually used, physically and verbally abused.

The most controversial example is 2 Live Crew, a group whose music has killed love and romance and has taken sex into the realm of perversion, violence, and pain. Many of their song titles can serve as examples of their sexist ideology: "We Want Some Pussy," "Me So Horny," "Head, Booty, and Cock," "Bad Ass Bitch," "Face Down, Ass Up," and "Dick Almighty." The cover of their album "As Nasty as They Wanna Be" flaunts the well-endowed buttocks of four black women in G-strings standing on a table with their backs turned and legs spread. Members of the 2 Live Crew position themselves in front of the women, each centered between a pair of legs, facing the camera. Luther Campbell, leader of the group, argues that his music is no worse than the work of Eddie Murphy or Andrew Dice Clay. In his defense he explains that "bitch" is an endearing term: "We're talking about a hell of a woman who ain't gonna take shit—one of those Dynasty, Alexis type motherfuckers. That's what I like in a woman. I want me a real Bitch, not some pushover."[28]

The hearings of Parents Music Resource Center (PMRC) have led to questions of censorship; however, it must again be noted that music is a business and that sex sells. Major record companies are currently dealing with the controversy of labeling sexually explicit and violent albums as they see fit. Geffen, for example, chose to drop The Ghetto Boys because of their obscenity, while Atlantic Records, in the midst of the media controversy, purchased an interest in the 2 Live Crew's Luke Records.[29]

In the profit-oriented music industry the success of sexually explicit acts is fantastic, considering the lack of radio and television airplay. The 2 Live Crew's album *Nasty as They Wanna Be*, with no video or other major advertising, made the *Rolling Stone* top fifty album chart. Because of the controversy created in their obscenity trials, the album leaped from number forty-four to sixteen in a two-week period.[30] It also outsold the clean version, *As Clean as They Wanna Be*, by nine to one.[31]

In all fairness it should be noted there is a significant number of male rap groups that do not advocate misogyny or violence toward women. Rappers like KRS One, A Tribe Called Quest, Jungle Brothers, and De La Soul are attempting to unify rappers and rap fans through positive information and education. Positive rap efforts are bringing male and female rap stars together to speak against gang violence and black-on-black crime, while empowering the black rap community as a whole.

While it is crucial to confront the perpetuation of sexism in rap music, Lewis suggests moving away from an emphasis on male attitude and behavior and instead focusing on the powerful messages and images of today's popular female stars.[32] Women as contrasting voices, "others," have created a new dialogue in rap music, challenging those negative, male-oriented perspectives. Their music reflects the same macho style and aggressive delivery, but it includes black feminist ideology that tests the line between socially accepted male and female roles.

According to Toop, male rappers were willing to accept female rappers but considered them lacking in the competitiveness necessary to survive and succeed in rap.[33] To compete in the male-dominated music industry, women are serious and hard-hitting in their lyrics and delivery style. The stereotypical portrayals of women as weak, stupid, and sexually out of control conflict with the new identity projected by female rappers. Their lyrical story line and performance style demonstrate an unyielding intelligence and strength.

The popularity of black female rappers comes as no surprise in light of the cultural experience of black women in the United States. The foundation of black music as a spoken song has always included women. Toop describes African women who also developed cultural legacies, such as lampoons and galla abusive poems. These expressions of hostility or hate were usually sung. In this tradition the hostile words of Yoruba women became lyrical poetry. Toop also mentions other prominent black women singers who serve as evolutionary examples of the black feminine voice in African American music: Dorothy Norwood, a prominent gospel storyteller; the sermonette singer Edna Gallman Cooke; the pioneer soul rappers Laura Lee and Irma Thomas; and finally, Millie Jackson, who was dubbed the mistress of musical raps. These women have all played a crucial role in the development of the rap music genre.[34]

In the late 1970s it was a female producer, Sylvia Robinson, who recognized and signed the first popular rap group, The Sugar Hill Gang. Their big hit, "Rapper's Delight," set the stage for today's rap music explosion.[35] Female rap artists have been phenomenally successful in proving their worth in the industry. Salt 'N Pepa strengthened the legacy started by the "Roxanne" hits when they vaulted up *Billboard's* pop charts, going platinum in 1987 with their first album, *Hot, Cool, and Vicious*, featuring the hit single "Push It."[36]

To better understand how female rappers are redefining the rap experience, this essay explores four pioneering female rap groups and their music—Salt 'N Pepa, MC Lyte, Queen Latifah, and Oaktown 3 5 7. This analysis of their powerful presence examines the use of image, fashion, performance, attitude, and lyrical context as a representative emergence of black feminist empowerment. One video was selected from each for critical analysis. Background information was obtained from secondary sources to better assess the group's views on black feminist issues and ideologies.

Salt 'N Pepa, "Express Yourself"

Salt 'N Pepa represents a historical turning point for the acceptance of females in rap. The Real Roxanne and Roxanne Shante were the first female rappers to break into the commercial market by knocking each other verbally, but their popular rap battles did not last. Salt 'N Pepa was the first female rap group to sustain true commercial success. Salt (Cheryl James), Pepa (Sandy Denton), and their DJ Spinderella (Dee Dee Roper) are all from Queens, New York. According to Ra'Chaun, female groups, especially Salt 'N Pepa, were under great pressure in the beginning to prove themselves because the "Roxanne" hits did not sustain their commercial success over time: "In the early days, they [female rappers] were dissed [put down] by male rappers who believed they were sisters who could rap, but were in their own words 'only females.' "37

In performance the group's style is strong, witty, and assertive. They move easily in and out of the variety of female roles and images established by their male counterparts and redefined by themselves. The balance between feminism and femininity seems to be a delicate one. Salt, Pepa, and Spinderella are often featured in magazines as stereotypically female, talking about hair, clothes, and makeup. Their efforts to maintain a duality between feminine and masculine roles is explained by Spinderella: "We're showing all of those guys that we can be just as hard, just as def [good] as they can and still be proud to be females."38

As women of the 80s, the group is known for its independent attitude and confident prowoman style.39 "We're feminists," Salt declares. "We're doing something that only guys are expected to do and doing it right. At our concerts, we'll do one hard core rap, then one where we'll be real sexy."40

"Expression" (1989) is about taking control. It explores the need for women to be themselves and to be able to do the things they want to do. As the video opens, Salt, Pepa, and Spinderella walk toward the camera in gangster-style suits and hats. This image is juxtaposed with a homeless man and woman on the street. The camera moves into the studio for candid shots of family interaction. These alternating ideas on screen reflect a changing image and consciousness for black women. The basic premise of the song and video is how important it is for women to express themselves.

The group goes on to model in traditionally feminine attire; they rap, in leather jackets and jeans, in the male-privileged space of the street; and then they dance in a studio setting in sleeveless blouses and low-cut tank tops, tastefully covered by jackets. In "Expression" Pepa rhythmically voices her understanding of who she is and her awareness of the dominant male system in rap:

> Yes, I'm blessed and I know who I am.
> I express myself on every jam.
> I'm not a man, but I'm in command.
> Hot damn, I got an all girl band.

The video's message focuses on change, as the homeless woman finds a hat, previously worn by Pepa, in the trash, which seems to give her renewed strength when she puts it on. This scenario further stresses the need to pass on positive black female identity. Salt has begun to produce for the group, crossing another crucial barrier in gender stereotyping in the music industry. She produced four of the thirteen tracks on their album *Black's Magic,* including "Expression," which subsequently has gone gold.[41]

MC Lyte, "Stop, Look, Listen"

MC Lyte (Lana Moore) was the first female rapper to perform on the Arsenio Hall show, opening a window across the nation on the potential of female rappers.[42] Writer Al Periera believes that her musical style and cultural background are interrelated in her music: "Part of the thrill of listening to one of Lyte's cut to the chase jams is that it neatly reflects the unpredictable, violent and funny Brooklyn streets."[43]

MC Lyte is also struggling with conflicting gender roles and labels. She has been described as "tough, yet tender," "one part soft, one part hard," and "a no-nonsense, straightforward lady, not the kind of girl who reminds you that girls are suppose to be all sugar and spice."[44]

"Stop, Look, Listen" focuses on the ability of MC Lyte to compete in the tough hard world of rap. The video begins with a transition from the airport to her concert. While riding in the limousine, she is informed about the logistics of the concert, given a good luck message from her mother, and readied by her hairdresser. Shots of the police escort, screaming audience, and waiting body guards are intercut.

When MC Lyte steps out on stage, she wears a loose-hanging pantsuit, covered by a floor-length, matching black-and-blue jacket. In opposition to the image of Salt and Pepa's all female band, MC Lyte is surrounded by two male dancers, a male disc jockey, and two male bodyguards. She is fully covered, while Leg One and Leg Two, her dancers, wear jackets that are unbuttoned, exposing their bare chests. Several times during the show, MC Lyte joins in with her dancers, moving smoothly in and out of their routine. When bragging about her rapping ability, she also proves she is worthy competition orally.

Her concert footage is intercut with black-and-white shots of MC Lyte in the privileged male space of the street. She further challenges tradition when she raps on the street corner, which traditionally is associated with negative images of women as prostitutes. MC Lyte uses her dynamic rhyming style to put male rappers in their place:

> Save all your crocodile tears, grin and bear it
> and with all your other brothers you're gonna share it.
> You hear me Junior, Junior.
> Be a grown man with the mic in your hand
> and understand it's not part of the plan.

Through her strong, positive, and aggressive delivery style, MC Lyte turns the idea of feminine weakness and dependency upside down. Her music speaks to her personal determination and individuality. The small gold ring in her nose is another fashionable sign of her confidence and control. MC Lyte believes "female rappers are coming out with something to say. And, it is all beginning to open up, slowly, but surely."[45]

Queen Latifah, "Ladies First"

Queen Latifah (Dana Owens) was a high school basketball star in her hometown of East Orange, New Jersey. Her 1990 debut album, *All Hail the Queen*, received considerable press coverage and quickly confirmed her title as the Queen of Rap. Queen Latifah continues her positive messages of Afrocentricity, black consciousness, and womanism in her second album, *The Nature of a Sistah*. She defines her success as the ability to write and deliver her own raps: "If you have rhymes written for you, you are not really a rapper. It's not like you possess any talent if you don't do it yourself."[46]

When asked about the negative images of women by male rap artists, Queen Latifah says she doesn't put herself into those categories: "No rapper who has made a record that has words like Bitch get out my face or stupid slut has ever applied to me. I think the people who they're referring to are females who play themselves like that."[47]

Queen Latifah's historic video of "Ladies First" contains rare footage of a South African rebellion led by women in the 1960s.[48] It is the most pointedly political video discussed in this essay. "Ladies First" features guest appearances by such female rap artists as Monie Love, Shelly Thunder, and Ms. Melody. It also spotlights such black female leaders as Harriet Tubman, Rosa Parks, Angela Davis, and Winnie Mandela.

The video begins with photographs of past and present black female leaders projected across the background. Queen Latifah and Monie Love then appropriate the male terrain of an empty road. Monie Love (Simone Johnson) uses her British accent and background to add an international flavor to female rap. According to David Thigpen, Love's music sends a lighter message to women, about trust, reconciliation, and relationships, because she believes "too many rappers are too serious."[49] Monie Love begins her lyrical exposition by defending the position of womanhood:

> Believe me when I say being a woman is great you see

> I know that all the fellas out there will agree with me
> Not for being one but for being with one
> Cause when it's time for loving it's the woman that
> gives some
> Strong stepping strutting moving on
> Rhyming cutting but not forgetting
> We are the ones to give birth
> To the new generation of prophets.

We see shots of unified women rappers juxtaposed against footage of the South African rebellion. The delivery style of Queen Latifah is passionate yet calm and confident as she challenges all rappers, no matter what sex:

> Laying down track after track
> Waitin' for the climax
> When I get there that's when I tax
> The next man or next woman
> It doesn't make a difference
> keep the competition coming

Queen Latifah and Monie Love use their public voice to exert messages about their newfound independence and equality. A full-blown black feminist consciousness develops as Queen Latifah explains her plan to change the stereotypical feminine roles she encounters:

> I break into lyrical freestyle
> Grab the mic, look at the crowd and see smiles
> Cause they see a woman standing up on her own two
> Sloppy slouching is something I won't do
> Some think that we can't flow—can't flow!
> Stereotypes they got to go—got to go!
> I'm gonna mess around and flip the scene into reverse
> With what
> With a little touch of ladies first

In "Ladies First" Queen Latifah dispels the traditional ideas of what being female means and confronts assumptions about her potential head-on:

> Who said that the ladies couldn't make it?
> You must be blind
> If you don't believe well here listen to this rhyme
> Ladies first, there's no time to rehearse
> I'm divine and my mind expands throughout the
> universe
> A female rapper with a message to send
> The Queen Latifah is a perfect specimen

Throughout the video Queen Latifah dresses in various uniform-style suits, with matching turbans and African headwear. She carries herself with an air of royalty, while playing a game similar to chess. The glass board includes a map of South Africa, and the pieces are clenched fists raised high in the air, a popular black power symbol in the 1960s, and figurines of men wearing suits and holding briefcases.

When the game is won, Queen Latifah raises her fist in the air. She is surrounded by several black males, who do the same. This gesture reinforces the reality of black female independence, yet the inclusion of black men in the victory scene reflects a shared struggle and triumph for black men and women.

"Ladies First" is a testimonial to the power of women around the world. It specifically challenges the negative male perspectives in rap, the male-oriented music system black female rappers have encountered, and male-dominated society as it exists today. As an ardent member of the women's movement, Queen Latifah is very defensive about her rise in popularity. She demands credit for her talent: "Me, MC Lyte, and Roxanne Shante got record deals because we're good and we deserve them, not because we happen to be women."[50]

Oaktown 3 5 7, "Juicy Gotcha Krazy"

Oaktown 3 5 7 is a different style of female rap group. The group originally consisted of Terrible T (Tabatha King) and Sweet LD (Djuana Johnican), who were former dancers for the popular rapper MC Hammer, now Hammer. In fact, Oaktown 3 5 7 is considered a product of MC Hammer. According to Greg Brooks, an executive with Hammer's Bustin' Productions, Hammer controls the packaging and selling of its image: "If MC Hammer had to be a couple of ladies, Oaktown 3 5 7 is the way he would be. The image he has for himself, they also portray . . . they're like female MC Hammers."[51]

The name Oaktown 3 5 7 was bestowed on the members by MC Hammer after he decided to promote them as his female group. They wear the unique, flared balloon-style pants that Hammer has made popular, along with the more traditional, male-preferred, female fashions, such as skintight jumpsuits and suggestive multicolored bra-style tops emphasizing the breast area.

Despite Hammer's obvious control, Oaktown 3 5 7 has managed to project its own feminine perspective in many of its musical rhymes. The members clearly believe in black female empowerment. As one Terrible T stated, "Our music is the California sound which speaks about one's taking a stand, believing in yourself, telling men the real story about women and not being a follower."[52]

One of their biggest hits, "Juicy Gotcha Krazy," was the first song they wrote.[53] It is a parody about male sexual politics. The words "juicy" and "juice" in the rap refer to sex, particularly sexual control. The video starts with the women bragging about controlling their men through sex:

> You know I'm fine, you can't deny,
> you gonna try, I'll tell you why.
> He's on his knees, he copped a plea,
> he wanna get a piece of me.

On the surface this may sound like a negative, calumnious statement, but in listening further it becomes obvious that the group has actually turned the tables on the traditional ideology of male sexual dominance:

> Get off my tip, don't give me lip,
> or succa you get pistol whipped.
> He lost his mind, the very first time.
> Just a little bit of juice keeps him in line.

To further display their sexual power and control, Oaktown 3 5 7 tests the fragile male ego by implying a lack of satisfaction with his lovemaking ability:

> You just tease me, you don't please me,
> Talk real big, but you sleep easy.
> Making lots of noise like the women I know.
> The juice is good, now he can't let go.

They go on to expand this reverse sexual domination into a rally cry for "fly" (fine) girls and all women in general:.

> Bust it, yeah discuss it, yeah, It's our time.
> Fly girls get served 'cause the juice is so prime.
> Ladies don't you worry if your man gets out of line,
> just ration out the juice till it gets pay time.

With clothes that hug every curve on their bodies, Oaktown 3 5 7 prove they can dance in the style of their mentor, Hammer. They gyrate suggestively as their explosive sexual movements interact with the potent rhythm. Several times in the song when they say the word *juicy*, they actually point to or reach for the pleasure spot, completely free of all stereotypical female inhibitions. They also dance in the forbidden male environment, the middle of the street, flanked by four male dancers. Their aggressive delivery style, oppositional lyrical content, and purposeful display of sensuality present an alternative feminine picture of full control and defiance.

Conclusion

The development of a rap music genre based on male-privileged domain and practice is breaking down. The popularity of and identification with this redefined feminine rap discourse are reshaping the rap music experience. As conflicting gender dialogues are created, rap music will continue to change. New extreme female rap groups have emerged to challenge extreme male rappers.

Bytches with Problems (BWP) and Hoes with Attitudes are pushing the definitions of feminine and masculine even further. Both groups feature explicit lyrics and an outrageous style to get their point across. Their motto is "If men can do it, we can do it too." Lyndah and Tanisia Michelle of the group BWP explain how they use the word *bitch* as a badge of honor: "There is a little bitch in all women and even some men. And, I'm just the bitch to say it. We feel like we can say anything we want 'cause men sure do."[54]

Black female rappers and their music illustrate many of the changes underway that challenge the socially mandated norm of female sex roles. Each group examined in this essay uses its songs and videos to present alternative practices and meanings for femininity.

Black women rappers project a dualistic message that is a direct result of their dualistic experience in American society. They are independent *yet* oppressed, equal *but* not the same, and black *and* female. As their popularity continues to grow, so too must the consciousness of social and political stereotypical roles; with that consciousness should come an eventual understanding and significant dismantling of the patriarchal business of rap music.

The presence of black female rappers has toppled the stereotypical ideas of what and where women are supposed to be. Their lyrics present positive feminine images and messages that have begun to overshadow or at least call into question the stereotypical negative images and messages imparted by many male rappers. Through their public rhythmic voices these women are glorifying female prowess, redefining male practice and domain, and revolutionizing the black feminist experience. They have entered the privileged space of men, and because of their unity, strength, and talent, they have earned the right to belong.

NOTES

1. hooks, *Talking Back*, 20–21.
2. Hare and Hare, *Endangered Black Family*, 139–41.
3. hooks, *Talking Back*, 23.
4. Smith, "Black Feminist Theory," 47.
5. hooks, *Talking Back*, 12.
6. See, for example, Lance and Berry, "Has There Been a Sexual Revolution?"; Zillman and Mundorf, "Image Effects"; and Abramson and Mechanic, "Sex and the Media."
7. Lance and Berry, "Has There Been a Sexual Revolution?" 162.
8. Endres, "Sex Role Standards."
9. Saucier, "Healers and Heartbreakers."
10. Hyden and McCandless, "Lyrics of Contemporary Music."
11. Butruille and Taylor, "Women in American Popular Song."
12. Sherman and Dominick, "Violence and Sex in Music Videos."
13. Vincent, Davis, and Boruszkowski, "Sexism on MTV."
14. Hansen and Hansen, "Influence of Sex and Violence."
15. Brown and Campbell, "Race and Gender in Music Videos."
16. See, for example, Thompson, "Gender Labels"; Weinraub, Clemens, and Sockloff, "Development of Sex Role Stereotypes"; and Masters and Wilkerson, "Consensual and Discrimination Stereotypy."
17. See, for example, Blakemore, Larve, and Olejnik, "Sex Appropriate Toy Preference"; Eisenberg, Murray, and Hite, "Children's Reasoning"; and Ruble, Balaban, and Cooper, "Gender Constancy."
18. See, for example, Masters and Furman, "Friendship Selection"; Lamb and Roopnarine, "Peer Influences on Sex Role Development"; and Langlois and Downs, "Mothers, Fathers, and Peers as Socialization Agents."
19. Harrison, *Black Pearls*, 63–113.
20. Ellison, *Lyrical Protest*, 111.
21. Carby, " 'It Jus Be's Dat Way Sometime,' " 241.
22. Ellison, *Lyrical Protest*, 107.
23. Ibid., 115.
24. Ibid., 113.
25. Garofalo, "Crossing Over," 115.
26. Toop, *Rap Attack*, 47, 94.
27. Lewis, "Female Address in Music Video," 75.
28. Quoted in Ressner, "On the Road," 20, 24.
29. See, for example, Dimartino and Rosen, "Labeling Albums," 6; and Newman, Lichtman, and Haring, "Atlantic Invests in Crew Label."
30. "Top Fifty Albums," 74.
31. Roberts-Thomas, "Say It Loud," 30.
32. Lewis, "Form and Female Authorship," 356.
33. Toop, *Rap Attack*, 94.
34. Ibid., 47–48.

35. Ibid., 78.
36. Small and Abrahams, "Salt 'N Pepa," 113.
37. Ra'Chaun, "Salt 'N Pepa," 73.
38. Quoted in Small and Abrahams, "Salt 'N Pepa," 113.
39. DiPrima, "Bad Rap," 36.
40. Quoted in Small and Abrahams, "Salt 'N Pepa," 113.
41. Periera, "Salt 'N Pepa."
42. Periera, "MC Lyte."
43. Ibid., 76.
44. Peters, "MC Lyte," 55.
45. Quoted in Turner, "First Ladies of Rap," 60.
46. Quoted in Gray, "All Hail the Queen," 46.
47. Quoted in ibid.
48. Ibid., 24.
49. Quoted in Thigpen, "Not for Men Only." The lyrics from "Ladies
First," © 1989 T-Boy Publishing, Inc./Queen Latifah Music/Forty-Five King
Music/Forked Tongue Music, are used by permission of the publisher.
50. Quoted in Light, "Queen Latifah," 30.
51. Quoted in Henderson, "Oaktown 3 5 7," 24.
52. Quoted in Brooks, "Oaktown's 3 5 7," 17.
53. The following lyrics from "Juicy Gotcha Krazy," written by Hammer,
© 1989 Bust It Publishing, are used by permission of the publisher. All rights
reserved.
54. Bytches with Problems, "Bitch Is a Badge," 46.

REFERENCES

Abramson, Paul, and Mindy Mechanic. "Sex and the Media: Three Decades
of Best Selling Books and Major Motion Pictures." *Archives of Sexual
Behavior* 12 (June 1983): 185–206.
Blakemore, Judith, Asenath Larve, and Anthony Olejnik. "Sex Appropriate
Toy Preference and the Ability to Conceptualize Toys as Sex Role Related."
Developmental Psychology 15 (May 1979): 339–40.
Brooks, Natasha. "Oaktown's 3 5 7: Rap Triple Threat Group." *Rap Master,*
October 1989, 17.
Brown, Jane, and Kenneth Campbell. "Race and Gender in Music Videos: The
Same Beat, but a Different Drummer." *Journal of Communication* 365
(Winter 1986): 94–106.
Butruille, Susan, and Anita Taylor. "Women in American Popular Song." In
Communication, Gender, and Sex Roles in Diverse Interaction Contexts,
edited by Lea Stewart and Stella Ting-Toomey. Norwood, N.J.: Ablex,
1987.
Bytches with Problems. "Bitch Is a Badge of Honor for Us." *Rappages,* October
1991, 46.
Carby, Hazel. " 'It Jus Be's Dat Way Sometime': The Sexual Politics of Wom-
en's Blues." In *Unequal Sisters: A Multicultural Reader in United States*

Women's History, edited by Ellen Dubois and Vicki Ruiz. New York: Routledge, 1990.

Dimartino, Dave, and Craig Rosen. "Labeling Albums Is Sticky Business." *Billboard,* 20 October 1990, 6.

DiPrima, Dominique. "Bad Rap." *Mother Jones,* September/October 1990, 32–36.

Eisenberg, Nancy, Edward Murray, and Tina Hite. "Children's Reasoning Regarding Sex-typed Toy Choices." *Child Development* 53 (February 1982): 81–86.

Ellison, Mary. *Lyrical Protest: Black Music's Struggle against Discrimination.* New York: Praeger, 1989.

Endres, Kathleen. "Sex Role Standards in Popular Music." *Journal of Popular Culture* 18 (Summer 1984): 9–18.

Garofalo, Reebee. "Crossing Over: 1938–1989." In *Split-Image: African Americans in the Mass Media,* edited by Janette Dates and William Barlow. Washington, D.C.: Howard University Press, 1990.

Gray, Gary. "All Hail the Queen: Queen Latifah." *Word Up,* April 1990, 24, 46.

Hansen, Christine, and Ronald Hansen. "The Influence of Sex and Violence on the Appeal of Rock Music Videos." *Communication Research* 17 (April 1990): 212–34.

Hare, Nathan, and Julia Hare. *The Endangered Black Family: Coping with the Unisexualization and Coming Extinction of the Black Race.* San Francisco: Black Think Tank, 1986.

Harrison, Daphne. *Black Pearls: Blues Queens of the 1920's.* New Brunswick, N.J.: Rutgers University Press, 1988.

Henderson, Alex. "Oaktown 3 5 7: Hammer's Girls Getting Started on Their Own." *Black Beat,* February 1990, 24.

hooks, bell. *Talking Back: Thinking Feminist-Thinking Black.* Boston: South End Press, 1989.

Hyden, Colleen, and N. Jane McCandless. "Men and Women as Portrayed in the Lyrics of Contemporary Music." *Popular Music and Society* 9 (Summer 1983): 19–26.

Lamb, M., and J. Roopnarine. "Peer Influences on Sex Role Development in Preschoolers: Characteristics, Effects, and Correlates." *Child Development* 51 (December 1980): 230–36.

Lance, Larry, and Christina Berry. "Has There Been a Sexual Revolution? An Analysis of Human Sexuality Messages in Popular Music, 1968–1977." *Journal of Popular Culture* 15 (Winter 1981): 155–64.

Langlois, Judith, and A. C. Downs. "Mothers, Fathers, and Peers as Socialization Agents of Sex Typed Play Behaviors in Young Children." *Child Development* 51 (December 1980): 1237–47.

Lewis, Lisa. "Female Address in Music Video." *Journal of Communication Inquiry* 11 (Winter 1987): 75.

———. "Form and Female Authorship in Music Video." *Communication* 9, no. 3–4 (1987): 355–78.

Light, Alan. "Queen Latifah." *Rolling Stone*, 22 February 1990, 30.

Masters, John, and Wyndol Furman. "Popular, Individual, Friendship Selection, and Specific Peer Interaction among Children." *Developmental Psychology* 17 (May 1981): 344–50.

Masters, John, and Alexander Wilkerson. "Consensual and Discrimination Stereotypy of Sex-Type Judgements by Parents and Children." *Child Development* 48 (March 1976): 208–17.

MC Lyte. "Stop, Look and Listen." In *Eyes on This*. Atlantic Records, 1990.

Newman, Melinda, Irv Lichtman, and Bruce Haring. "Atlantic Invests in Crew Label." *Billboard*, 7 July 1990, 72.

Oaktown 3 5 7. "Juicy Gotcha Krazy." In *Wild and Loose*. Capitol Records, 1989.

Periera, Al. "MC Lyte: Takes on the Boys of Rap." *Black Beat*, June 1990, 76, 78.

———. "Salt 'N Pepa." *Black Beat*, August 1990, 22, 78.

Peters, Jan. "MC Lyte: Tough yet Tender." *Word Up*, April 1990, 55.

Queen Latifah. "Ladies First." In *All Hail the Queen*. Tommy Boy Records, 1990.

Ra'Chaun. "Salt 'N Pepa: Raps Leading Ladies Are Here to Stay." *Black Beat*, February 1989, 20–21, 73.

Ressner, Jeffrey. "On the Road with Rap's Outlaw Passee." *Rolling Stone*, 9 August 1990, 20, 24.

Roberts-Thomas, K. "Say It Loud, I'm Pissed and Proud." *Eight Rock*, Summer 1990, 27–31.

Ruble, Diane, Terry Balaban, and Joel Cooper. "Gender Constancy and the Effects of Sex Typed Televised Toy Commercials." *Child Development* 52 (June 1981): 667–73.

Salt 'N Pepa. "Expression." In *Black's Magic*. Next Plateau Records, 1989.

Saucier, Karen. "Healers and Heartbreakers: Images of Women and Men in Country Music." *Journal of Popular Culture* 20 (Winter 1986): 147–66.

Sherman, Barry, and Joseph Dominick. "Violence and Sex in Music Videos: TV and Rock and Roll." *Journal of Communication* 36 (Winter 1986): 79–93.

Small, Michael, and Andrew Abrahams. "Salt 'N Pepa: Shake It up, Laying a Cold Rap on Men." *People Weekly*, April 18, 1988, 113.

Smith, Valerie. "Black Feminist Theory and the Representation of the 'Other.'" In *Changing Our Own Words: Essays on Criticism, Theory, and Writing by Black Women*, edited by Cheryl A. Wall. New Brunswick, N.J.: Rutgers University Press, 1989.

Thigpen, David. "Not for Men Only." *Time*, 27 May 1991, 72.

Thompson, Spencer. "Gender Labels and Early Sex Role Development." *Child Development* 46 (June 1975): 339–47.

Toop, David. *The Rap Attack*. Boston: South End Press, 1984.

"Top Fifty Albums." *Rolling Stone*, 9 August 1990, 74.

Turner, Renee. "First Ladies of Rap." *Ebony*, October 1991, 59–60.

Verna, Paul. "NWA Disk Is No Go at Waxworks Web." *Billboard,* 15 September 1990, 5.

Vincent, Richard, Dennis Davis, and Lilly Boruszkowski. "Sexism on MTV: The Portrayal of Women in Rock Videos." *Journalism Quarterly* 64 (Winter 1987): 750–55.

Weinraub, Marsha, Lynda Clemens, and Alan Sockloff. "The Development of Sex Role Stereotypes in the Third Year: Relationships to Gender Labeling, Gender Identity, Sex Typed Toy Preferences, and Characteristics." *Child Development* 55 (August 1984): 1493–1503.

Zillman, Dolf, and Norbert Mundorf. "Image Effects in the Appreciation of Rock." *Communication Research* 14 (June 1987): 316–34.

10

"Cursed Was She": Gender and Power in American Balladry

Susan C. Cook

The ballads of ages gone by
that harped on the falseness
Of women, will cease to be sung . . .
If only Apollo,
Prince of the lyric, had put
in *our* hearts the invention
Of music and songs for the lyre,
Wouldn't I then have raised
up a feminine paean
To answer the epic of men?
                    —Euripides, *Medea*,
                    translated by Paul Roche

Ballads, the musico-literary genre of sung stories, are perhaps best known to us as part of the ancient epic tradition through works like *The Illiad* and *The Odyssey*. Set to music, so scholars think, and performed by soloists for others, these epic tales were passed on through oral transmission and subsequently provided the source material for the dramas of Euripides and others. Musical epic traditions similar to those of ancient Greece have been found in many cultures. A particular North American variety, derived from the vibrant and long-lived tradition of the British Isles, thrived well into this century. Settlers from Scotland, England, and Ireland brought their balladry along with other representations of their cultural identity. In this new setting, the repertory changed through the retention of older songs and the simultaneous creation of new ballads, stimulated by current events and indicative of North American experiences and ideology.

Balladry thrived in North America among members of the so-called middling classes, typically in agriculturally based communities both in the settled areas of the East and on the westward-moving frontiers of the United States and Canada. Not confined to just white Anglo-Americans, ballad repertory benefited from African American contributions, perhaps the best-known example being "John Henry." Balladry existed side-by-side with mass-marketed repertories and religious music, and it was a predominant force in American popular music until the early years of this century, when it waned with the introduction of new media, such as the radio, which supplanted communal music making. Today the genre exists largely in remnants or revival.

My essay title is a line from "Fuller and Warren," an Anglo-American ballad created in response to events that happened in Lawrenceburgh, Indiana, from December 1819 to August 1820, when Amasa Fuller shot Palmer Warren and was hanged for the crime. The ballad retells these events and in doing so becomes, as Nelly Furman notes of other plot summaries, "an interpretative act, a forceful muting of some voices of the text, an option between reading strategies, the evidence of an ideological stance."[1] The ballad's narrative presents its own story and becomes a social transaction with vested interests in the hearing and the telling. "Fuller and Warren" transcended its appeal to a local audience and was passed on across the continental United States and into Canada for well over 150 years. Its retelling across time and place proves both the wide appeal of its interpretation of the murder and its function as a kind of "canonical tale," encoding values and behavior for its tellers and hearers.[2]

One version of the "Fuller and Warren" text follows (used by permission of the Indiana Historical Society). Part of the appeal of the ballad was no doubt its story of murder and execution, involving, as might be guessed from my title, a woman and a love triangle. The woman is cursed, a strong judgment in the context of the nineteenth century, and the ballad calls for her death in retribution for the deaths of the two men. The ideological stance and the behavior and beliefs the narrative valorized were misogynistic and patriarchal.

Execution of Fuller

O, ye sons of Columbia! your attention I crave,
While a sorrowful ditty I tell,
Which happened of late, in the Indiana State,
Of a hero who none could excel.

Like Sampson, he courted and made choice of a fair,
Intending to make her his wife;
But she, like Delilah, his heart did ensnare,
And cost him his honor and his life.

A gold ring he gave her in token of true love,
On it was engraved the image of a dove—
They mutually agreed to marry with all speed—
They were promised by the powers above.

But this fickled [sic] minded maid, had vowed again to wed,
With young Warren, a resident of this place;
This was a fatal blow, for it proved his overthrow,
And added to her shame and disgrace.

Now Satan thro' the hands of this woman, laid a snare
To deprive these two heroes of their lives;
Young gentlemen, be cautious, be wise, and beware
Of your vows, while you're courting for your wives.

When Fuller came to hear, he was depriv'd of his dear,
Whom he'd promised by the powers to wed,
With his heart full of woe, unto Warren he did go,
And smiling, unto him thus said:

"Young man, you've injured me to gratify your cause,
By reporting that I left a prudent wife;
Now acknowledge you have injured me, although I break the laws,
Or, Warren I'll deprive you of your life."

Then Warren thus replied, "your request shall be denied,
For my heart to your dear one is bound—
And further, I will say, this is my wedding day,
In spite of all the heroes in the town."

Then Fuller, in a passion of love, and anger, too,
Brought tears to many an eye,
For, at one fatal shot, he killed Warren on the spot,
Then smiling, said "I am willing now to die."

Then Fuller was condemned by the honorable court
Of Lawrenceburgh, and then doomed to die
The ignominious death, to hang above the earth,
Like Haman on the gallows so high.

Now the minutes draweth nigh, when Fuller was to die;
With a smile he bade the world adieu—
Like an angel he did stand—he was a handsome man,
And on his breast he wore a ribbon of blue.

The great God of love, looked with anger from above,
And the rope broke asunder at His command;
Two doctors, for their prey, murdered him we may say,
For they hung him by the main strength of hand.

The body then was buried—the doctors lost their prey,
And the harlot was deprived of her groom.
While ten thousand spectators smote upon their breasts,
And solemnly lamented his sad doom.

'Tis not a realizing spirit, nor an avaricious mind,
Nor it really was not my design—
Look in Genesis and Joshua, Kings, Samuel and Job,
And the truth of my story you will find:

That marriage is a lottery, and few that gain the prize,
That is pleasing to the heart and the eye;
And those who never loved, may be well considered wise,
So gentlemen and ladies, all good bye.

On the surface balladry appears to be equally accessible to men and women, existing for a mixed-sex and mixed-age community. A closer examination reveals that North American balladry has been largely a male-dominated form of discourse that privileged the male voices and experiences of the community while muting, or even silencing, its women. Although both men and women sang ballads, they did so often in very different circumstances across the public and private continuum and with different results.[3] Male-only occupations, such as lumbering or cowboy life, took men away from their families and communities for months at a time, providing segregated forums, in which certain men achieved particular fluency as performers or creators, and common sources of experiences and events to retell. When men returned home, they brought new songs to share with their families, though some songs were reserved as a gendered repertory, considered appropriate only for an all-male audience.[4]

Women's experiences in balladry as performers or creators have been difficult to document, because women lacked these occupational ties and their listeners were often other women, family members, or underage children. Certainly women contributed much to the continuance of the genre and gained proficiency in it, but they often did so in a less public forum or in a male-identified way. Almeda Riddle, for example, a highly regarded traditional singer from the Ozarks, described herself as the son her father never had. She was therefore allowed to travel and to become an active participant in the genre in an atypical fashion, in essence as a nonwoman.[5] Riddle, however, also recognized a gendered repertory; she refused to sing some songs because she considered them too violent for a woman to *sing*, yet she *heard* them performed by men.

Much of the fascination of working with a ballad is exploring its transmission—how many times and in how many places it can be "found," either in human memory or written down or even published as a broadside. The multiple versions of one narrative allow for an intertextual examination of its transmission process. What are the elements most often remembered and retained, and, likewise, what can be forgotten, changed, or personalized through human agency? Inquiries, however, into larger issues of ideology, particularly gender ideology and construction, have been of little concern for scholars of folk song. Typically less interested in the "why" of the narrative, scholars have chosen instead to occupy themselves with cleaner and safer issues of transmission, regional variants, and tune studies and to ignore messier issues of intent. My focus here is on the text and its intent, providing a close reading through the lens of feminist criticism.

"Fuller and Warren" is well represented throughout the United States, appearing in almost all regions where collectors have done fieldwork.[6] As appendix 10.1 shows, I have found forty-four versions of the ballad from fifteen states, one Canadian province, and the West, as part of the cowboy tradition. All versions appear to come from white Americans of Anglo descent, both male and female, thus suggesting the predominant audience for this particular social transaction. The earliest datable version is from around 1870, some fifty years after the incident occurred;[7] however, two broadsides, or published texts, in the archives of the Indiana Historical Society may well represent much earlier versions created and marketed shortly after the events took place. The most recent version was uncovered in Indiana in 1963. Of these forty-four retellings, thirty-three provide enough text for a feminist reading of the narrative transaction.[8]

Palmer Warren's murder and the events leading up to and following it can be documented in newspaper coverage from Indiana, Ohio, Vermont, and Massachusetts, as well as in the published memoirs of two noted Indiana judges. A. J. Cotton wrote a fifty-eight-verse poem about Fuller's execution for his *Cotton's Keepsake*, and Oliver H. Smith recalled the case in his *Early Indiana Trials and Sketches;* both appeared in 1858. None of these accounts—newspaper or personal— provides all the information we might wish to have today to judge for ourselves what took place on 10 January 1820 and why.

Here is Judge Smith's interpretation of what precipitated the deaths of Fuller and Warren and stimulated the subsequent creation of the ballad: "These young men it seems, became attached to a young, though not handsome girl, with a broad English accent, and both proposed marriage. The young lady preferred Warren, and rejected Fuller."[9] Smith's summary is succinct and has a minimum of interpretative detail, yet he pronounces a judgment against the third party as "not handsome," and though he does not blame her for Fuller's actions, as does the ballad, his judgment of her attractiveness suggests his bewilderment as to why the tragedy happened at all.

While judging against her appearance, Smith does not give her name, and the woman's namelessness remains true in other accounts as well. Only one newspaper story, a personal letter from a Lawrenceburgh resident reprinted in the Corydon *Indiana Gazette* shortly after the murder, notes that Fuller had made "overtures of courtship to a Miss Catharine Farrar, and as is reported, had got her consent for marriage."[10] All other accounts, even those subsequently published in the *Indiana Gazette*, referred to the woman as Judge Smith did: "a young lady." This omission of her name reflects the nineteenth-century practice of "protecting" a woman's modesty, a practice that also abridged her selfhood and autonomy.

The particular misogynistic framing of the ballad occurs through the characterization of the three individuals involved and more completely in a concluding moral found in almost two-thirds of the texts.[11] Even though not all retellings share the same elements of the narrative, all contain some aspect of the judgment against womankind and thus maintain the misogynistic intent of the ballad's story. It is here that the omission of the woman's name has ramifications beyond modesty. Her namelessness removes her from the discourse, "forcefully muting" her experience, and allows the narrative to slide without question from a discussion of *a woman* and her actions, which she can neither substantiate nor contradict, to generalize about and condemn *all women*.

I will compare two versions of the ballad, the broadside from the Indiana Historical Society entitled "The Execution of Fuller," provided earlier, and one sung by Charles Finnemore of Bridgewater, Maine, in 1941, given below, and use them to make references to the remaining texts and textual variants. The undated broadside contains key plot aspects, rhyme schemes, and phrases found in an overwhelming number of all other versions. Helen Hartness Flanders, whose ballad collection is housed at the Middlebury College Starr Library, collected the version from Finnemore when he was in his seventies, and she subsequently transcribed and published both text and tune.[12] Finnemore's telling is shorter than the broadside's by four stanzas and contains a key element—the "cursed" line—not found in the broadside but present in two-thirds of the remaining versions.[13]

Susan C. Cook

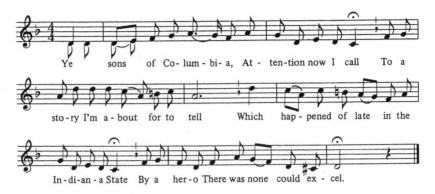

Ye sons of Co-lum-bi-a, At-ten-tion now I call To a
sto-ry I'm a-bout for to tell Which hap-pened of late in the
In-di-an-a State By a her-o There was none could ex-cel.

Fuller and Warren

Ye sons of Columbia, attention now I call
To a story I'm about for to tell
Which happened of late in the Indiana State
By a hero there was none could excel.

Like Samson he courted the fairest of the sex
Intending to make her his bride
But like young Delilah fair, O she did his heart ensnare
And she robbed him of his honor and his pride.

When Fuller came to hear he was deprived of his dear
How she promised by the powers to wed,
To Warren he did go with his heart full of woe
And those words unto Warren he said.

"Now, Warren, you have wronged me for to gratify your cause
By reporting I've left a prudent wife,
Now acknowledge you've wronged me, or I will break the law,
Warren, I'll deprive you of your life."

Then Warren he replied, "Your request must be denied
For my heart unto your darling is bound.
Furthermore, let me say that this is our wedding day
In spite of all your heroes of this town."

Then Fuller in a passion of love and anger flew
And then he began for to cry.
With one fatal shot he killed Warren on the spot
Then smiling says, "I'm ready now to die."

Then Fuller he was taken by the honorable board
By the laurel of Auburn to die
Such an ignominious death for to swing above the earth
Like Homer on the gallows so high.

Now the time was drawing nigh when poor Fuller he had to die.
To his friends he bid them all adieu;
On the gallows he did stand and he was a handsome man.
On his breast he wore a ribbon of blue.

Ten thousand spectators they smote upon their breast
And the guards they dropped tears from their eyes
Saying, "Curs-ed was she—she has caused his misery
And she ought to in his stead have to die."

Come all you young married men who has got a prudent wife,
Be loving, be true and be kind.
You may look in the book of Moses, of Genises [sic], and Job
And the truth of my story you'll find.

For love it is a lottery and he who wins the prize.
She may be pleasing to his mind and his eyes
But the man that never marries is the man that's counted wise
So ladies and gentlemen "Good-bye."

The opening stanza's call to an audience—"ye sons of Columbia"—
is present in all versions of the ballad and is a formal technique
common in British broadside ballads. The specific designation of the
listeners as male is shared with other ballads about soldiers and particularly lumberjacks and suggests that this ballad is of particular interest to men; it speaks to their experience, not in their occupations
but in the domestic arena. The first stanza further situates the narrative
as tragic and based on an actual event. The final line begins the central
characterization of Fuller as a hero.

The second stanza reveals the ballad's rhetorical strategy: its reliance
on biblical and religious imagery. The majority of versions call up the
story of Samson and Delilah from the Book of Judges in reference to
Fuller's courtship of Catharine Farrar. Samson's story was misread
throughout Judeo-Christian history to show the evil of women's sexuality and desire rather than as a warning against marriage outside the
faith.[14] The biblical allusion thus casts this story as another example
of this female seduction plot. The woman in the ballad "ensnares"
Fuller as a seductress, "robs" him of his name, and "costs" him his
life. She acts on her desires, and, like Delilah, she destroys heroes.

Omitted from Finnemore's telling, but present at least partially in
many other versions, are the three stanzas in the broadside that describe
Fuller's intention to marry the woman and her subsequent involvement with Warren. Fuller gives her a ring, and they are described as
being "promised by the powers above." According to newspaper cov-

erage of the trial, Fuller gave Farrar a ring "in pledge" before leaving Lawrenceburgh in the fall of 1819 to work in nearby Brookville, Indiana.[15] Some weeks after his departure, Farrar returned the ring to Fuller with a note that was in Warren's handwriting, renouncing "all feelings of attachment towards him."[16] After Fuller received the letter, he returned to Lawrenceburgh on 7 January and took up residence in a rooming house under the same roof as Warren's office and near Farrar's home.

The ballad's description of the betrothal as being "promised by the powers above" defines the relationship as already blessed, a virtual marriage in the eyes of God. The woman's subsequent involvement with Warren is a sinful betrayal of her solemn vow. Fuller's revenge can thus be later justified as the permissible response of an offended husband.

The next stanza, present in the ballad and in over two-thirds of the texts, echoes the earlier characterization of the woman as Delilah.[17] She is judged "fickle-minded," and her actions cause the deaths of both men and bring her shame. The broadside's fifth stanza expounds on woman's inherent evil, with a religious reference recalling Eve's original sin through the temptation of Satan in the guise of the serpent. This extra stanza disappears from all but two other versions; its substance, however, returns in the concluding moral. The presence of the elaboration at this point in the broadside breaks the dramatic progression and betrays the ideological stance. It is as if the broadside author cannot wait until the end to deliver the moral, which was the standard practice.

After preparing us for Fuller's revenge and alluding again to the heavenly promise, the next two stanzas allow each man to speak for himself, something not accorded the woman. Fuller accuses Warren of having lied about him and demands that he confess to his actions or suffer the consequences. After Fuller returned to Lawrenceburgh on 7 January, the newspaper accounts reported, he sought out Farrar at her home and then quarreled with Warren. The following day Fuller borrowed a pair of pistols from a friend, and on 10 January followed Warren to his office and demanded that he sign a letter, found at the scene, "to renounce all pretensions to the young lady, and acknowledge himself to be a base liar and a scoundrel."[18]

When Warren refused—as he does in the next stanza of the ballad— Fuller challenged him to a duel, and when Warren again refused, Fuller shot him. The newspapers noted, "It does not appear that Warren had ever taken an undue advantage of Fuller, or even spoke a disrespectful word of him to the young lady, or any other person."[19] Yet in Warren's stanza in the ballad, he denies injuring Fuller and refuses to call off his impending marriage to Farrar. (In actuality, Warren and Farrar were to have been married the following day.) Warren's refusal is the closest the ballad comes to holding him responsible for anything that happens.

In the ballad the murder is framed further in terms of gender. All the ballad texts describe Fuller as in a "passion" of love, anger, or rage following Warren's refusal. In the newspaper account of the trial, Fuller was quoted as having said at the scene of the crime, "I am a man, and have acted the part of a man! I have been ridding the earth of a vile reptile!! I glory in the deed!!!"[20]

Natalie Zemon Davis, in her study of sixteenth-century French pardon letters, notes that a defense of murder on the grounds of passionate anger was an old one, coming from Judaic law, but had gendered implications.[21] In the understanding of the bodily humors or passions, men were by nature hot and dry whereas women were cold and wet. Men, in anger, could suffer from a condition of "hot bile" (*chaude colle*) that might cause irrational behavior. Since they had not acted in "cold blood," a concept we still acknowledge, they could petition for remission of a death sentence. Female humors did not allow for such passions, "their anger thickened by phlegm and compromised by melancholy."[22] Women's pardon letters pleaded other circumstances, often with less success. British common law and U.S. legal statutes similarly allowed a distinction between murder and manslaughter, or killing without malice aforethought, on the grounds of "heat of passion," an anger or rage so great that a person loses normal capacity for self-control. Although women can plead manslaughter, one has only to read of the struggles of women who kill their spouses after years of abuse and are charged with murder to realize a gender bias remains.[23]

Causes of such uncontrollable rages upheld by U.S. courts into this century were suspicion of a wife's unfaithfulness (so-called passion killings) and being falsely accused. Both grounds are provided for Fuller in the ballad. Fuller's beloved has proven fickle, and Warren has falsely accused him, of all things, of having deserted a first and "prudent" wife. Fuller has a right to his anger; the ballad agrees that he has only "acted as a man."

Yet Fuller claims in the ballad that he is ready to die for what he has done, acknowledging that in the eyes of the state he does not have grounds for manslaughter. Indeed, witnesses testified that Fuller planned the murder—obtaining pistols, practicing with them, and borrowing a coat that would conceal them—at least two days before he shot Warren. The ballad narrative plays it both ways, giving Fuller moral grounds for his actions yet blaming Farrar for causing these actions to begin with.

Fuller pleaded not guilty on grounds of insanity. The broadside and Finnemore versions succinctly recount Fuller's trial and sentencing, without lingering on a potentially compromising courtroom scene. The form of execution, this "ignominious death," contains another biblical reference: hanging "like Haman" (changed through transmission to "Homer" in Finnemore's version and in several others). This move from describing Fuller as the heroic Samson to the villain Haman from the Book of Esther is odd. Yet Esther's story presents images of good and bad women and wives. Queen Vashti refused to come to her husband when commanded, and he retaliated by seeking virgins for a harem. Esther, a Jew in exile, is chosen and through her humility and beauty becomes queen. Through more acts of submission Esther saves her people from Haman's gallows, and he is hanged instead. Esther's story presents a good woman and the hanging of a bad man, providing an ingenious irony to the ballad's narrative of the hanging of a good man through the actions of a bad woman.

Fuller's final moments as described in the ballad maintain his heroic characterization. He bids farewell to his friends cheerfully, and on the gallows he is handsome, even angelic. The ribbon of blue, like a medal on his chest, suggests his bravery in the face of death, as if a martyr for his cause.

According to Cotton's memoirs, Fuller was baptized and received communion prior to his execution and was attended by several church elders, one of whom delivered a sermon from the gallows.[24] A notable feature of a second broadside in the Indiana Historical Society's collection, entitled "A New Song on the Unhappy Fate of the Late Mr. Fuller," is its verse declaring Fuller's salvation through baptism. Although clearly based on the "Execution of Fuller" broadside, this "New Song" has entirely different rhyme schemes throughout. Yet stanzas recounting Fuller's spiritual redemption appear in about one-third of the texts that are otherwise similar to the "Execution of Fuller." Three of these versions, two from the memories of women, give Fuller's salvation as the sole conclusion and thus transform somewhat the ballad's moral from woman's guilt to promises of Christian forgiveness.

The rope broke during the execution, and Fuller was hanged on a second attempt. The broadside and half of the other texts contain a stanza describing this event as an act of God, who thus judged Fuller innocent by a code clearly higher than that of the state of Indiana. To make Fuller's end even more tragic and to account for the fact that he was hanged, the ballad adds the chilling and unsubstantiated image of doctors, wishing to obtain a cadaver for dissection, strangling Fuller with their bare hands.

The final three stanzas in both the broadside and Finnemore versions conclude the drama and provide the moral. A huge crowd, consistently recorded at ten thousand, is present for the execution and mourns Fuller's death. Finnemore gives the death curse—"cursed was she"— on Catharine Farrar to the prison guards, while other versions put the curse in the mouth of the judge or the assembled crowd or leave it pronounced by the balladeer alone. The broadside, which does not carry the "cursed" line, judges her instead as a harlot, a characterization found only in two other texts. The lack of the "cursed" line in the first broadside version yet its presence in other versions sharing the broadside's features suggests that either an influential singer inserted the new verse or another version of the ballad with the "cursed" line existed alongside the "Execution of Fuller" broadside.

The moral found in the last two stanzas of the Finnemore and broadside versions contains a judgment on both marriage and women, reflecting the misogyny of Pauline theology and later church views of celibacy. In the Finnemore version it also returns to the audience— "sons of Columbia," now "you young married men"—in directing the moral specifically to men. Finnemore tempers the moral somewhat by noting that some women, those "prudent" wives, can escape the judgment against all womankind, an escape provided in other versions as well. The narrative can thus claim some leniency; women who act in accordance with their place, like Esther, may be read or read themselves into this one line.

All versions sharing the moral about marriage once again resort to biblical references to supply the proof for their story and what it teaches. Finnemore calls on Moses, Genesis, and Job, while the broadside adds Joshua, Kings, and Samuel, together referring to the stories of Eve, Jezebel, Job's wife, Solomon and the Queen of Sheba, and David and Bathseba. Other texts merely refer to "ancient history" or the "scriptures" as their source of proof. Thus, the ballad ends proclaiming the truth of its narrative.

Certainly Fuller's case aroused much interest and discussion; both Smith and Cotton emphasized the importance of Fuller's trial not only to themselves personally (it was the first case Smith observed) but to the entire state. They noted that the crowd witnessing the execution was in the thousands, which could well have been most of the inhabitants of the county given that the census, taken in 1816 when Indiana attained statehood, gave the population of Lawrenceburgh and surrounding Dearborn County as 4,424.[25] There is, however, conflicting testimony as to what the predominant public sentiment was regarding Fuller's innocence. Newspaper accounts immediately following Warren's murder describe Fuller as "a villain" or the murder as "of the most cold-blooded nature."[26] After the trial, Fuller's good character was commented on regularly.

Fuller won a gubernatorial stay of execution so the defense's appeal, on procedural grounds, could be examined; the state supreme court upheld the original verdict. The *Franklin Herald* of Greenfield, Massachusetts, reprinting a dispatch from Cincinnati, maintained that the temporary pardon was unpopular; the jail guards protested it by walking off the job.[27] Smith later claimed, however, that the entire citizenry of Lawrenceburgh signed a petition asking for a stay of execution and that Fuller was so sure of receiving a pardon that he did not escape from jail when he might have. This difference of opinion surrounding the case is evidence of why the ballad was created; if public opinion was not unanimous, it could at least keep alive its particular reading of the evidence.

The misogyny expressed in "Fuller and Warren" can be understood in the larger context of not only gender but also class conflict in the nineteenth century, as the roles of men and women, particularly in the white middle class, changed in the face of growing industrialization.[28] Class tensions are present in the ballad. Both men were described in the press and by Smith and Cotton as well liked and well respected in their community. Warren was twenty-three at the time of his death; Fuller was his senior. Although neither man's occupation is given, Warren, a native of New York State, worked in an office. In attendance at his funeral were members of his local lodge as well as members of the light infantry company in which he had served.[29] Fuller had left town to seek work and had returned in January on foot; his family was known in the area.[30] Warren, however, may well have made more money or had more professional prestige in Lawrenceburgh than Fuller did.

In 1820 Indiana had been a state for only four years. Part of the ballad's need to prove Fuller's innocence therefore may reflect the clash of rural and settled society and, with it, social stratification. Fuller was a frontier working man, while his younger rival represented the growing regularity of settled towns, where individuals no longer could settle disputes by taking the law into their own hands. This clash would account for the tension in the ballad between the law of the state and the story's support of Fuller's actions as an individual motivated by a different moral code. The ballad's biblical references suggest that the state betrayed Fuller, as did the professional doctors. This sympathy for the frontier working man may well account for some of the ballad's continued popularity, particularly when occupations, such as lumbering, forced economic and domestic hardships on men and their families.

G. Malcolm Laws, Jr., in his germinal study of American ballads, *Native American Balladry*, tried to isolate all works he decided had been created in the United States and to organize them by plot following the model James Francis Child set forth in his monumental study *The English and Scottish Popular Ballads* (1882–98). (Laws created a kind of North American ballad canon, and although his work remains of central importance, his methodology, such as how he distinguished between authentic and doubtful works, is under question.) Laws discusses "Fuller and Warren" under the category "murder ballads," where it is only one of five ballads in which men alone are killed.[31] The twenty-five remaining plots—or five times as many—have female victims, all murdered by men, most of whom they know as lovers, husbands, or other family members. In folklore research they are designated as a distinct plot subcategory—"murdered-girl" ballads. Ballads recount male homicides too, but, as Laws recognized, they typically occur in conjunction with the hazardous activities of outlaw life.[32] When all of the ballad plots are examined, regardless of Laws's further distinctions, sixty-seven recount murders, of which the overwhelming number of victims—forty-three—are women, compared with twenty male victims (four ballads recount the murder of entire families).

Anne Cohen, in her major study of the "Pearl Bryan" ballads, has shown how the plot conventions of the "murdered-girl" ballad influenced not only the ballads written about Bryan following the 1898 investigation of her murder but the attending newspaper coverage as well.[33] Such conventions included the victim's innocence, although it was understood that she was pregnant, and her absolute passivity in the face of her lover/seducer's actions to silence her. Cohen, however, does not question the very presence of such an archetype. What kind of "cultural work," to use Jane Tompkins's image, was being done by a musical genre that memorializes domestic violence?[34] Do these tales somehow legitimate violence toward women as a result of such transgressive behavior?

Not only have these questions been left unexamined, but the way such ballads have been treated often shows a marked callousness toward the gender implications of the violence. "The Lexington Murder," known in England as "The Berkshire Tragedy," tells the story

of a woman lured by her lover to a secluded spot; he beats her to death
and dumps the body in a river. Liner notes to a commercial release of
a field recording of this ballad state, "Throughout all the relocations
from town to town, certain gory and beloved details are faithfully
retained: the girl is beaten to death with a stick or a fence-stake; the
blood-spattered murderer attempts to explain his appalling appearance
by blaming it on a nose-bleed."[35] Would anyone call the details "beloved" if these murders were delineated on racial or ethnic grounds?

The gender issues of "murdered-girl" ballads become even thornier
when brought up against those of "Fuller and Warren." Together the
"murdered-girl" ballads and "Fuller and Warren" leave little space for
women to maneuver. If passive, we may be murdered by our sweet-
hearts; if we act, we can be held accountable for the subsequent actions
of others. In both cases they promise punishment for desire and legitimate men's need to control women's sexuality. In their distinction
between active and passive victims, as well as in the Delilah/"prudent
wife" dichotomy already identified in "Fuller and Warren," these nar-
ratives yet again replicate that timeworn duality of woman as the
passive "angel of the house" or the active "angel of death": the virgin
or the whore.

Of the forty-four known versions of "Fuller and Warren," twenty-
one contain a tune either as sung in field recordings or notated by the
collector. These twenty-one tunes yield three melodies of similar con-
tour and minimal variation.[36] Finnemore's modal tune, shared by other
singers from Maine and New England, reflects the influence of the
Irish fiddling and ballad tradition that thrived in the lumbering camps.
All three tunes have similar first halves, with greater differences in
range and direction of movement coming toward the end; indeed, they
may all be from the same tune family.

The ballad's tune is a crucial element in the narrative transaction,
acting as a powerful fixative, sticking, as it were, the story in the minds
of the singer and listener and aiding in later recall. Furthermore, the
musical nature of the ballad emphasized its particular communal function as entertainment. Ballads were regularly repeated in a community
as a diversionary activity, and this repetition provided individual stories with more opportunities to teach their codes of behavior. Indeed,
in the case of "Fuller and Warren" the ballad's ideological interpretation, when set to music, outlived other judgments of the events.

Ballad tunes may work in much the same way that Catherine Clément says operatic scores do, as transitional objects that allow the stories
to pass unnoticed.[37] Likewise, the relatively simple harmonic structure
of these tunes underscores key aspects of the narrative. The second

line of all three tunes described above ends on the dominant or dominant harmony and thus sets off the third line of text as it resolves to
the tonic.[38] It is in the third line of text that we get the image of
Delilah, of Fuller being wronged, the fatal shot, Fuller's "ignominious
death," the curse, the biblical proof of the story, and the moral, key
issues, and images in the story.

There are more versions of "Fuller and Warren" that come from
the memories of men than from women, suggesting that it was part
of a male-identified ballad repertory. In judging, however, it would
help to know whether the women collected here sang it by choice and
whether they learned it from male or female relatives. Nonetheless,
both in singing and in hearing this ballad, women adopted the male
point of view, in which they cursed themselves and pronounced judgment against marriage, the institution they were, by nature, supposed
to hold most dear and in which they exercised some power.

Throughout history our popular songs, in managing our private and
public selves, have defined women's place.[39] The evidence of Cohen's
study, as well as the work of feminist and African American literary
criticism, powerfully illustrates that we shape and are shaped by the
stories we tell and that we come to believe them even in the face of
other evidence.[40] Those of us who love music's language and its emotional and affective power need to acknowledge as well the power it
wields in social transactions and how its relegation to "entertainment"
effectively masks narrative ideology and sanctions violence towards
women.[41] We must become resisting listeners, adding our textual ri-
postes and dissonant countermelodies to these same old songs.

APPENDIX 10.1: Versions of "Fuller and Warren"

The following lists the versions of "Fuller and Warren" known to me from
published collections, archival holdings, and field or commercial recordings.
The texts are arranged geographically according to the location of the individual informant (or the source itself if a broadside) and in order of the number
of versions per area. In each location the sources are listed chronologically,
using the year the individual recording or text was taken from the informant.
When that date is unknown, the date is given as before the date of publication
of the collection containing the version.

The data for each version are listed in the following order: the date; the
name of the informant, if known; the kind of source (e.g., broadside, field
recording, published text, or manuscript); the version's source, using the abbreviations below; and the number of stanzas of the text, a stanza being defined
as a four-line completed rhyme scheme. Then follows a judgment about

whether the text was considered complete by the informant, designated "cc." If a version was truncated by mechanical failure during the field recording process, the designation "mf" follows. In some cases collectors chose not to publish an available text or to reproduce only part of it; "nt" indicates no text at all was given, and "pt" designates a partial text. Finally, there is an indication as to whether the source provides a published tune, "t," or whether the version was sung, "s."

Abbreviations Used

AFC   Archive of Folk Culture, American Folklife Center, Library of Congress, post-1950 catalog.

Barry   Phillips Barry. "Fuller and Warren." *Bulletin of the Folk-Song Society of the North East* 9 (1935): 7, 14–17.

Belden   Henry M. Belden, ed. *Ballads and Songs Collected by the Missouri Folk-Lore Society. The University of Missouri Studies: A Quarterly of Research* 15 (1 January 1940).

Brewster   Paul G. Brewster. *Ballads and Songs of Indiana*. Bloomington: Indiana University Press, 1940.

Buford   Mary Elizabeth Buford. "Folk Songs of Florida and Texas." M.A. thesis, Southern Methodist University, 1940.

Burt   Olive Woolley Burt. *American Murder Ballads*. New York: Oxford University Press, 1958.

Check-list *Check-List of Recorded Songs in the English Language in the Archive of American Folk Song to July, 1940.* Washington D.C.: Library of Congress, Music Division, 1942.

Cox   John H. Cox. *Folk-Songs of the South*. Cambridge, Mass.: Harvard University Press, 1925.

Dunn   Caroline Dunn. "An Indiana Ballad of Hapless Love." *Year Book of the Society of Indiana Pioneers*, n.p., 1947, 16–20.

Finger   Charles J. Finger. *Frontier Ballads*. Garden City, N.Y.: Doubleday, 1927.

Flanders   Helen Hartness Flanders, ed. *Ballads Migrant in New England.* New York: Farrar, Strauss, and Young, 1953.

FS   *Fine Times at Our House.* Folkways Recording FS 3809.

Gordon   R. W. Gordon Collection of Recordings, Archive of Folk Culture, Library of Congress.

Gordon 2   R. W. Gordon. "Old Songs That Men Have Sung." *Adventure*, 10 March 1924, 191.

HHFBC   Helen Hartness Flanders Ballad Collection, Middlebury College, Middlebury, Vt.

Hubbard   Lester A. Hubbard, ed. *Ballads and Songs from Utah*. Salt Lake City: University of Utah Press, 1961.

Hudson   Arthur Palmer Hudson. *Folksongs of Mississippi*. Chapel Hill: University of North Carolina, 1936.

IHS   Printed Collections, Indiana Historical Society Library, Indian-
               apolis, Ind.
Ives   Edward D. Ives Tapes. Northeast Archives of Folklore and
               Oral History, University of Maine at Orono.
Larkin   Margaret Larkin, ed. *Singing Cowboy: A Book of Western
               Songs.* New York: Alfred A. Knopf, 1931.
Lomax   John A. Lomax. *Cowboy Songs.* New York: Sturgis and Walton,
               1910.
Musick   Ruth Ann Musick. "The Old Album of William A. Larkin."
               Journal of American Folklore 60 (July-September 1947): 201–
               51.
NAFOH   Northeast Archives of Folklore and Oral History, University of
               Maine at Orono.
Pound   Louise Pound. *American Ballads and Songs.* New York: Charles
               Scribner's Sons, 1922.
Randolph   Vance Randolph, ed. *Ozark Folksongs II.* Columbia: State
               Historical Society of Missouri, 1948.

Versions

INDIANA: 9 versions (1 man, 6 women, 2 broadsides)
    after 1820, broadside "Execution of Fuller," IHS/Dunn, 15 stanzas, cc.
    after 1820, Thomas Thompson?, broadside "A New Song," IHS,
        16 stanzas, cc.
    1892, Dora McNeely, published text, Brewster, pt.
    1925, Kate Milner Rabb, published text, Brewster, 16 stanzas, cc.
    1935/1938, Mrs. T. M. Bryant, published text and field recording,
        Brewster and Check-list (1736B), 12 stanzas, cc, 1938 s.
    1935, Ada Fenley, Brewster, nt.
    1935, Mrs. James Williams, Brewster, nt.
    before 1958, Max Egly, published text, Burt, 12 stanzas, cc, t.
    1963, Anna Mae Underhill, commercial recording, FS, 13 stanzas, cc, s.
MAINE: 8 versions (7 men, 1 woman)
    1934, James A. Buckley, published text, Barry, 13 stanzas, cc, t.
    1934, Herbert L. Merry, published text, Barry, 12 stanzas, cc, t.
    before 1935, Perley L. Quigg, Barry, nt, t.
    1941, Irish Alton, field recording, HHFBC, 13 stanzas, cc, s.
    1941, Charles Finnemore, field recording, HHFBC, 11 stanzas, cc, s.
    1941, Jack McNally, field recording, HHFBC, 11 stanzas, cc, s.
    1957, Mrs. Lidelle W. Robbins, field recording, Ives (tape 1.6), 6
        stanzas, pt.
    1962, Stanley Finnemore, field recording, NAFOH, 11 stanzas, cc, s.
MISSOURI: 4 versions (2 men, 2 women)
    1905, Finis Dean, published text, Belden, 11 stanzas.
    1912, W. T. Street, published text, Belden, 16 stanzas, cc, t.

1927, Mrs. L. A. Thomas, published text, Randolph, 10 stanzas, cc, t.
1928, Kate Stubblefield, published text, Randolph, 2 stanzas, pt.
ARKANSAS: 3 versions (1 man, 2 women)
1905, Miss Lowry, published text, Belden, 1 stanza, pt.
1930, F. M. Goodhue, published text, Randolph, 1 stanza, pt.
1936, Emma Dusenbury, field recording, Check-list (864B), 12 stanzas,
cc, s.
ILLINOIS: 3 versions (2 men, 1 woman)
c. 1866–72, William A. Larkin, ballet book, Musick, 12 stanzas, cc.
1935, M. L. Lasher, published text, Brewster, 1 stanza, pt.
1935, Mary J. Shriver, Brewster, nt.
NEW HAMPSHIRE: 3 versions (2 men, 1 woman)
1942, Belle Luther Richards, field recording, HHFBC, 14 stanzas, cc, s.
1942, David Shatney, field recording, HHFBC, 14 stanzas, cc, s.
1942, Abe Washburn, field recording, HHFBC, 13 stanzas, cc, s.
WEST/Cowboy Tradition: 3 versions (3 men)
before 1902, Joe Stafford, published text, Finger, 14 stanzas, cc.
before 1910, informant unknown, published text, Lomax, 12 stanzas,
cc.
before 1931, informant unknown, published text, Larkin, 14 stanzas,
cc, t.
CALIFORNIA: 2 versions (2 men)
1941, Bill Jackson, field recording, AFC (5101 B2), 2 stanzas, mf, s.
date unknown, unknown male informant, field recording, Gordon (Cal
184 18,996:A), 1 stanza, mf, s.
KENTUCKY: 1 version (1 man)
1918, Sam Turman, published text, Cox, 7 stanzas, cc, t.
MISSISSIPPI: 1 version (1 man)
before 1936, A. H. Burnette, published text, Hudson, 12 stanzas, cc.
FLORIDA: 1 version (1 woman)
before 1941, Ella Miller, published text, Buford, 12 stanzas, cc.
NEBRASKA: 1 version (1 woman)
1915, Jane Andrews, published text, Pound, 11 stanzas, cc.
KANSAS: 1 version (1 man)
1920, Earl Cruickshank, published text, Belden, 7 stanzas, pt.
IDAHO: 1 version (1 woman)
1949, Mrs. S. P. Cardon, published text, Hubbard, 12 stanzas, cc.
TEXAS: 1 version (1 woman)
1937, Minta Morgan, field recording, Check-list (1328 A2), 5 stanzas,
mf, s.
MICHIGAN: 1 version (1 man)
1924, A. C. DeRemer, published text, Gordon, 14 stanzas, cc.
CANADA, New Brunswick: 1 version (1 man)
1961, James Cameron, field recording, Ives (tape 1.111), 10 stanzas,
cc, s.

Criminal Brought to Justice Variant

CALIFORNIA: 1 version (1 man)
 1938, George Vinton, field recording, Check-list (3813 A2 A3), 10
 stanzas, mf, s.

NOTES

Versions of this essay were given as papers at the 1989 meeting of the American Musicological Society and the 1990 Berkshire Conference on the History of Women. I wish to acknowledge the considerable assistance of Leigh Darbee, curator of Printed Collections, Indiana Historical Society, and John Selch, newspaper librarian, Indiana State Library, as well as Jennifer Post and Elizabeth Wood, who read earlier drafts of this essay and supplied insightful comments. The lines from "Medea" in the epigraph are reprinted from *Three Plays of Euripedes: Alcestis, Medea, The Baccahe*, trans. Paul Roche (New York: W. W. Norton, 1974). Copyright © 1974 by Paul Roche. Used by permission of W. W. Norton and Company, Inc.

 1. Furman, "Languages of Love in *Carmen*," 170–71.
 2. See B. Smith, "Narrative Versions," 232; and Gates, "Narration and Cultural Memory," 17.
 3. Post, "Ballad Tradition," has identified differences between men and women in the repertories they sang, particularly the treatment of gory details in songs they shared (women frequently omitted such details), and in the approach to ornamentation in shared tunes (men ornamented more than women).
 4. Bethke, *Adirondack Voices*; Ives, *Joe Scott.*
 5. Abrahams, *Singer and Her Songs*, 4, 16.
 6. I did not collect any of the texts myself but instead relied on many different sources and kinds of materials, as indicated in the appendix.
 7. See Musick, "Old Album."
 8. I have been unable to obtain a copy of Almeda Riddle's text for this ballad; hers would increase the available texts to thirty-four and would provide a woman's telling of the story.
 9. O. H. Smith, *Early Indiana Trials*, 8.
 10. "Horrid Murder."
 11. Twenty-one of the thirty-three texts retain this concluding moral.
 12. Flanders, *Ballads Migrant*, 174–75. The ballad transcription is reprinted here with permission of the Flanders Ballad Collection, Middlebury College, Middlebury, Vt. Finnemore's son Stanley remembered the ballad some twenty-one years later in a version almost identical to his father's.
 13. The line "cursed was [or be] she" appears in twenty-three of the thirty-three texts.
 14. See Rogers, *Troublesome Helpmate*, 5ff.

15. "Trial for Murder."

16. Ibid.

17. The woman's fickle-mindedness (sometimes remembered as "frickle-minded") appears in twenty-five of the thirty-three texts.

18. "Trial for Murder."

19. Ibid.

20. Ibid.

21. Davis, Fiction in the Archives, 37, 81. See also Moi, "Jealousy and Sexual Difference," 134–53.

22. Davis, Fiction in the Archives, 81.

23. For a recent study of judicial double standards in the nineteenth century, see Ireland, "Fallen Females."

24. Cotton, Cotton's Keepsake, 445. Unfortunately, I have not been able to locate newspaper coverage of the execution that took place on 14 August 1820. It would be especially helpful to corroborate whether a sermon was given and whether anyone commented on its content. Cotton notes that the sermon warned "young gentlemen and ladies to be careful how they trifle with 'won affections and plighted vows.' " This ballad, with its unusual reliance on biblical imagery and heavy moralizing, suggests a sermon.

25. Esarey, History of Indiana, 215.

26. "Shocking Murder"; "Horrid Murder."

27. Franklin Herald, 25 April 1820, quoted in Phillip Barry's notes on the ballad contained in "Fuller and Warren" file, Flanders Ballad Collection.

28. Evans, Born for Liberty, 76.

29. "Distressing Event."

30. In fact Cotton, Cotton's Keepsake, 445–46, reported on the unhappy ends two of Fuller's relatives met: his brother Daniel, who claimed Fuller's body after the execution, was shot and killed shortly thereafter by his brother-in-law, and Fuller's father was accidentally killed after being taken into custody for murder.

31. Laws, Native American Balladry, 199. His categories, focusing as they do on occupations and such activities as soldiering, privilege male experience over female.

32. "Frankie Silvers" is one of two ballads in the Anglo-American repertory in which a wife kills a husband; the other is "Frankie and Albert," also known as "Frankie and Johnny." Laws discussed the latter in his questionable separate chapter on "ballads of the negro." Laws, however, elected to put "Frankie Silvers" in the category "ballads about criminals and outlaws," not "murder ballads," even though Frankie, like Amasa Fuller, had no prior history of criminal activity.

33. Cohen, Poor Pearl, Poor Girl!

34. Tompkins, Sensational Designs.

35. McCormick, liner notes.

36. The one exception is the tune given by Larkin from the cowboy tradition. This tune runs over two verses, although it too shares characteristics of the other three melodies.

37. Clément, Opera, 179.

38. I am most grateful to Suzanne Cusick for this observation on the harmonic implications of the tune.

39. Frith, "Aesthetic of Popular Music," 141.

40. I have been particularly influenced by Heilbrun, Writing a Woman's Life, and "What Was Penelope Unweaving?"

41. For example, the postmodernist composer John Zorn opens his composition Spillane with a woman's scream that most certainly means she is being murdered or raped.

REFERENCES

Abrahams, Roger D., ed. A Singer and Her Songs: Almeda Riddle's Book of Ballads. Baton Rouge: Louisiana State University Press, 1970.

Bethke, Robert D. Adirondack Voices: Woodsmen and Woods Lore. Urbana: University of Illinois Press, 1981.

Clément, Catherine. Opera, or the Undoing of Women. Translated by Betsy Wing. Minneapolis: University of Minnesota Press, 1988.

Cohen, Anne B. Poor Pearl, Poor Girl! The Murdered-Girl Stereotype in Ballad and Newspaper. Austin: American Folklore Society, 1972.

Cotton, Alfred Johnson. Cotton's Keepsake. Cincinnati: Applegate, 1858.

Davis, Natalie Zemon. Fiction in the Archives: Pardon Tales and Their Tellers in Sixteenth-Century France. Stanford, Calif.: Stanford University Press, 1987.

"Distressing Event." Cincinnati Western Spy, 22 January 1820.

Esarey, Logan. A History of Indiana. Vol. 1, From Its Exploration to 1850. Indianapolis: W. K. Steward, 1915.

Euripides. "Medea." In Three Plays of Euripides, translated by Paul Roche. New York: W. W. Norton, 1974.

Evans, Sara M. Born for Liberty: A History of Women in America. New York: Free Press, 1989.

Flanders, Helen Hartness. Ballads Migrant in New England. New York: Farrar, Straus, and Young, 1953.

Frith, Simon. "Towards an Aesthetic of Popular Music." In Music and Society, edited by Richard Leppert and Susan McClary. Cambridge: Cambridge University Press, 1988.

Furman, Nelly. "The Languages of Love in Carmen." In Reading Operas, edited by Arthur Groos and Roger Parker. Princeton, N.J.: Princeton University Press, 1988.

Gates, Henry Louis, Jr. "Introduction: Narration and Cultural Memory in the African-American Tradition." In Talk that Talk: An Anthology of African-

American Storytelling, edited by Linda Goss and Marian E. Barnes. New York: Simon and Schuster, 1989.

Heilbrun, Carolyn G. "What Was Penelope Unweaving?" In *Hamlet's Mother and Other Women*. New York: Columbia University Press, 1990.

———. *Writing a Woman's Life*. New York: W. W. Norton, 1988.

"Horrid Murder." *Indiana Gazette*, 20 January 1820.

Ireland, Robert M. "Frenzied and Fallen Females: Women and Sexual Dishonor in the Nineteenth-Century United States." *Journal of Women's History* 3 (Winter 1992): 95–117.

Ives, Edward D. *Joe Scott, the Woodsman-Songmaker*. Urbana: University of Illinois Press, 1978.

Laws, G. Malcolm, Jr. *Native American Balladry: A Descriptive Study and a Bibliographical Syllabus*. Philadelphia: American Folklore Society, 1964.

McCormick, Mack. Liner notes for *Songs of Death and Tragedy*. In *Folk Music in America*, vol. 9. Washington, D.C.: Library of Congress, Music Division, 1976–78. Record number LBC 9, 77–750128.

Moi, Toril. "Jealousy and Sexual Difference." In *Sexuality: A Reader*. London: Virago, 1987.

Musick, Ruth Ann. "The Old Album of William A. Larkin." *Journal of American Folklore* 60 (July-September 1947): 201–51.

Post, Jennifer C. "Women in a New England Ballad Tradition, 1930–1960." Unpublished paper, 1983.

Rogers, Katharine M. *The Troublesome Helpmate: A History of Misogyny in Literature*. Seattle: University of Washington Press, 1966.

"Shocking Murder." *Cincinnati Inquisitor/Advertiser*, 18 January 1820.

Smith, Barbara Herrnstein. "Narrative Versions, Narrative Theories." *Critical Inquiry* 7 (Autumn 1980): 213–36.

Smith, O. H. *Early Indiana Trials and Sketches: Reminiscences by Hon. O. H. Smith*. Cincinnati: Moore, Wilstach, Keys, 1858.

Tompkins, Jane. *Sensational Designs: The Cultural Work of American Fiction, 1790–1860*. New York: Oxford University Press, 1985.

"Trial for Murder." *Indiana Oracle* (Lawrenceburgh), 7 March 1820. Reprinted in the *Brookville Enquirer*, 16 March 1820.

Zorn, John. *Spillane*. New York: Elektra/Nonesuch, 1987. Record number 79172.

Contributors

LINDA PHYLLIS AUSTERN is an assistant professor of music and fine arts in the Program of Liberal Studies at the University of Notre Dame. She is the author of *Music in English Children's Drama, 1597–1613* (1993) and numerous articles on music and culture in sixteenth- and seventeenth-century England. She is currently completing a work entitled "Music in English Life and Thought, 1558–1649."

JANE L. BALDAUF-BERDES, a musicologist and arts journalist, is the coauthor of *But What Is Greatness* (1963) and the author of *The Women Musicians of Venice: Musical Foundations, 1525–1855* (1993) as well as numerous articles. At the time of her death in 1993, she was in residence as an honorary fellow at the University of Wisconsin–Madison Women's Studies Research Center, where she was completing an archival study of the life, times, and works of composer Maddalena Laura Lombardini Sirmen (1745–1818).

VENISE T. BERRY is an assistant professor in the Journalism and Mass Communication Department at the University of Iowa. Using a historical, social, and cultural approach to examine images of African Americans in the media, she has published several articles and is currently at work on a manuscript entitled "Mediated Messages: Issues in African American Culture."

ADRIENNE FRIED BLOCK is codirector of the Project for the Study of Women in Music at CUNY's Graduate Center. She coedited (with Carol Neuls-Bates) *Women in American Music: A Bibliography of Music and Literature* (1979) and is currently writing a biography of Amy Beach.

MARCIA J. CITRON is a professor of music at Rice University and the author of *Letters of Fanny Hensel to Felix Mendelssohn* (1987), *Cécile Chaminade: A Bio-Bibliography* (1988), and *Gender and the Musical Canon* (1993).

SUSAN C. COOK is an associate professor of music and women's studies at the University of Wisconsin–Madison. She is the author of *Opera for a New Republic* (1988) and the coeditor (with Judy S. Tsou) of *Anthology of Songs* (1988), a volume of nineteenth-century French songs. She is currently working on a biography of the American social dancer Irene Castle and a study of Billie Holiday.

PATRICIA HOWARD is a tutor and lecturer in music at the Open University and the author of numerous articles and books on Britten, Gluck, and Lully, including *Gluck and the Birth of Modern Opera* (1963) and Cambridge Opera Handbooks on Gluck's *Orfeo* and Britten's *Turn of the Screw*.

SUSAN MCCLARY is a professor of musicology at McGill University. Her publications include *Feminine Endings: Music, Gender, and Sexuality* (1991) and a study of Bizet's *Carmen* for the Cambridge Opera Handbook series. She is currently completing a study on desire in seventeenth-century music.

BONNY H. MILLER, a native of Los Angeles, has studied and performed widely in the United States as a pianist and chamber player. Her doctoral research at Washington University in St. Louis on the atonal music of Arnold Schoenberg evolved into a study of music published in literary journals and household periodicals, an investigation that has taken her to more than forty major university collections and private archives in the United States and Canada.

JENNIFER C. POST is curator of the Flanders Ballad Collection at Middlebury College. Her principle research has involved extensive studies on women in Indian music and women in the traditional music of New England.

CATHERINE PARSONS SMITH is a professor of music at the University of Nevada, Reno. She is the coauthor (with Cynthia S. Richardson) of *Mary Carr Moore, American Composer* (1987) and is currently working on a study of music in Los Angeles before World War II. She is also principal flute of the Reno Philharmonic.

JUDY S. TSOU is the assistant head and archivist of the Music Library at the University of California–Berkeley. She has cataloged the Women's Music Collection at the University of Michigan Music Library, coedited (with Susan C. Cook) *Anthology of Songs* (1988), and contributed several articles to the forthcoming *New Grove Dictionary of Women Composers.*

Index

Abbott, John, 112
Absolute music, 22, 23–24. *See also*
  Music: instrumental; Symphony
Addams, Jane, 9
Afghanistan, 40, 41, 43
Africa: Kpelle, 38; Vai, 41; West Africa,
  186–87; women's roles in, 188–89
African American culture, 186–87, 188;
  musical traditions in, 42, 45, 96,
  185–86, 188–89; social and political
  movements in, 183; and "signifying,"
  187; black consciousness in, 192. *See
  also* Rap
African Americans. *See* Black men; Black
  women
Afro-American feminist theory. *See* Fem-
  inist consciousness and criticism:
  black feminist criticism
Afro-American literary criticism, 217
Afro-American Studies, 4
Afrocentricity: influence on Queen Latifah, 192, 194
Albania, 38, 41
Amateurs: male performers and composers, 44, 161, 166; female performers
  and composers, 156, 159, 161, 166
Americanism: musical, during romantic
  period, 90, 93, 94, 98. *See also* Mod-
  ernism: in American music
American Musicological Society, 15
American Studies, 4

American Women Composers, Inc., 3, 4
Ammer, Christine, 4
Anna Maria della Pietà: biography of, 8,
  134–35, 136–37, 139, 144, 146, 147,
  148–49; concertos for her by Anto-
  nio Vivaldi and others, 137–39, 141;
  treatment and daily life of, at the
  Pietà, 139–40, 142–43; instruction
  with Vivaldi, 140–41; as solo violin-
  ist and teacher, 141–43. *See also*
  Orphanages
Anne of Austria, 70
Antheil, George: *Ballet Mécanique*,
  96–97
Anthropology, 2, 7, 35
Antifeminism, 90, 92, 94, 100. *See also*
  Antiwoman sentiments; Misogyny
Antiwoman sentiments, 51, 90–91, 95,
  99. *See also* Antifeminism; Misogyny
Aristocracy, French, 70, 71
Aristotle, 53
Art music: European, 95. *See also* Abso-
  lute music
Asay, Mrs. Mary A., 164, 167, 169, 170
Astrology, 55
Astronomy, 62
Auerbach, Susan, 37–38, 39, 40
Austern, Linda Phyllis, 7, 9

Bach, Johann Christian, 20
Bach, Johann Sebastian, 120

Baermann, Carl, 120
Bailey, Nancy Gisbrecht, 5
Bailey, Walter, 5
Baldauf-Berdes, Jane, 8, 9, 11n9
Balkans, 39
Balladry: North American, 6–7, 8, 9, 202–3, 205–6, 216; of British Isles, 202, 216; African American contributions to, 203; in Canada, 203, 206; in U.S., 203, 206, 215; as narrative, 203, 207; gender encoding in, 205, 217, 221n8; women as performers and creators of, 205, 221n8; transmission of, 206, 212; British broadside ballads, 209; "murder ballads," 215; "The Lexington Murder" or "The Berkshire Tragedy," 215–16; "murdered-girl ballads," 215–16. See also "Fuller and Warren" ballad
Ballads: as house music genre, 165
Ballet Mécanique (Antheil), 96–97
Bandora, 58, 63
Barnard, Charlotte Allington (Claribel), 162, 164, 166, 167, 169, 173, 181n23
Barthes, Roland, 25–26, 78
Bauer, Marion, 97–98
Bayly, Mrs. Thomas Haynes, 163, 164, 166, 167, 168, 169, 171
Beach, Amy Cheney: as composer, 8, 11n9, 92, 98, 111–12, 113–14, 116, 125–26, 162, 167, 171, 180n9; and relationship with mother, 8, 107, 117–18, 126–27; childhood of, 107–8, 110, 113, 115, 117; autobiography of, 107–8, 111, 112–13, 114, 121–22, 124–25; and relationship with the piano, 108, 111, 113, 115; education of, 115–16, 118–21; as public performer, 116, 119–20, 124, 125–26; piano debut of, 121–24; marriage of, 124–26
Beach Collection, University of New Hampshire, 117, 123. See also Cheney, Charles Abbott; Cheney, Clara Imogene (Marcy); Clement, Emma Frances (Marcy)
Beach, Henry Harris Aubrey, 125–26
Beethoven, Ludwig van, 19, 23–24, 116, 161; attacked by Charles Ives, 95

Berckman, Evelyn, 93
Bergersen, Marie, 93
Bernasconi, Andrea, 137
Berry, Christina, 184
Berry, Venise T., 7, 8, 9
Biblical analysis and references, 53, 54, 60, 61
Biblical imagery. See "Fuller and Warren" ballad: biblical imagery in
Billboard Magazine, 189. See also Music journalism
Bingen, Hildegard of, 30n30
Biography, 107; of women, 5, 6, 8, 10n9, 107
Bizet, Georges: Carmen, 17
Black American culture. See African American culture
Black consciousness, 192
Black feminist theory. See Feminist consciousness and criticism: black feminist criticism
Black men, 184, 186–87, 190, 191, 194–95
Black music, 185–86, 188–89; blues, 185–86; gospel, 189. See also Rap
Black women, 8, 9, 183–86, 187–88, 192, 196. See also Feminist consciousness and criticism: black feminist criticism; Rap: women as performers in
Black, Jenny Prince, 180n9
Blackwell, Alice Stone, 131n80
Blackwell, Anna, 162, 167, 171
Blackwood, Mrs. Price (Lady Helen Dufferin), 164, 167, 168, 169, 171, 174
Bliss, Mrs. J. Worthington, 164, 166, 168, 169, 171, 175
Block, Adrienne Fried, 4, 8, 11n9
Blues, 185; women in, 185–86
Bodily humors, 87n19, 211
Bok, Edward, 159
Borroff, Edith, 30n33
Boruszkowaki, Lilly, 185
Boston, 116, 117; Handel and Haydn Society in, 122
Boston Symphony Orchestra, 98, 122
Boulanger, Nadia, 92
Bouquet-Boyer, Marie-Thérèse, 137, 148
Bourgeois society, 20, 22, 71
Bowers, Jane, 4, 6

Brégy, Charlotte de, 72–73, 81
Britain, Radie, 5
Brown, Jane, 185
Browne, Augusta, 162, 164, 165, 167, 170, 172
Brusa, Giovanni, 137
Bruts, G. M. (Giovanni Bruto), 60, 61
Burtis, Mrs. Sarah R., 164, 167, 169, 172
Bushnell, Horace, 109–10
Butler, Charles, 55
Butruille, Susan, 185

Caffi, Francesco, 140
Campbell, Kenneth, 185
Campbell, Luther, 187
Canon: musicological construction of "great work," 4, 5
Carby, Hazel, 5, 186
Carmen (Bizet), 17
Carminati, Lorenzo, 141
Caroline, Norton, 164, 168, 169, 176
Carreñno, Teresa, 119
Castiglione, Baldessar, 58
Castle, Irene, 11n9
Cecilia, Saint, 1, 10
Celibacy, 213; women and, 74–76, 78
Chamber music, 18
Chaminade, Cécile, 5, 165, 169, 173, 180n10; piano music of, 26, 98
Chansons, 156
Chastity, 74. See also Celibacy
Cheney, Charles Abbott, 108, 114, 118, 122
Cheney, Clara Imogene (Marcy): as Amy Beach's mother, 107–8, 113, 125, 126; child-rearing methods of, 107–11, 113, 114, 116–17, 119, 120, 124, 126; as pianist, 108, 115, 118. See also Beach, Amy: and relationship with mother
Child, James Francis: ballad study, 215
Childbearing, 73
Child-rearing practices, 8, 108–11, 116. See also Beach, Amy: childhood of
Chopin, Frédéric, 116, 122, 161
Christianity, 52, 54, 55–56; symbolism in, 145
Church: women's participation in, 42. See also Christianity

Citern, 58, 63
Citron, Marcia J., 5, 7, 9, 11n9
Claribel. See Barnard, Charlotte Allington
Class: as analytic category, 7, 8, 9, 24, 25, 37, 54, 58, 71, 90, 92, 98, 118, 119, 158, 159, 183, 214–15
Classical antiquity, 54, 60
Clay, Andrew Dice, 187
Clément, Catherine: on opera, 5, 70, 76, 216
Clement, Emma Frances (Marcy), 113, 117, 126
Clement, Ethel, 117
Clement, Lyman, 117
Cohen, Aaron, 4
Cohen, Anne, 215, 217
College Music Society, 5
Collins, Laura Sedgwick, 180n9
Composers. See Women: as composers
Composition, 4. See also Women: as composers
Concert hall, 22, 23
Concerto, 18
Controversy on women. See Women: debate on
Cook, Susan C., 8, 9, 11n9
Cooke, Edna Gallman, 189
Coolidge, Elizabeth Sprague, 93
Coote, Mary P., 39, 40
Copland, Aaron: on women composers, 92
Corneille, Pierre, 71, 78
Corner, Marietta, 141
Cosmetics, 59
Cott, Nancy, 42
Cotton, A. J.: relation to ballad "Fuller and Warren," 206, 212, 213–14
Country bands, 45
Country music: women in, 185. See also Vernacular music
Court, French, 72
Courtesan: women musicians as, 45
Courtly love, 74
Cowell, Henry, 94
Cowell, Miss A., 164–65, 167, 169, 173
Cowell, Sydney Robertson, 94
Creativity: as cultural construct, 1
Cross-cultural patterns in research, 35. See also Interdisciplinary method

Cross-dressing, 58. *See also* Transvestism
Croxall, Mrs., 162, 168, 173
Crozet, Cordelia C., 162, 168, 173
Culler, Jonathan, 27
Cushman, Charlotte Saunders, 164, 167, 172

Dadaism, 96
Dahl, Linda, 42
Dahlhaus, Carl, 22, 99
D'Alaij, Mauro, 137
Dalby, Liza Crihfield, 44
D'Angennes, Julie, 74
Dance, 43, 44, 45, 58, 59, 60, 96, 190, 191, 195; instructions, 161
Dance music, 41, 49n31; in periodicals, 159–60, 161, 165
Davis, Angela, 192
Davis, Dennis, 185
Davis, Natalie Zemon, 211
Deacon, Miss E. L., 165, 167, 169, 173
Denton, Sandy. *See* Salt 'N Pepa
De Vere, Leila A., 165, 169, 173
Dickens, Charles: and Amy Beach, 111–12
Dickinson, Emily, 30n32
Difference: as analytic category, 1, 5, 24
D'Indy, Vincent, 20
Domesticity: female, 9, 22, 24, 36–37, 38–39, 42, 54, 56, 64, 156; male, 56, 209, 215. *See also* Gender: ideologies; Public-private spheres or duality
Domestic music. *See* Music making, domestic; Vernacular music
Domestic violence. *See* Violence: against women
Dominick, Joseph, 185
Don Juan: literary theme, 23
Don Quixote: literary theme, 23
Drinker, Sophie, 3
Drums, 58, 63
Duets: in periodicals, 159, 165. *See also* Periodicals: music in
Dufferin, Lady Helen. *See* Blackwood, Mrs. Price
Dunn, Ginette, 41
Dupree, Mary Herron, 94
Dvořák, Anton, 98

Ebel, Otto: on women composers, 3

Edel, Leon, 107
Education: music education for women, 18, 60, 159; general, 53, 55; for women, 55, 59, 60, 157; mother's role in, 112; musical training at the Venitian *ospedali*, 139–44, 146–47, 149. *See also* Beach, Amy: education of
Effeminacy, 61, 88n24, 95, 98, 115; music as feminizing, 58
Eliot, T. S., 91, 95
Elizabethan England, 55
Ellison, Mary, 185, 186
Elson, Arthur: on women composers, 3
Elson, Louis C., 120
Emancipation: women's, 75, 76
Emerson, Ralph Waldo, 158
England: rural music traditions, 41; Elizabethan, 55
English Renaissance: and music, 8
Ensembles: all-women, 45
Epic tradition, 202
Ericson, Margaret, 5
Erudition, 56, 57, 62, 63; musical erudition as unfeminine for women, 160
Essentialism, 3, 22, 24, 25, 31
Essipoff, Annette, 119
Ethnomusicology, 6, 7, 35; feminist method in, 5, 10n7, 37
Euripides: *Medea*, 202
Eve. *See* Women: representations of
Eversole, Rose Mansfield, 180n9

Fabbri, Cora, 111
Farmer, John, 55
Farrar, Catherine: in ballad "Fuller and Warren," 207, 209, 210, 212, 213
Faust: literary theme, 23
Fay, Amy, 119. *See also* Keyboard: women performers of
Female aesthetic, 17
Female creativity. *See* Women: as composers
Female culture, 17
Female nature. *See* Feminine attributes and behavior; Gender roles
Female seduction, 209. *See also* Women: representations of
Female subjectivity, 7, 26–27

Feminine attributes and behavior, 7, 9;
in choice of instruments, 40, 95; in
English Renaissance views, 52, 55,
57–59, 61, 63–64; in eighteenth-century France, 74, 76, 83; in nineteenth-century U.S., 114–15, 121,
157, 160, 165, 207, 211, 217; for
black women, 184, 188, 190–91,
193, 196. See also Gender roles
Femininity, 1, 8, 19, 21, 54, 58, 90, 96,
157, 160, 190, 192, 193. See also
Feminine attributes and behavior;
Masculinity
Femininization: of women, 92, 98; of
music, 93–94
Feminism: as political movement, 3, 90–
91, 97, 98–99, 116, 118, 186. See
also Woman suffrage movement
Feminist consciousness and criticism, 1,
2, 4, 9, 35, 37, 48n2, 183–84, 206;
feminist literary criticism, 2, 7, 90–
92, 93, 95–96, 99; black feminist
criticism, 2, 8, 183–84, 188, 190–91,
192–96. See also Reader-response
theory; Women's history
Feminist musicology. See Musicology:
feminist method in
Fine, Vivian, 101n14
Finnemore, Charles, 207–9, 212, 213,
216
Flanders, Helen Hartness, 207–9
Flute, 159; associated with women, 115
Folkes, Martin, 145
Foscarini, Pietro, 147
Franklin, Aretha, 186
French Revolution, 70, 71, 85n3
Freudian theory, 18, 21; "female affiliation complex," 91–92
Fuller, Amasa: relation to ballad "Fuller
and Warren," 203, 207, 209–11, 212,
213, 214, 217, 222n30. See also
"Fuller and Warren" ballad
"Fuller and Warren" ballad, 203, 206,
214–17; broadside versions of, 203–
5, 206, 207, 210, 212–13; newspaper
coverage of ballad events, 206, 214;
biblical imagery in, 209, 212, 213,
214, 217, 222n24; appendix of all
versions, 217–21

Funeral music, 39. See also Life cycle:
music in
Furman, Nelly, 203
Futurism, 92, 96, 100

Gabrieli, Andrea, 144
Gabrieli, Giovanni, 144
Gadamer, Hans-Georg, 25
Garofalo, Reebee, 186
Gaynor, Jessie Love, 180n9
Gender: defined, 1; ideologies, 1, 2, 3, 5,
8, 22, 53, 54, 61, 121, 184, 206; as
analytic category, 1–2, 5, 7, 8, 9, 16,
17, 25, 52, 53, 60, 211, 214; relations, 2, 7, 37, 185; bias against
women, 5, 25, 156, 211; and race, 9,
11n12, 184
Gendered discourse, 7, 94–95; in the
sonata aesthetic, 18–21
Gender encoding in music, 1, 2, 5, 7, 8,
17, 29n8, 38, 41, 43, 205, 217,
221n3. See also Public-private spheres
or duality
—in American music, 91, 95–96, 100
—in balladry, 205, 217, 221n8
—by Charles Ives, 94–95
—in French opera, 70–71, 78–85
—in house music genres and music in
periodicals, 156–60, 165–66, 179n6
—in northern India, 37–38
—in music videos, 190, 191, 192, 195,
196; through "male-privileged" space,
186, 190, 191, 192, 195, 196
—in popular music, 184–86
—in rap, 8, 9, 186–89, 196
—in sonata aesthetic, 16, 20, 21, 22, 24,
26
Gender roles, 1, 2, 5, 7, 24, 36, 38, 45,
71, 92, 94, 160, 184, 196; in English
Renaissance, 53–55, 61; and Amy
Beach, 111, 114, 115, 116, 118, 119,
121, 126–27; in nineteenth-century
America, 205, 207, 217
Genius: as cultural construct, 1
Gibson, Anthony, 62, 63
Gideon, Miriam, 101n14
Gilbert, Sandra M.: feminist literary criti-
cism of, 7, 90–92, 93, 95–96, 99
Giuntini, Maestro, 96
Glanville-Hicks, Peggy, 5, 92

Gluck, Christoph, 85
Godey's Lady's Book: as household peri-
    odical, 158–59; music in, 161–65,
    167–68. *See also* Periodicals: music in
Godey, Louis, 158
Goethe, Johann W. von, 151*n21*
Gossec, François Joseph, 85
Gottschalk, Louis Moreau, 113
Gourd rattle, 41
Gourmont, Remy de, 97
Greek musical traditions, 38–39, 40
Green, Mildred Denby, 4
Greene, Robert, 55
Greenwood Press Biobibliographies, 5
Grey, Gertrude, 162, 167, 174
Griswold, Gertrude, 180*n9*
Gro, Josephine, 180*n9*
*Grove's Dictionary of Music and Musi-
    cians* (1954), 92
Gubar, Susan: literary criticism of, 7,
    90–92, 93, 95–96, 99
Guitar, 159; as feminine instrument, 40

Hale, Sarah, 158
Hall, Arsenio: show, 191
Hammer, Marie S., 180*n9*
Hammer (MC Hammer), 194, 195. *See
    also* Oaktown 3 5 7
Handel and Haydn Society, 122
Handy, D. Antoinette, 4
Hansen, Christine, 185
Hansen, Ronald, 185
Harp, 159; as feminine instrument, 40
Harrison, Annie Fortescue, 164, 168,
    169, 174
Harrison, Daphne, 185–86
Hawes, Maria Billington, 164, 167, 168,
    169, 174
Hawthorne, Nathaniel, 158
Hayes, Deborah, 5
Hegelian thought, 28, 30*n19*
Hemans, Felicia Browne, 163–64, 168,
    175
Hennessee, Don, 4
Hensel, Fanny Mendelssohn, 30*n32*,
    166, 176
Herndon, Marcia: research on Malta, 37,
    39, 41, 43
Heyman, Katherine Ruth, 93
Hill, Junius Welch, 120

Hirsch, E. D., 25
Hirsch, Marianne, 117–18
Hixon, Don L., 4
Hoby, Thomas, 58
Hodges, Faustina Hasse, 180*n9*
Hofmann, Josef, 93
Homosexuality. *See* Lesbian identity
Hood, Helen, 180*n9*
hooks, bell, 183–84
House music. *See* Music making, domes-
    tic
Howard, Ella C., 180*n9*
Howard, Patricia, 7
Hughes, Harriet Mary Browne, 163–64,
    167, 168, 169, 172, 175
Hull, Mrs. C. L., 162, 164, 167, 168,
    170, 175
Humanism: in English Renaissance, 53,
    55, 60, 61
Hyden, Colleen, 185
Hymns, 112–13, 165

Immigration: in U.S., 98–99
Imray, Linda, 37
India, 39, 40, 43, 44, 45, 47; northern,
    37–38; Maharashtra, 39, 41; Hindu,
    43, 44; Muslim, 44
Indiana, state of, 203, 212, 213, 214
Indiana Historical Society: versions of
    "Fuller and Warren," 203, 206, 207,
    212, 221
Indiana State Library, 221
Industrialization, 21, 22; effects of, 214
Instruments: gender associations of, 115;
    string, 58. *See also* Gender encoding
    in music
Interdisciplinary methods, 2
International Congress of Women in
    Music, 4
International League of Women Com-
    posers, 3, 4
International Year of the Woman, 3
Iser, Wolfgang, 25–26, 29*n7*
Ives, Charles: use of gendered discourse,
    94–95

Jackson, Millie, 186, 189
James, Cheryl. *See* Salt 'N Pepa
James, Henry, 107

Japan: Geisha tradition in, 43–44, 45,
  49n31
Jauss, Hans-Robert, 25
Jazz, 96; women in, 42, 45
Joan of Arc, 70
Johnican, Djuana. *See* Oaktown 3 5 7
Johnson, Rose-Marie, 5
Johnson, Simone. *See* Monie Love
Jones, Grace, 186
Jones, Mrs. A. Wedmore, 162, 169, 175
Joseffy, Raphael, 120
Journals. *See* Periodicals
Joyce, James, 91, 97
Junghare, Indira, 39, 41

Kamuf, Peggy, 27
Kellogg, Clara Louise, 114, 122
Kerber, Linda, 8, 9
Keyboard: as acceptable instrument for
  women, 40, 41, 49n31, 95, 119, 159;
  women performers of, 108, 119, 120.
  See also Beach, Amy: and relation-
  ship with the piano
King, Tabitha. *See* Oaktown 3 5 7
Kneisel Quartet, 95
Koskoff, Ellen, 5, 6
Kramer, Lawrence, 95

Ladies' Companion: household periodi-
  cal, 158; music in, 163, 164, 168. *See
  also* Periodicals: music in
Ladies' Home Journal: household period-
  ical, 158–59; music in, 161–62, 165,
  168–69. *See also* Periodicals: music
  in
Lance, Larry, 184
Lang, Margaret Ruthven, 98, 180n9
Latifah, Queen. *See* Queen Latifah
Lawrenceburgh, Indiana: location of bal-
  lad "Fuller and Warren," 203, 204,
  213–14
Laws, G. Malcolm, 215
Learning. *See* Education
Lears, T. J. Jackson, 93
Lederman, Minna, 93
Lee, Gerald Stanley, 108–9
Lee, Laura, 189
Leonarda, Isabella, 30n30
Lesbian identity, 9; and music, 6
Lewis, Lisa A., 187, 188

L'Hermite, Tristan, 71, 72
Liberal sciences, 56–57. *See also* Educa-
  tion
Liebe, Teresa, 119, 120
Life cycle: music in, 39–40, 49n35
Lind, Jenny, 161
Lindsay, Mary. *See* Bliss, Mrs. J. Worth-
  ington
Literary criticism. *See* Feminist con-
  sciousness and criticism: feminist lit-
  erary criticism; Reader-response
  theory
Llewellyn-Fitch, Kate, 162, 169, 175
Logic, 56
London, 53
Longfellow, Henry Wadsworth, 119–20,
  158
Louis XIV: reign, 70; opera libretti and,
  83–84; mistresses of, 84, 88n26
Love: as *précieux* topic, 72. *See also
  Précieuses*
Lully, Jean-Baptiste: operas, 7, 70, 73,
  85, 87–88n24; *Armide,* 70, 74, 77,
  84, 87–88n24; *Proserpine,* 73, 74, 77,
  84; *Alceste,* 73, 75, 76–77, 84; *Atys,*
  73, 76–77, 84; *Persée,* 73, 77; *Thésée,* 74, 75, 76, 78–83, 84; *Phaëton,*
  74, 77, 84; *Isis,* 74–75, 76–77; *Cadmus,* 76; *Poland,* 77
Lute, 58, 59, 63, 137

McCandless, N. Jane, 185
McClary, Susan, 5, 17, 22
MacDowell Colony, 126
McLeod, Norma: research on Malta, 37,
  39, 41, 43
Magazine music. *See* Periodicals: music
  in
Magazines. *See* Periodicals
Maintenon, Madame de, 84
Malaysia, 38, 41
Male hegemony, 21. *See also* Misogyny
Malibran, Maria: as performer, 161; as
  composer, 162, 163, 164, 166, 168,
  169, 176
Malta: musical traditions in, 37, 39, 41,
  43
Mandela, Winnie, 192
Mandolin, 137
Manslaughter, 211

Marches, 161
Marinetti, Filippo T., 96
Marriage: institution of, 39, 55, 56, 73–75, 117, 118, 143–44, 149, 213, 217
Marriott, Annette, 165, 166, 169, 176
Martinez, Isidora, 162, 169, 176
Marx, A. B.: on the sonata, 19–20
Mary. *See* Women: representations of
Masculine attributes and behavior, 24, 38, 58, 60, 61, 62, 64, 114–15, 184, 188, 196, 211; "male-privileged" space in music videos, 186, 187, 190, 191, 192, 195, 196
Masculinism: defined, 91, 96
Masculinity, 1, 9, 19, 21, 60, 64, 93, 94. *See also* Masculine attributes and behavior
Mason, William, 120
Materna lingua: defined, 91; in music, 92
Maud, Constance, 180n9
Mazarin, Cardinal, 70
MC Lyte (Lana Moore), 189, 191–92, 194; "Stop, Look, Listen" music video, 191–92. *See also* Rap: women as performers in
Medea (Euripides), 202
Media studies, 2
Meggett, Joan M., 5
Melody, Ms., 192
Meyer, Ernst, 20
Michelle, Lyndah, 196. *See also* Rap: women as performers in
Michelle, Tanisia, 196. *See also* Rap: women as performers in
Middle class, 7, 9, 90, 92, 98, 118, 119, 158, 159, 183, 202, 214. *See also* Class
Middleton, Audrey, 37
Militarism: in futurism, 96
Millard, Mrs. Philip, 163, 166, 167, 168, 169, 176
Miller, Bonny H., 8, 9
Misogyny, 7, 8, 52, 57, 63, 90, 95–96, 188, 203, 207, 213, 214. *See also* Antifeminism; Antiwoman
Modernism: in American music, 7, 8, 17, 91–95, 97–100; literary, 7, 90–91, 93, 96–97, 99; modernist com-

posers, 92, 93; in European music, 96, 99
Molière, Jean-Baptiste, 74, 75
Monie Love (Simone Johnson), 192–93. *See also* Rap: women in
Monk, Meredith, 31n37
Monologue: in Lully operas, 78–83
Montaigu, Comte de, 135
Monteverdi, Claudio, 144
Montpensier, Mademoiselle de, 70, 85
Monts, Lester P., 41
Moore, Frances J. (or Hatton-Moore), 162, 165, 169, 176
Moore, Lana. *See* MC Lyte
Moore, Mary Carr: operas, 98
Morality, 54
Morelli, Giovanni, 148
Morini, Lorenzo (Reggiano), 137
Morley, Thomas, 55
Moscheles, Ignaz, 122
Mother-daughter relationships, 117–18; in Amy Beach's life, 8, 107, 117–18, 126–27
Motherhood: duties of, 112
Mozart, Wolfgang Amadeus, 95, 161
MTV (Music Television), 185, 187. *See also* Music videos
Murder: grounds for, 211
Murphy, Eddie, 187
Music: controversy about, 7, 54, 58; instrumental, 16, 17, 18; gender restrictions in, 40–41, 47; religious, 41; merits of, 54; and love, 55; as feminizing influence, 58. *See also* Absolute music; Art music; Balladry; Black music; Blues; Country music; Funeral music; Gender encoding in music; Greek musical traditions; Jazz; Music videos; Periodicals: music in; Popular songs; Rap; Ritual music and activity; Salon music; Secular music; Singing; Songs; Symphony; Vocal music
Music editors, 161
Music education. *See* Education: musical
Musicians: male, 35, 41–42, 56, 57, 61, 62, 120. *See also* Women: as musicians and performers
Music industry, 45, 187–88, 191, 194, 196
Music journalism, 93–94

Music Library Association, 5
Music making, domestic, 58, 99, 156–57, 159–60
Musicology, 7, 26; feminist method in, 1, 2, 3, 5, 6, 7, 15–17, 27–28, 28n2, 99, 148–49; paradigms of, 16, 18, 19
Music publishers, 159, 160–61
Music teachers: female, 92, 98–99, 139, 142, 146, 148, 156; male, 93. *See also* Education
Music theory: in English Renaissance, 55; in nineteenth century, 20
Music videos, 185; "male-privileged" space in, 186, 187, 190, 191, 192, 195, 196; depiction of women in, 187, 189; Salt 'N Pepa's "Expression," 190–91; MC Lyte's "Stop, Look, Listen," 191–92; Queen Latifah's "Ladies First," 192–94; Oaktown 3 5 7's "Juicy Gotcha Krazy," 194–96
Mythology, 7, 146; references in English Renaissance, 54, 55, 58, 61, 63; in French opera, 73, 76–77, 84

Narrative content in music, 16, 22
Narrative theory, 203, 206, 216
Nationalism: in American music, 98. *See also* Americanism
Nemeitz, Joachim Christoph, 135
Neoclassicism, 91–92
Neo-Platonism, 53, 55
Neuls-Bates, Carol, 4
New England: musical traditions of, 38–39. *See also* Balladry
Norwood, Dorothy, 189

Oaktown 3 5 7, 189, 194–95; "Juicy Gotcha Krazy," 195–96. *See also* Rap: women as performers in
Occupations: male, 9, 38, 41, 205, 215, 216
Opera, 5, 8, 18, 31n37, 70, 76, 78, 97, 216; eighteenth-century French, 70–71, 73, 76–77, 85; seventeenth-century Italian, 76–77; libretti, 83. *See also* Lully, Jean-Baptiste
Orchestras, women's, 44
Orphanages: *ospedali grandi*, 8, 9, 134, 140, 146, 147, 148, 149, 150n2; fig-

lie del *coro*, 134, 139–40, 141–44, 146–47, 148–49, 151n21; Ospedale della Pietà, 134–36, 139–41, 142–43, 145–46, 149–50n1, 152n24; descriptions of *coro* performances, 135–37; and Venetian welfare policy and civic pride, 139–40, 147; musical education of *coro*, 139–44, 146–47; music faculty at the Pietà, 140–44; duties of *coro*, 142–44
Orpheus, 55
Ospedali grandi. *See* Orphanages: *ospedali grandi*
Overbury, Thomas, 55
Owens, Dana. *See* Queen Latifah

Paisiello, Giovanni, 85
Pallavicino, Gasparo, 58
Parents Music Resource Center (PMRC), 187
Paris, 96
Parks, Rosa, 192
Parlor songs. *See* Songs: parlor and home use
Passion killings, 211
Patriarchy: beliefs and practices of, 2, 3, 71, 124, 127, 157, 184, 186, 196, 203. *See also* Misogyny
Patrius sermo: defined, 91; in music, 92
Pauline theology, 213
Pelous, Jean-Michel, 75
Pendle, Karin, 4, 6
Perabo, Ernst, 119–20
Periera, Al, 191
Periodicals: household, 156–66; male readership of, 157; female readership of, 157–58, 160
Periodicals: music in, 7, 8, 9, 156–57, 159–60, 164; female composers of, 156–57, 161–66, 166–79; and gender encoding, 156–58, 160, 154–66; 179n6. *See also* Godey's Lady's Book; Ladies' Companion; Ladies' Home Journal
—Albion, 163, 164, 166
—Arthur's Home Magazine, 158, 164, 166
—Boston Miscellany of Literature and Fashion, 163, 166
—Boston Pearl, 163, 167

—*Boston Weekly Magazine*, 164, 167
—*Christian Parlor Magazine*, 158, 163, 167
—*Columbian Lady's and Gentleman's Magazine*, 162, 164, 165, 167
—*Graham's Monthly Magazine*, 158, 168, 164
—*Harmonicon*, 163, 164
—*New-Yorker*, 164, 169
—*New York Mirror*, 163, 164, 169
—*Peterson's Magazine*, 158, 162–63, 164, 169
—*Sartain's Union Magazine*, 158, 163, 170
Petrovic, Ankica, 37
Philidor, André Danican, 85
Phonograph, 165
Piano: as suitable for women, 30*n*27, 157, 165; music for, 98, 156, 159–60. *See also* Keyboard
Piccinni, Niccolo, 85
Pisan, Christine de, 53
Pisendel, Johann Georg, 138
Pitman, Alice L., 180*n*9
Placksin, Sally, 4
Poe, Edgar Allan, 158
Poetry, 111, 160
Pöllnitz, Baron Karl Ludwig von, 135
Popular music. *See* Vernacular music
Popular songs, 96, 184. *See also* Vernacular music
Positivism: in musicology, 16, 28*n*2
Post, Jennifer C., 7, 37
Poststructuralism, 29*n*6
Pound, Ezra, 91; and George Antheil, 96–97
Powell, Maud, 129*n*50
Power: and music, 5, 8, 19, 42, 59, 217; and gender, 9, 16, 37, 72, 217; of love, 95; political and women, 70. *See also* Music: and love; Music: merits of
Pratella, B. F., 96
Précièuses: French literary movement, 71–76, 78, 80, 83–85. *See also* Quinault, Philippe
Protestantism: New England child-rearing practices of, 107–9, 112, 115, 126. *See also* Cheney, Clara Imogene (Marcy)

Pseudonyms: in composition, 163
Public-private spheres or duality, 7, 8, 9, 11*n*62, 21, 35–42, 54, 95, 112; duality seen as a continuum, 36, 43, 205; encoded in musical practices, 37–43, 47, 119, 125, 156, 165–66, 185, 205, 221*n*3; women's presence in public sphere, 43–46, 93; women in "male-privileged" space in music videos, 186, 187, 190, 191, 192, 195, 196. *See also* Gender roles
Pure, Abbé Michel de, 71, 75
Puritanism: English, 53, 54, 55
Pyrrye, C., 62

Quantz, Johann Joachim, 135, 138, 152*n*37
Queen Latifah (Dana Owens), 183, 189, 192–94; "Ladies First" music video, 192–94. *See also* Rap: women as performers in
Querelle des Femmes. *See* Women: debate on
Questions d'Amour, 72–73. *See also* *Précièuses*
Quilting as metaphor, 6, 7
Quinault, Philippe: as librettist for Lully, 7, 72, 73–78, 80, 84–85; as benefactor of *précieux* support, 7, 74–75, 83; settings of his libretti by other composers, 85. *See also* *Précièuses*

Race: as analytic category, 7, 8, 9, 11*n*12, 24, 25, 90, 92, 98–99, 183–84, 216; and gender, 9, 11*n*12, 184
Ra'Chaun: rap critic, 189–90
Racine, Jean Baptiste, 78, 85; *Phèdre*, 70
Racism, 5, 9, 25, 96; in feminist movement, 9; in American music, 95, 98
Radio, 165
Rainey, Gertrude ("Ma"), 185–86
Rand, Josephine, 180*n*9
Rap, 6, 7, 8, 9, 187–88, 192, 196; women as performers in, 8, 9, 184, 186–89, 192, 193, 196; other rap groups, 187–90 passim, 196; MC Lyte, 189, 191–92; Queen Latifah, 189, 192–94; Oaktown 3 5 7, 189, 194–96; Salt 'N Pepa, 189–91

Ravenscroft, Thomas, 55
Reader-response theory, 16, 25–27. See
    also Feminist consciousness and criti-
    cism: feminist literary criticism
Recitative: in Lully opera, 81
Reformation, 55, 60
Reich, Nancy B., 5
Reis, Clare, 93
Reitmeyer, Wilse, 162, 168, 176
Religion. See Christianity
Representations of women. See Women:
    representations of
Rhetoric, 18, 53, 56, 63
Richardson, Cynthia S., 5
Riddle, Almeda, 205, 221n8
Rieger, Eva, 5, 17
Riemann, Hugo, 20
Ritournelle: in Lully opera, 80
Ritual music and activity, 37, 38, 41, 42,
    43
Rivé-King, Julie, 180n9
Robinson, Sylvia, 189
Rock music: treatment of women, 185.
    See also Vernacular music
Rogers, Clara Kathleen, 120, 180n9
Rolling Stone Magazine, 188. See also
    Music journalism
Roman law, 53
Romanticism: German, 17, 21, 22; nine-
    teenth-century American, 91–92, 93,
    98
Rondeau: in Lully opera, 81
Roper, Dee Dee. See Salt 'N Pepa
Roseman, Marina, 37–38, 41
Rosen, Charles, 19–20, 22
Rösenmuller, Johann, 140
Rossetti, Christina, 30n32
Rousseau, Jean-Jacques, 135
Russolo, Luigi, 96
Ryom, Peter, 138

Sakata, Hiromi Lorraine, 40, 41, 43
Salon music, 6
Salons: précieux, 71, 72, 73–74, 75, 83
Salter, Thomas, 60–61
Salt 'N Pepa, 189–91; "Expression" mu-
    sic video, 190–91. See also Rap:
    women as performers in
Sawyer, Harriet P., 180n9
Schmidt, Cynthia, 37–38

Schoenberg, Arnold, 92
Schumann, Clara, 5, 30n32
Schuyler, Georgina, 180n9
Schweickart, Patrocinio, 26–27
Schwörer-Kohl, Gretel, 37–38
Scott, Joan Wallach, 2
Scott, Joyce, 76
Scudéry, Madeleine de, 71, 74, 75
Secular music, 38. See also Ritual music
    and activity
Seeger, Ruth Crawford: and modernism,
    93
Sensuality. See Sexuality
Separate spheres. See Public-private
    spheres and duality
Serbo-Croatia, 39, 40
Serialism, 92
Sex: biological, 1, 35, 47, 76, 92, 96. See
    also Gender
Sexism, 5; in rap music, 186, 187–88.
    See also Gender bias; Misogyny;
    Women's oppression
Sex roles. See Gender roles
Sexual aesthetics, 5
Sexual difference, 1
Sexual exploitation: of women in music,
    184–85, 187
Sexuality, 5, 25, 97; female, 7, 8, 52,
    57–60, 62, 64, 76, 77, 83, 186, 195,
    215–16; male, 60, 187, 195
Sexual linguistics: defined, 91
Sexual orientation, 9. See also Lesbian
    identity
Shakespeare, William, 55
Shamisen, 44
Shante, Roxanne, 189–90, 194
Sheet music, 162. See also Periodicals,
    music in
Shehan, Patricia K., 39
Sherman, Barry, 185
Shevelow, Kathryn, 161
Showalter, Elaine, 6, 27
Sicard, Mlle., 156
Singing: women as singers, 38–40, 41,
    42, 44, 45, 60–61, 62, 108, 113, 114,
    118, 120, 122, 135, 148. See also
    Songs: parlor and home use; Vocal
    music
Slavery: in the U.S., 183, 186

Sloman, Anne, 162, 164, 165, 167, 168, 170, 177
Slonimsky, Nicolas, 97–98
Smith, Bessie, 185–86
Smith, Catherine Parsons, 5, 7, 8
Smith, Oliver H.: relation to ballad "Fuller and Warren," 206–7, 213, 214
Smith, Patrick, 83
Smith, Penelope, 164, 166, 168, 169, 177
Smith, Valerie, 184
Social class. See Class
Sociology, 2
Somaize, Antoine-Baudeau de, 72, 73, 75
Sonata aesthetic, 7, 16–19. See also Women: as composers
Sonata form, 16, 18–20, 22, 30n19
Songs: women's performance of, 39, 40, 41, 45; parlor and home use, 44, 156, 157, 159–60, 163–64, 165. See also Singing
Soranzo, Tommaso, 141
Sorcery, 59
Spada, Bonaventura, 140
Spencer, Fanny M., 180n9
Spivey, Victoria, 185–86
Stair, Patty, 180n9
Storytelling: by women, 37; in West African tradition, 186–87
Stowe, Harriet Beecher, 158
Strauss, Johann, 160
Stravinsky, Igor, 97
Sugarman, Jane C., 37–38, 41
Surian, Elvidio, 148
Swetnam, Joseph, 58, 63
Symphony, 17–18, 23–24

Talma, Louise, 101n14
Tartini, Giuseppe, 137
Taylor, Anita, 185
Taylor, Deems, 94
Tchaikovsky, Peter, 17, 161
Ternary form, 20
Tessarini, Carlo, 137
Thailand, 38
Theorbo, 137
Thigpen, David, 192
Thomas, Irma, 189
Thomson, Virgil, 96, 97

Thunder, Shelly, 192
Tick, Judith, 4, 5, 6, 160; on Charles Ives, 94–95
Tompkins, Jane, 215
Tonality, 20
Toop, David, 186, 188–89
Tovey, Donald Francis, 20
Transcendence, 22
Transvestism, 95. See also Cross-dressing
Truette, Everett Ellsworth, 3
Tubman, Harriet, 192
Turkey, 40
Tuvil, Daniel, 59, 60

Upton, George, 3
U.S. Bicentennial, 3

Valladier, André, 71
Vandervelde, Janika, 17
Varèse, Edgard, 98
Venice: musical life in, 7, 9, 134, 137, 144, 148–49; state welfare policy of, 139–40, 145–47; liturgical role for women in, 144–48. See also Orphanages
Venus, 55, 62
Vernacular music, 6, 184–86, 188–89, 203, 217. See also Balladry; Periodicals: music in; Rap; Salon music
Vice, 53, 61
Victoria, Queen, 160
Videos. See Music videos
Video Soul, 185
Vincent, Richard, 185
Violence: against women, 97, 185, 187–88, 215, 217, 223n41; gang violence, 188
Violin, 159; as acceptable instrument for women, 115, 119, 120, 129n50. See also Anna Maria della Pietà
Virgin/whore dichotomy. See Women: representations of
Virtue, 53, 61
Vivaldi, Antonio: relation with Ospedale della Pietà, 134, 136, 140–41, 149–50n1, 152n37; concertos for Anna Maria della Pietà, 137–39, 141
Vocal music, 23, 44, 160. See also Singing

Wade, Bonnie, 39
Walther, Johann G., 135
Warren, Elinor Remick, 101n14
Warren, Palmer: relation to ballad
    "Fuller and Warren," 203, 206, 207,
    209–11, 214. See also "Fuller and
    Warren" ballad
Webb, George, 160
Weber, Carl Maria von, 161
Webster, James, 20
Weill, Irving, 94
Wesley, John, 109
White women, 7, 9, 90, 92, 98, 158,
    183, 185
White, Elizabeth Anne, 162, 167, 178
Whitmer, T. Carl, 93
Whittemore, William L., 120
Wilder, Laura Ingalls, 158
Wilson, Mrs. Cornwall Baron, 164, 166,
    169, 178
Winner, Septimus, 163
Woloch, Nancy, 42
Woman: as other, 18, 21; as subject, 53.
    See also Women: representations of
Womanism, 192. See also Feminist con-
    sciousness and criticism: black femin-
    ist criticism
Woman suffrage movement, 3
Women: status of, 61; and celibacy, 74–
    76, 78. See also Black women; White
    women
—as composers: 3, 4, 5, 8, 15, 17, 18,
    24, 26, 27, 30n30, 30n32, 31n37, 54,
    64, 92; of sonata form, 18, 22, 23–
    24; in American music, 90, 92–93,
    95, 98–100, 119, 120; in Venetian
    ospedali, 139, 146; of magazine mu-
    sic, 156, 160–66, 166–79. See also
    Beach, Amy: as composer
—debate on: in English Renaissance, 52,
    53, 54, 56, 57; Querelle des Femmes,
    85
—as musicians and performers: 1, 4, 8,
    9, 35, 39–41, 43–47, 98, 99, 118,
    161–62, 166; in rap, 8, 9, 184, 186–
    89, 192, 193, 196; in English Renais-
    sance, 54, 56, 57, 58, 59, 60, 61, 62,
    63, 64; in American music, 114, 120,
    122, 129n50; in Venetian ospedali,
    134–37, 139–42, 144–49; in black

music, 185–86, 188–89; in balladry,
    205, 221n8. See also Anna Maria
    della Pietà; Rap: women as perform-
    ers in
—as music teachers, 92, 98–99, 156; at
    Venetian ospedali, 139, 142, 143,
    146, 148
—in other professions: as authors and
    writers, 91, 93, 165; as patrons, 93;
    as conductors, 142; as editors, 158,
    165; as artists, 165; as record produc-
    ers, 189, 190–91
—representations of: as whore, 58, 59,
    62, 185, 187, 196; as siren, 62; as
    Mary, 71; as Eve, 71, 76; as saint,
    185; as sex object, 185; as "bitch,"
    187, 192, 196; as Delilah, 210, 216;
    virgin/whore dichotomy, 216
Women in music, 2, 4, 5, 17; research
    on, 2, 4, 48n2. See also Musicology:
    feminist method in
Women of color, 8, 9. See also Black
    women; Feminist consciousness and
    criticism: black feminist criticism
Women's equality, 57
Women's history, 2, 3, 8, 9. See also
    Feminist consciousness and criticism
Women's music, 35. See also Women: as
    composers; Women: as musicians and
    performers
Women's oppression, 2, 8, 183
Women's orchestras. See Ensembles; Or-
    chestras, women's
Women's sphere. See Public-private
    spheres and duality
Women's studies, 2, 3. See also Feminist
    consciousness and criticism; Women's
    history
Wood, Elizabeth, 148
Wood, Mary Knight, 180
Working class. See Class
World War I, 90, 98, 99, 159, 165
Worrell, Edna Randolph, 162, 165, 169,
    178–79

Yocum, Margaret, 37
Yugoslavia, 37

Ziegler, Susanne, 40
Zorn, John, 223n41